THINKING STRAIGHT

Prentice-Hall English Literature Series

Maynard Mack, EDITOR

PRENTICE-HALL INTERNATIONAL, INC., *London*
PRENTICE-HALL OF AUSTRALIA, PTY. LTD., *Sydney*
PRENTICE-HALL OF CANADA, LTD., *Toronto*
PRENTICE-HALL OF INDIA (PRIVATE), LTD., *New Delhi*
PRENTICE-HALL OF JAPAN, INC., *Tokyo*

third edition

THINKING STRAIGHT

principles of reasoning
for readers and writers

MONROE C. BEARDSLEY
Swarthmore College

Prentice-Hall, Inc., Englewood Cliffs, New Jersey

Current printing (last digit):
10 9 8 7 6 5

Library of Congress Catalog Card Number:
66-16388

Printed in the United States of America
[91816-C]

PREFACE

In this third edition of *Thinking Straight,* as compared to the previous edition, the similarities are more basic than the differences. The topics are introduced in a somewhat different order. Improvements have been made in several points of doctrine. The text has been completely rewritten with an eye to greater conciseness, and all the earlier examples, in the text and in the exercises, have been replaced by fresh material.

I would again like to thank those who gave helpful counsel for the first edition. I owe an extra debt to my wife, Elizabeth Lane Beardsley, for her critical reading of the manuscript; to Antony Flew, for his detailed comments on the second edition; and to Richard M. Gale, for his good suggestions. I wish I were able to express my gratitude individually to the many students who have pointed out, in class discussion or in letters, ways of making the book better.

M. C. B.

CONTENTS

THINKING STRAIGHT

PREVIEW

One of the difficult issues confronting our society today concerns the use of certain chemical compounds known as pesticides in controlling undesirable animals and plants. Since the introduction of DDT in 1942, the use of these chemicals has increased enormously: today there are more than 50,000 varieties, of which over a billion pounds are produced each year. Those who believe pesticides to be one of the greatest inventions of man point out that without them, production of apples, citrus fruits, cotton, and potatoes would be 50 per cent less—that before their wide use, blight destroyed half the crop of tomatoes in 1946, and in other years the corn borer ruined millions of acres of sweet corn—that DDT has virtually wiped out malaria and typhus in this country. On the other hand, conservationists and biological ecologists point out that millions of birds and fish have been killed off by heavy use of pesticides —that these compounds build up in the fatty tissues of the body, where their ultimate effect is unknown—that allergic reactions to them may be increasing as our diet contains more and more of them, since once they are sprayed on a plant, they are nearly impossible to dislodge.

As public debate widens and grows more intense, the ordinary citizen finds it difficult to get his bearings on the matter. He does not know how to vote, or what to write his senator, or whether to support or oppose his local borough council when it is considering a campaign of spraying mosquitoes. In the emotional atmosphere, there is danger that an excessive fear of consequences will lead to unwarranted restrictions on the use of pesticides and on the development of further types. On the other hand, there is also a danger that ignorance or apathy, or the propaganda campaigns of the pesticide industries, will make us think that all is well, and that ten or twenty years from now, when the long-range consequences become clear, our children will curse us for spreading these chemicals through our topsoil and our rivers.

It is a situation that calls not for hysteria or for smug complacency, but for *thinking.*

In a popular sense, almost anything that passes through the mind can be called thinking—including memories and daydreams. But I am using the word in a narrower sense. Thinking is a series of ideas that is directed, however vaguely, toward the solution of a problem. When what goes on in our minds is initiated by some question that we want to answer, then it takes on purpose and direction: it has something to aim at, and its course is under the control of the question that started it off. Pesticides are a problem, undoubtedly. There is the *practical* problem: What are we going to do about them? But this also involves a *theoretical* problem: Will the controlled use of pesticides produce benefits without corresponding evils? As soon as we ask ourselves this question, all sorts of leads suggest themselves, for there is much that we will want to know: about the chemistry of the compounds, about their immediate and long-range physiological effects, about the balance of nature, and so on. But even if the inquiry takes us far afield, we will have a standard of relevance, for we will be guided all along by a desire to find what we need in order to answer the original question.

What thinking is after is simply the truth. When it results in truth, the thinker acquires new knowledge. That is the measure of its success. That is what makes thinking *good* thinking.

When we consider the nature of thinking more closely, as it might develop, for example, in the pesticide problem, we find that it has two fundamentally different aspects: a *creative* aspect and a *critical* aspect.

Creative thinking gives us new ideas. At some point—and it is to be hoped at many points—along the line, someone will come up with ingenious suggestions for new experimental studies. For example, what is the best way to find out how much pesticide material there actually is in the food we eat? And, again, how can we predict the long-range effect of pesticides, without waiting around until it is too late? Moreover, some of those working on the problem will come up with original ideas about possible alternatives to the use of pesticides. These may be radical, yet they may be worth trying: for example, importing or breeding special insects to attack the ones we want to get rid of, or killing the pests with high-pitched sounds or luring them to their death with artificial female-insect scents.

This kind of thinking is an exercise of imagination, which is needed in biology and engineering just as it is in writing poetry or music. So one task before us, if we are interested in good thinking, is to discover how we can make thinking more creative. Unfortunately, we do not yet know very much about this matter. Psychologists have studied creative thinking, and can say something about the personality factors and environmental factors that seem to favor it or hinder it. And teachers of literature have long contended that one of the values of the arts, especially of literature, is to enlarge and free our imaginations. But there is no handy set of rules to follow to make our thinking more creative. Perhaps there is even something a little paradoxical in the very notion of rules for creative thinking—since this is thinking that leaps out in new directions to unexplored territory, and moves in sudden, unexpected, and unpredictable ways.

Critical thinking comes into play after we have an idea to try out, a theory to test, a proposition that someone wants to prove or to refute. Are we sure that all the evils sometimes attributed to DDT really are due to it? And what about the benefits? Granted that between 1940 and 1962 the average farmer increased his productivity from providing enough for himself and ten others to providing enough for himself and twenty-six others—how much of this increase is due to pesticides and how much to other factors? Whenever a claim is made to knowledge, there is an occasion for critical thinking—that is, for a careful and serious effort to test that claim, as far as possible.

To judge the worth of any kind of claim—whether to knowledge or to an estate—we must have some standards, some principles of legitimacy that can be applied to the case at hand. There are many different kinds of thing in the world to think about, and there are different ways of thinking about them. What makes good critical thinking in economics, for example, is not exactly what makes good critical thinking in engineering or literary criticism or psychology or storekeeping. But there are some general principles of critical thinking that apply in every field. These are the principles of *logic*. It is the business of the logician to discover what conditions must be satisfied by any critical thinking if it is to be considered a success.

This book is concerned with critical thinking, and especially with good critical thinking, which is *straight thinking*—though we shall have to look frequently at examples of crooked thinking, in order to see clearly what to avoid. The first half of the book concentrates on the most fundamental and general principles of logic. Our effort will be, not to cover them all, but to understand many of the principles that are most readily applicable to the kinds of problem we are likely to meet in the ordinary affairs of life, as citizens of a modern democracy.

These everyday problems come to us very often in the medium of words—the spoken words of our families and friends and the written words that we see everywhere we go. At our present stage of civilization, language plays a more dominant and decisive role than ever before in history. I am not referring primarily to what might be called the person-to-person message, which exists in every culture, civilized or not: the lullaby, the love-letter, the greeting, the family quarrel. These can be of great moment to us, but in sheer quantity they do not match the flow of those more public, more impersonal, more civic messages that impinge upon us through nearly every waking hour. We live in a sea of words: the insinuating or insistent drone of transistor radio, television, public-address system, record player; the billboard, traffic sign, newspaper editorial, magazine article, book, box top, directions for assembling, and monthly letter from the Fair Housing Council or the American Reactionary Society.

We must get the data for much of our thinking through language, since our range of direct experience is small compared to that of all mankind. And we must carry on a good part of our thinking in the medium of language; for we cannot be sure that we understand an idea clearly, and that we see what is right and what is wrong with it, until we have put it into words. Therefore, critical thinking requires skill in handling language: in analyzing and grasping meanings, as readers or listeners, and in managing and communicating our own meanings, as writers or speakers. The second half of this book is concerned with the basic difficulties that arise when we use language as a vehicle of critical thinking, and what we can do to overcome them.

I do not mean to suggest that we shall consider all the various aspects of language. Words have many uses besides the one that concerns us here: for example, in poetry or religious worship. But there is one set of uses—including such activities as persuading, convincing, informing, briefing, reporting, enlightening—that can be set apart from the others as *cognitive* uses, that is, as having to do with knowledge, or at least with the formation of belief. These cognitive uses are those that come into play when language is made an instrument of thought, and the aim of studying language as a part of (or a partner to) logic is to master them, so that when we need to think straight, words will work with us and not against us.

Since this book is primarily designed to be practical, it contains a good many quizzes and exercises, the materials for which are taken, with as little change as necessary, from newspapers, magazines, advertisements, sermons, and so forth. If you do most of this work, you should be pretty familiar with the principles set forth in the text; but it will be even better to make your own collection as you study the book. By keeping your eyes open, you will find many examples of odd or dubious reasoning in your favorite periodicals, and there is no better way to make sure you are mastering the subject than to take the principles of logic, so to speak, outside the laboratory and into the field.

To get the most from your study of this book, you should have some idea of what you are looking for in it. You might begin by trying the following Preliminary Quiz. See what you think about the twenty-five examples, before you turn to Chapter 1—and later, when you have come to the end of the book, you can look back and see how much more clearly you understand what (if anything) is wrong with these examples.

A Preliminary Quiz How good is the thinking in the passages below? Read each passage carefully. If you find that the thinking is confused or crooked, explain briefly, in your own words, what is wrong.

A. Should the Death Penalty be Abolished?

In recent years, more and more states have seriously considered doing away with capital punishment (as at least nine states have done so far). Wherever this proposal has been advanced, it has been hotly disputed. Here are some comments that have been made:

1. Sir: If capital punishment is in fact a logical method of crime deterrence, then executions should be held in public and should be as grisly as possible. The head should be exhibited on a pole, as in eighteenth-century England, and every citizen should be required to view at least one execution before the age of twelve, so the full force of the deterrence will strike him.
2. Sir: If individual *A* murders individual *B*, then is apprehended and put to death, he cannot kill individuals *C*, *D*, *E*,

and so on. The deterrent effect on individual *A* has been 100 per cent. This is such simple logic that even a sociologist should be able to grasp it.

3. You can't get around the statistics, if they are properly used. True, Alabama has the highest rate of murders per 100,000 people, Vermont the lowest; but remember that Alabama has a younger population than Vermont. All other states have more unrelated individuals per 100 families than Alabama, while only four other states have proportionately more unrelated individuals than Vermont.
4. I'm against capital punishment because as long as we have these do-gooders around, it gets in the way of society's taking its just revenge on the murderer. Somebody commits a murder, and is brought to trial. Then what happens? The bleeding-hearts set up a cry about the cruelty of killing. They forget about the poor guy that got murdered; they have no consideration for him at all. So, far too often, the jury acquits the murderer or else convicts him of manslaughter, out of sympathy. If we got rid of capital punishment, we might get more convictions, and that's what society demands. The whole secret of justice is exacting the full measure of the law.
5. Opponents of the death penalty argue that the number of executions in the United States has gone down from 200 a year 25 years ago to 68 in 1962 (more than half of them in California, Texas, and Florida), while at the same time the number of homicides a year has continued to fluctuate between 7,000 and 8,000. The explanation of this is obvious: as our standard of living rises, and we grow more law-abiding, the deterrent effect of executions constantly increases—so that fewer executions have the same deterrent effect as more used to do.
6. If we cannot abolish the death penalty, at least we should have as few executions as possible. For the Constitution forbids cruel and unusual punishments, and when there are few executions, then they are certainly unusual, and seem especially cruel, which would be a good argument for not having many of them.
7. The theory of capital punishment is tied up with a whole system of punishment based on violence, torture, and brutality, which is gradually being replaced by a more humanitarian one. If the original system (say, as it existed in the Middle Ages and early modern period) were valid, capital punishment would be justified; but since it is not valid, capital punishment is not justified.

8. I don't care what you call it, but I call capital punishment legalized murder—that is, the deliberate taking of life under color of law by government officials. The emperors of ancient Rome had to satisfy the appetite for violence, when the populace screamed for blood; so they threw the Christians to the lions and turned thumbs down on the gladiators. Today, when twelve good men and true, reflecting the same blood-lust of their neighbors, turn thumbs down on the defendant—without understanding, in most cases, anything about how he became what he is, or what he might become with proper treatment—we call it justice, but actually it is simply an institutionalized and ritualized revenge.
9. It is essential to be clear about the exceptions we propose to our general law abolishing the death penalty. The exceptions may be classified as (1) homicides committed in the course of kidnapping a child, (2) rape of a minor, (3) rape with aggravated assault, and (4) treason during a military emergency.
10. It is in accordance with Christian teaching that every man is responsible for all men; in other words, either by our action or inaction, we all have some effect on others, and help to make them what they are. But when we execute a criminal, we are washing our hands of all responsibility for him; we are putting him out of our mind. Therefore capital punishment is unchristian.
11. Let's be practical about this business; after all, it's the pocketbook that we have to think about, not these fuzzy notions of morality or these tricky statistics. Why should you pay out your hard-earned money through higher taxes for the sake of some murderer? I have calculated that it costs society more to execute a murderer (if he has an opportunity to carry his appeal through several higher courts, over several years, as many have done) than it does to keep him in prison for the rest of his life, where he can pay at least part of his own upkeep by useful labor. Therefore, I'm against capital punishment. It's as simple as that.
12. Some say that the distinction between first- and second-degree murder is not understood by many juries, so that convictions vary, and the law cannot be applied equally. But the definition is clear and exact, provided the other relevent qualifications are borne in mind. The principal variety of first-degree murder is homicide with malice aforethought and with premeditation and deliberation. But remember that, in the first place, legally speaking the malice does not have to be directed against the victim, in the sense

of hate or dislike; and, in the second place, premeditation may be a matter of a few seconds, so long as it takes place before the actual killing.

13. I admit the sincerity of those who deplore capital punishment. However, a realistic approach to the problem demands that they weigh the right of innocent persons to live their lives free from fear of bestial killers against statistical arguments which boast of how few murderers kill again after "rehabilitation" and release (for example, that the 169 first-degree murderers paroled in Ohio since 1945 have made the best "adjustment" of any group among the 6,000 paroled convicts). No one, unless he can probe the mind of every potential killer, can say with any authority that capital punishment is not a deterrent. As one police officer has asked, how can we possibly know how many people are not on death row because of the deterrent effect of executions?

B. Should Prayer be Permitted in Public Schools?

On June 17, 1963, the United States Supreme Court ruled eight to one on two cases that had involved prescribed religious activity in public schools. The Schempp case, which came from Abington Township, near Philadelphia, involved a challenge to a Pennsylvania state law requiring the reading of ten verses of the Bible each day; the Murray case challenged a Baltimore school-board requirement that opening exercises include either the reading of a Bible chapter or the recitation of the Lord's Prayer. The Court held that these requirements violated the establishment clause in the Bill of Rights. In the wake of the decision, as at the time of the first District Court decision in favor of the Schempps, there was much public discussion of the principles involved in these cases. Here are some views that were expressed:

14. Those who scorn the very foundations of our democratic way of life are those who have never heard prayers in school. And now, alas, our own little children will not ever hear prayers in school, so they, too, must inevitably scorn our way of life.
15. We know from Jefferson's famous letter of 1802 that the First Amendment to the Constitution provides a "wall of separation between Church and State"—that is, it is like a stone wall separating different fields, to keep the activities apart so that government leaves religion free to go its own way, and religion keeps its hands off government. But, just as a wall cannot allow any crossing between the two areas,

or any contact between, say, the sheep on one side and the cows on the other, it follows that the First Amendment does not allow the government to aid religions in any way whatsoever, even to give subsidies in the form of tax exemption or loans for schools and hospitals.

16. Anyone who thinks that a few minutes of Bible-reading and school prayers fosters religion is confused; what it fosters is not religion but *religiosity.* This is an excessive reliance upon empty formal activity and gesture, in the place of substantial meaningfulness and genuinely deep commitment and conviction.
17. The choice is clear: either we will amend the Constitution to put the Bible back in the schools (and get the progressive educators out), or we are in for it: we will produce a generation of atheists whose rampant materialism will bring the decline and fall of America. I am here to tell you, gentlemen, that the Bible will return; and therefore, thank God, that generation of atheists will never materialize.
18. There are two basic reasons why I, as a teacher, hold a brief religious ceremony at the beginning of each day. First, because of its moral effect; reading those fine Biblical words and saying a sincere prayer gives each pupil a sense of right and wrong, and of deep spiritual uplift. Second, when they come in from the playground they are always noisy and unruly, and it is necessary to have some kind of ritual to quiet them down and make them shut up for a bit. They realize that if it's a religious ceremony, they have to be quiet. And what harm can it do them? They don't have to understand or believe what they say, so long as they repeat the words; they can believe anything they like, but they have to be solemn and quiet.
19. I don't know whether you realize it or not, but a Pandora's box has been opened by the Court, and there is nowhere it can stop. They took God out of the schools; yes, and to be logical they will take God out of the courtroom and the legislative hall. No more chaplains to invoke the blessings of the Supreme Being on the work of our senators and congressmen—no longer will they have the strength to do God's work in their legislation. Then they will take words out of the national anthem, and "In God We Trust" off the coins, to debase the currency; finally, it will even be illegal to have special postage stamps for Christmastime.
20. It is obvious that the Supreme Court's decision would not hold up for a minute if it were put to a vote; and that is enough to condemn it.

21. Speaking of religious toleration is all very well, but this word must be carefully defined. Toleration strictly means letting others have their way; and since the majority wishes to read the Bible in the schools, it is clear that the minority, in practicing toleration, should let them do it. Majorities have rights, too, you know—not just the psychoceramics, or crackpots.
22. Why don't they just let people pray at home and in their churches? I'll tell you why. Those defenders of school religious ceremonies will tell you they are only interested in the spiritual welfare of the average citizen, but I know better: their secret motive is simply to promulgate their own sectarian religions, gain new converts, brainwash the young. It follows that we can't put any trust in anything they suggest.
23. The first Bible reading case was in Maine, in 1854, when a Catholic pupil was expelled from public school because of her refusal to read the King James version of the Bible, and the supreme court of the state upheld the right of the school board to use any version it chose. There have been similar cases over the years, and the lesson is plain: the more the schools are used for religious purposes—which in our pluralistic religious society can never be acceptable to all believers—the more social conflict and social injustice will ensue.
24. I can only agree with Cardinal McIntyre's statement that "The decision . . . seems to interpret our Constitution as an entirely different document from the content of the original and from the spirit that obviously prevailed amongst our Founding Fathers and which stimulated their thinking regarding justice and truth.

    "The apparent flight from the principles of the natural law, from the distinction between good and bad and between right and wrong revolutionizes our philosophy and our historical background.

    "In embracing the materialistic concepts of life as the religion of man and denying the almost universal acceptance that creation was divine, and the necessary consequences flowing therefrom, the effect of the decision can only mean that our American heritages of philosophy, of religion, and of freedom are being abandoned in imitation of Soviet philosophy, of Soviet materialism, and of Soviet-regimented liberty."
25. The problem can be settled in a rational way, merely by applying logic. In Pennsylvania, for many years, every

school child has been required to hear ten verses of the Bible every day; in New York State, on the other hand, this has not been required. A comparison of the crime statistics for the two states shows no constant and significant difference. Therefore, the Bible-reading has not been of any moral benefit, as claimed by the school administrators who defend it.

chapter one | ANALYZING AN ARGUMENT

It will be convenient to have a very general term to refer to the varied pieces of language that come our way. Any series of words that are organized into sentences by the grammatical rules of some language I shall call a **discourse.** I include not only Descartes' *Discourse on Method* and Leibniz's *Discourse on Metaphysics,* but also the sermons of John Donne, *The Great Gatsby, The Politician,* "Ode to a Nightingale," the report of the Warren Commission on the assassination of President Kennedy, the broadcast of a game between the Phillies and the Mets, the Civil Rights Act of 1964.

Discourses, as these examples suggest, may differ in many ways. They may be put to many different uses by the sender (the writer or speaker) and the receiver (the reader or hearer). They may stir a frenzy of action or bore to sleep, stimulate used-car sales or waken the noblest sentiments, point out injustice or conceal it behind a screen of misrepresentation. Moreover, any particular discourse, because it is made of words and these words must have some syntactical order, presents many aspects to the curious and attentive perceiver. We may be interested in its rhythm, its wit, its beauty—its grammatical errors, its tactlessness, or its indications that the speaker is on the point of cracking up. Or we may be interested in whether or not we ought to believe it.

It is this last concern that is central to this book; all the others we shall set aside. There are books on grammar, on aesthetics, on metrics, on psychiatry, on how to be a successful after-dinner speaker, and so forth—and they deal with important aspects of discourses. But this is a book on logic. It deals with what we may call the **acceptability** of a discourse—that is, the quality in virtue of which it, or some part of it, deserves to be believed, is worthy of belief.

What makes a discourse acceptable? That is the logical question.

Sometimes, no doubt, we can give a pretty good answer without taking time to reflect. We can see right away what is wrong, or that nothing is wrong. At least, we *think* we can see this right away, though perhaps we will discover later that we were fooled. But very often when we are confronted with a particular discourse, and wonder whether it is acceptable, the answer is not forthcoming at once. We have to think. Now the first step in thinking is analysis. A discourse may be a whole, but it is a complex whole—a whole with parts. Before we can judge how well those parts fit together to make a whole that is acceptable, we must be sure we understand what those parts are and how they are actually related.

Let us begin by considering the basic working parts of a discourse, namely the individual statements of which it is composed.

§1. statements

A discourse can be considered, on one level, a string of words and, on another level, a string of sentences. (For convenience, let us include among sentences those units of discourse, such as exclamations, that some grammarians would call "nonsentences.") The second way of analyzing a discourse is the more interesting one from the point of view that we have adopted here, for it permits a distinction that is very fundamental from this point of view.

Let us begin with extreme examples, to make the distinction plain:

(1) Ouch!

(2) The average American housewife washes 24,825 dishes a year.

One very obvious difference between these two sentences is that the second one (from *The New York Times*) is either true or false, but the first one (no particular source) is neither true nor false. When we hear someone say "Ouch!" we can reply in many ways: "Too bad!" or "Be brave, little man!" or "Excuse me; I forgot I had left my teeth on the chair." But we cannot sensibly say, "That's true," or "I think you've got a point there," or "Surely you are mistaken." The exclamation shows how the speaker feels, and enables us to make some rough guesses about what has happened to him, but it is not, like the second sentence, a statement. A **statement** is a sentence, or a sentence part, that is either true or false. (Statements are also called "propositions" by some writers.)

I say "sentence part" because, of course, a complex or compound sentence may consist of more than one statement. A nonrestrictive clause that is introduced by a relative pronoun, for example, is an independent unit that can even be detached and made into a sentence on its own. "The police arrested the demonstrators, who had sat down in the street." This sentence contains two statements, and might, for some purposes, be rewritten this way: "The police arrested the demonstrators. The demonstrators had sat down in the street." I don't want to imply that the second version means exactly what the first version means, but it brings out the fact that there are two statements here.

This example points up the importance of the comma in marking the difference between a nonrestrictive and a restrictive clause. If the comma were omitted, we would have "The police arrested the demonstrators who sat down in the street." Here the clause "who sat down in the street" does not make another statement, but serves to explain more fully which of the demonstrators were arrested. Thus this sentence contains only one statement.

Whether a sentence is, or contains, a statement cannot always be decided without external help. A sentence may be incomplete. For example, if it contains pronouns that require an antecedent if they are to have a reference, then its meaning will depend on the circumstances under which it is uttered. "I was there" is not true or false taken just by itself, but when we know the speaker's name and where "there" is, the sentence is completed, and becomes a statement. The sound "Fire!" is a statement when shouted by someone who stands up at the back of a motion picture theater; but it is not a statement when shouted by an officer who has just said "Ready! Aim!" to a firing squad.

Most interrogative sentences, or questions, are neither true nor false ("How many dishes does the average American housewife wash in a year?"), though the answers will be. Most imperative sentences, or commands, are neither true nor false ("Vote for O'Reilly!"), though the reply that the command will, or will not, be obeyed is a statement. Most exclamations are neither true nor false, though true or false statements may be inferred from the fact that they are uttered ("Since you said 'Ouch!' I suppose you must have felt a sudden sharp pain").

I have said *most* of these sentences are not statements, but not that none of them are. In the first place, there are two kinds of question, direct and negative. If you ask, "Does life have a meaning?" the question is direct, and is neither true nor false. But if you ask, "Doesn't life have a meaning?" you seem to be saying—however tentatively and cautiously—that it does (that it is not absurd, or futile, or valueless). To say "Didn't I see you at the races yesterday?" is like saying, "I *think* I saw you at the races yesterday (though knowing your moral disapproval of racing, I may be mistaken)." Negative questions *include* statements. To make the statement explicit, you drop the negative and change the order of the words. "Doesn't life have a meaning?" includes the statement "Life does have a meaning."

There are also two kinds of command: simple direct commands, and complex descriptive ones. "Vote for O'Reilly, the ideal candidate" includes the statement that O'Reilly is the ideal candidate. "Don't forget your promise to take me to the circus" includes the statement "You promised to take me to the circus."

There are even two kinds of exclamation. The simple expletive is nothing more. But other exclamations contain descriptive clauses, which can be extracted and taken as statements by themselves. "How that bee stung!" goes beyond "Ouch!" by including the statement "The bee stung [me]." And "How lovely you are tonight, my dear!" contains the obvious compliment.

Questions, commands, and exclamations, then, are not, as such, statements, but some of them contain statements, and these statements may be very important to the discourses in which they appear. Sometimes it is best to draw them out and put them openly by themselves, so their full force becomes evident—even if it seems a little artificial to do so.

On the other hand, we cannot quite say that all declarative sentences are statements. There is one odd sort of declarative sentence that turns up occasionally, and it will get us into difficulties if we try to treat it as either true or false. Suppose someone asks you whether or not your car is red, and you don't happen to own a car. You don't want to say your car is red, and you don't want to say that it is *not* red, because in either case you will be committing yourself to saying that you have a car, and this is a false statement.

If your car, so to speak, is nonexistent, then the question of its color does not arise, and statements about its color are neither true nor false. The trouble with the celebrated question put to the alleged wife-beater suffers from exactly this fault, for the question "Have you stopped beating your wife?" makes its illegitimate imputation of guilt by not admitting of an answer; one who has not been beating his wife can neither stop nor continue.

So I shall make one exception to the generalization that all declarative sentences (when completed, if necessary, by information concerning their circumstances of utterance) are statements. If the subject of a sentence refers to a nonexistent thing ("In 1966, the fifty-first state of the Union had the highest proportion of Spanish-speaking citizens"), the sentence cannot be either true or false, and so is not a statement.

This is the only exception that I shall allow, however. Some declarative sentences express judgments of value, and it might be said that these are neither true nor false. "Modern art," its critics have remarked with some heat, "is fakery, and has no aesthetic worth." That is certainly a normative judgment, like judgments about right and wrong, about rights and duties, about goodness and badness. And difficult philosophical questions—too complex to take up here—can be raised about what it means, and how it might be defended or refuted. But I assume that it is a statement; it is either true or false.

Other declarative sentences are unsatisfactory in other ways as topics of discussion or as subjects of investigation. They are the ones we call "matters of opinion," as opposed to "facts," because we do not regard them as susceptible of any very final determination, and we think that anyone who professes certainty about them is guilty of dogmatism. "The cold war could be ended by unilateral disarmament," says one man; and another strongly disagrees with him. Then a third man comes along and suggests that the claim is not true, and not false, either, but simply an expression of "personal opinion." Now, this sentence is an extremely oversimplified summary of a complex matter; it is loose as it stands; and it would be very hard (perhaps even impossible) to prove, even by a direct test. But it is not senseless. There are certainly declarative sentences of which we will never know whether they are true or false (for example, "The 1,777,999th visitor to the New York World's Fair in 1965 had dark hair")—but still they *are* either true or false, whether or not we can ever know which. There may be many things wrong with saying, "The cold war could be ended by unilateral disarmament" (we shall consider these difficulties in Chapter 4), but I see no reason to deny that it is a statement.

The contrast between opinions and facts is often misleadingly put. A fact is, by definition, a true statement whose truth is judged (in calling it a fact) to be well established. It is a fact, we say, that Alaska is larger than Texas; or that eighteen tons of aspirin are consumed every day in the United States. These things can be measured. Facts are thought to be clear-cut, and decisively determinable.

Opinions are, on the other hand, by definition tentative and subject to doubt or denial or rebuttal. But to have an opinion is to believe something to be true, however hesitantly; and today's opinion may be tomorrow's fact. When I use the word "fact" here, I shall simply mean a statement that is known to be true; the point of calling something a "fact" is to contrast it in a given context with other statements that are (presumably) not known to be true *or* known to be false.

Truth and falsity are the most fundamental concepts that we use in approaching a discourse from a logical point of view. We want to know, as I said earlier, what to believe—that is, whether the discourse, or any statement it contains, is true. And the aim of our study in this book is to learn how to tell, as far as we *can* tell, whether or not a statement, or group of statements, is true.

Now, you may question the relevance of this logical point of view to every discourse. It is a single-minded interest in the truth, and makes the same demand of any discourse. It is not interested in humor, or beauty, or elegance, or eloquence, or inspiration, or any of the other valuable and delightful qualities that a discourse may have. That does not mean, of course, that *we* cannot be interested in these qualities as well, but only that the logical point of view must be distinguished from the aesthetic, the moral, the religious, the political, and all the other points of view. But aren't there many discourses that it is impossible, or inappropriate, to approach from the logical point of view? What about a lyric poem, a joke, a novel, or even a sermon or Fourth-of-July oration?

Some discourses *cannot* be approached from a logical point of view. If a discourse consists wholly of nondeclarative sentences that contain no statements, it cannot be considered logically. There are few such discourses. Or, if it consists wholly (or almost wholly) of declarative sentences concerning nonexistent persons, places, and things, then it cannot be considered logically, for it contains no statements. There are more than a few such discourses—they are works of prose fiction (though many works of prose fiction do contain some statements, often true, about real people, places, and objects).

Aside from these two exceptions, I don't see why we cannot, if we wish, ask of any discourse whether it is true or contains some truth. Keats's "Ode to a Nightingale," for example, not only beguiles us with a deep look into the dramatic speaker's mind and heart, but adumbrates some general reflections on man and society, on the nature of life, and art. You may say that these are not stated explicitly, and this is an important point, which we shall have occasion to deal with more systematically in Chapter 5. Where there are implicit statements, presumably we can discuss their truth or falsity, if we have a mind to.

But though this response is possible, it may not be *appropriate*. This distinction has important implications for aesthetics and literary criticism, which we cannot follow out here. There is a significant difference (though perhaps no sharp line) between those discourses that seem to invite, or demand, or require, or encourage, or promise a reward for, an approach from the logical point of view, and those that do not. The distinction may be complicated, but one element of it seems fairly plain: the discourse to which a logical consideration is appropriate is assertive discourse.

To *utter* a statement, in a broad sense, is to produce or exhibit it in some fashion—to pronounce the words, or write them on the blackboard or in the sand or across the sky. To **assert** a statement is to utter it in such a manner as to show (or pretend) that you believe it and to invite your hearer or reader to believe it. An assertion, in short, evinces belief and solicits belief. It may be false; it may even be deliberately false and designed to deceive; but it is still an assertion if it claims or purports to be true, if it is offered as true.

Assertion is probably the usual and normal mode of utterance: when you answer a question about the way to get out of Boston, or write a letter applying for a job, your statements will be assertions. The tone of voice, the air of sincerity and seriousness, the importance of the circumstances or the purpose at hand, the conventions of certain types of discourse (such as the sermon or the speech on a ceremonial occasion), and many other features of a discourse are cues to assertiveness—they make it evident that the statement is an assertion. A statement made under ordinary circumstances will be, and will be taken to be, an assertion, unless a warning is given. You can't say, "I wrote a vigorous letter to the newspaper protesting the Urban Redevelopment Authority's plans to tear down the houses on my block, but I wasn't making an assertion." If the letter, as printed, was a vigorous protest, then it showed, or at least pretended, belief on the writer's part and invited the reader to share that belief.

There are, however, ways of removing the assertiveness of an utterance, for special purposes. Sometimes the occasion sets the scene: when people sit around telling jokes to each other, they all understand that the statements ("Two astronauts landed on Venus, and when they opened the hatch . . .") are not supposed to be facts. We can put a statement into indirect discourse ("Henry Ford believed that history is bunk") or between quotation marks ("Henry Ford said, 'History is bunk' "). We can utter the statement in a sarcastic or ironic tone. Or we can simply assert, by one statement, that other statements are not asserted. The newspaper publisher may label part of a page "advertisement" if he thinks the advertisement is in danger of being taken for a news story; this is his way of indicating that *he* is not asserting the statements in the advertisement, even if the advertiser is. On the other hand, the radio or television announcer does his best to make his utterances seem like genuine assertions ("This is the best bargain that Sonny ['Hole-in-the-head'] Stein has ever offered"), and his producer uses a burst of theme music to indicate that what follows—the drama itself—is a tale, not necessarily to be believed. To label a book "a novel" or "a ghost story" is to say that it is a work of fiction, and that any resemblance to actual persons, living or dead, does not make it a piece of history or biography.

Because assertiveness depends on so many conditions, which may exist in various degrees, there is no sharp line between asserted and unasserted statements. Sometimes you can't tell whether someone is serious or is kidding. Consider, for example, the famous Orson Welles broadcast of H. G. Wells' science-fiction novel, when thousands of people leaped into their cars and drove headlong out of New Jersey under the impression that the state had been invaded by Martians.

A discourse that consists of, or contains, assertions may be called an **assertive discourse.** And it is this sort of discourse that we are to be concerned with in this book: editorials rather than lyric poems, magazine articles rather than short stories, campaign speeches rather than dramas. For these are the discourses that we are constrained to approach from a logical point of view, because they are most likely to reward our search for knowledge when they are true and to lead us dangerously astray when they are false. Therefore, they are the ones that it is most important to think straight about.

From this point on, unless explicit exception is made, let it be understood that when I speak of discourses, I shall be referring to assertive discourses.

A Check-up Quiz Which of these sentences either are or include statements? If part of a sentence is a statement, rewrite that part as a sentence.

1. STEE-RIKE!
2. Do you know why Denver is called "the mile-high city"?
3. Come to me all ye who are weary and heavy-laden, and I will give you rest.
4. Calories don't count!
5. Who is Sylvia? What is she, that all the swains commend her?
6. Tomorrow's weather: increasing cloudiness and a 47 per cent probability of precipitation.
7. There is no one on whom the President depends more than those advisers who meet with him frequently during periods of crisis.
8. What a strange man he is!
9. Never send to know for whom the bell tolls.
10. Extremism in the defense of liberty is no vice.

For Further Study Morris Cohen and Ernest Nagel, *An Introduction to Logic and Scientific Method,* Ch. 2, Sec. 1. New York: Harcourt, Brace & World, Inc., 1934. L. M. Myers, *American English,* Part III. Englewood Cliffs, N.J.: Prentice-Hall, Inc., 1952. David Mitchell, *An Introduction to Logic,* Ch. 5. London: Hutchinson University Library, 1962.

§2. exposition and argument

The first question—or one of the first questions—that we must ask when we find ourselves confronted with a discourse is whether or not it is assertive. If it is, then the second question is this: Which of the two basic types of assertive discourse is it?

For example, you might pick up the report of the President's Commission on Registration and Voter Participation (November 1963), and read:

> American elections have not always been characterized by low voter participation. Turnout was consistently high in the later 1800's, with a peak of 85.8 per cent of adult enfranchised males voting in 1876. Yet in the early 1900's, voter participation declined steadily, dwindling to 44.2 per cent in 1920. It never reached 60 per cent in the era of Franklin D. Roosevelt, and has only slightly exceeded that percentage in the past decade.
>
> Still fewer people vote in congressional elections. Since 1920, the national turnout in nonpresidential election years has never touched 50 per cent, ranging from a low of 30.1 per cent in 1926 to a high of 48.9 per cent in 1962 . . . [p. 6].

This passage, as you see, consists of a series of assertions, strung together because they are about the same topic. The tone is straightforward and fairly detached; the facts are simply presented for your inspection.

But now read on in a later part of the report:

> The Commission supports permanent, personal registration. Some registration systems force people who vote only in Presidential elections to re-register every year they plan to vote. Such provisions make little sense. It is unreasonable for a would-be voter, who thinks he is still registered, to be told on Election Day that his name has been removed from the roster for failure to vote in the last election and that, as a result, he cannot vote . . . [p. 37].
>
> . . . The Commission is not impressed by the argument that only those who can read and write or have a sixth-grade education should have a voice in determining their future. This is the right of every citizen no matter what his formal education or possession of material wealth. The Commission recommends that no literacy test interfere with the basic right to suffrage . . . [p. 40].

Here the assertions are not only presented; they are connected in a new way. Some of the statements are offered as *reasons* for other statements. The connections are not explicitly marked, but it is quite apparent that the writer is doing more than simply stating ("The Commission supports . . ." "The Commission is not impressed by the argument that . . ."). And with the help of a single word, "therefore," we can bring out this feature of the two paragraphs:

> It is unreasonable for a would-be voter . . . to be told on Election Day that his name has been removed from the roster . . . [*Therefore,* there should be] permanent, personal registration.

[The right to vote] is the right of every citizen. [*Therefore,* there should be] no literacy test.

When a discourse not only makes assertions but also asserts that some of those assertions are reasons for others, we shall call it an **argument.** Assertive discourse that does not give reasons we shall call **exposition.** Note that it is not a question of whether or not the assertions are *arguable* or debatable. It's true that the rejection of literacy tests in the second passage above was dissented from by some of the Commission members. But we might also want to challenge the correctness of the figures in the first passage, if we happened to have superior evidence. The difference is that in the second passage, the statement that there should be no literacy tests is actually *argued:* that is, reasons are given to support it and make it acceptable.

The word "argument" is used here in a careful way. In common speech, it often means a dispute or altercation, as when someone says, "Let's not get into an argument." In the language of logic, it means simply a discourse that includes the claim that one statement ought to be believed because one or more other statements are true. To believe one statement because you think it is well supported by another is to make an *inference.* And making inferences is *reasoning.* Reasoning is a mental process; the argument is its verbal record.

The word "exposition" is used here in a broad but useful sense. Books on rhetoric often classify discourses as "exposition," "argument," "description," and "narration." Some description and narration, as in poems and stories, are of course not assertive discourse. But within the category of assertive discourse, it seems more logical to let the word "exposition" cover all discourse that asserts but does not argue. Then *description* will be a special kind of exposition. It is exposition that deals, in the main, with fairly concrete matters: we describe a sunset, a mugger, a lost dog, an automobile accident. *Narration* will be a special kind of description. We narrate a happening, or a series of happenings: a mugging, a baseball game, a trip, or the rise of an executive from rags to riches.

Arguments come in all degrees of complexity, but the minimum requirement, as in the examples just given, is that there be at least two assertions, plus the claim, implicit or explicit, that one logically supports the other. "Then conquer we must, for our cause it is just," says one currently popular version of "The Star-Spangled Banner."

That is an argument, of the simplest possible form. The statement before the word "for" is the *conclusion:* that is, the statement we are invited to accept. The statement after the word "for" is the *reason* that is supposed to support the conclusion. The word "for" itself, which signals that an argument is in process, we shall call a *logical indicator*. And this two-statement argument can be set up in this way:

Our cause is just.
Therefore:
Conquer we must.

Reason; *therefore,* conclusion.

Francis Scott Key's original words were "Then conquer we must when our cause it is just" (when Congress adopted this song as the national anthem, in 1931, it never got around to making clear which is the official version, and so numerous ones have been used). It is important to see that, though the change may seem slight, the original version is not an argument at all. It is hypothetical or conditional; it does not say that our cause is just and so we must conquer, but only that we must conquer if ever and whenever our cause is just. To make the point clear, let us recast it as "If *our cause is just,* then *we must conquer.*" This cannot be an argument, because it makes only one assertion. Three statements are involved, one of which contains the other two—which is more than enough statements to make an argument. They are: (1) "Our cause is just," (2) "We must conquer," and (3) "If our cause is just, then we must conquer." But neither the first nor the second statement is *asserted* in this context, and therefore there is only one assertion, and no argument.

In prose that is written with some care, it is the logical indicators that usually (though not always) tell us that the discourse is an argument, and also tell us which way the argument is going—whether from reason to conclusion or from conclusion back to the reason. We must above all be alert to them. I have chosen "therefore" as perhaps the plainest and most direct logical indicator, and it will be convenient to use this one whenever we find it necessary to set out an argument in formal fashion for very close scrutiny. But there are many other words and phrases in our language that do the same job of signaling that inference is afoot and pointing out the direction in which it is moving.

Each of the following words or phrases, like "therefore," usually shows that the statement that follows is a conclusion:

hence . . .
thus . . .
so . . .
implies that . . .
entails that . . .
which shows that . . .
proves that . . .
indicates that . . .
consequently . . .
allows us to conclude that . . .
we may deduce that . . .
points to the conclusion that . . .
suggests very strongly that . . .
leads me to believe that . . .
bears out my point that . . .
from which it follows that . . .

And each of the following words or phrases usually shows that the statement that follows is a reason:

for . . .
since . . .
because . . .
for the reason that . . .
in view of the fact that . . .
on the correct supposition that . . .
assuming, as we may, that . . .
may be inferred from the fact that . . .
may be deduced from . . .
as shown by . . .
as indicated by . . .
as is substantiated by . . .

This does not pretend to be a complete list of logical indicators, but it does contain most of the words and phrases that can do the job of marking an argument. Nor do I mean to imply that they are all identical in meaning. Each has its subtle individual uses; but there is a particular logical function that they can all serve, and this function can be represented explicitly by substituting "therefore" for these other logical indicators—except that when we substitute it for the ones in the second list, we must of course turn the two assertions around. ("We should turn the clocks ahead, *because* it is the last Sunday in April" becomes "It is the last Sunday in April; *therefore*, we should turn the clocks ahead.")

The main difficulty in recognizing a discourse as an argument appears when the logical indicators are omitted. Look again at the two arguments selected from the report of the President's Commission. How did we know that they were arguments? The first one starts out in a tone of firm assertiveness. "The Commission supports permanent, personal registration." We naturally ask why, and then we look to see whether the statements that follow could at least plausibly be offered by the writer to back up his first assertion. That doesn't mean that the argument will necessarily turn out to be a good one, but only that from the general tone and the logical relationships between the statements, we can take the passage as an argument. This is even clearer in the second paragraph, which begins by stating that the Commission rejects an argument; after that, we are free to take the next statements as the Commission's reasons for rejecting that argument.

In cases like these, where the logical indicator is left out and yet we are given other clues to the nature of the discourse, we cannot say that the passage *states* that one assertion is a reason for another, but only that it *suggests* this connection. (This term will be clarified later, in Chapter 5.) There is an implicit "therefore" (or, in reverse, an implicit "because"). If the hint is too subtle or vague, we cannot be sure whether we are confronted with an argument or with pure exposition. If a writer doesn't take the trouble to provide clear guideposts so that we can see when he claims to be reasoning and when he does not, we ourselves may not find it worth the trouble to try to follow him. But, in our own writing and speaking, we can bear in mind the importance of being clear about this important matter. Sometimes it may seem a bit tedious to sprinkle your essay with "therefore" and "since" and other logical indicators. And, indeed, on rereading the essay you may be able to omit some of them where the context makes clear that you are giving a reason. But when you are in doubt, be explicit.

Another borderline case is the discourse that hovers on the verge of coming to a conclusion without quite coming out with it. The statements may be highly tendentious, and quite clearly pointed in a certain direction. And in that case we are justified in saying that there is an implicit conclusion, and even stating it in our own words for the purpose of examining it. When a writer says, "The proposed location of the expressway destroys an irreplaceable wildlife refuge and a historic building, and it is both less efficient and less economical than the alternate routes," it is no very dangerous leap to supply the implicit conclusion, "The proposed route should not be adopted." Certainly we must be cautious about imputing to others conclusions they may not wish to draw, but we must also be on the lookout for conclusions that are merely hinted at or insinuated. For sometimes these are the most influential ones.

In this book we shall be especially (though not exclusively) concerned with arguments. That covers more ground than you might think, for there is hardly any long passage of sustained exposition that doesn't move over into argument, and most of the discourses that affect our thinking about important matters (about our children, our government, our career, our religion) are full of argument—sound or unsound.

In this book we shall be interested in whether an argument is a sound one—that is, whether its reasons are good reasons, or, to put it more carefully, *how* good they are. When a reason is very good, we say that an argument amounts to a *proof*. And a critical reader or listener is one who makes an effort, when he encounters an argument about things that really matter, to find out whether or not that argument comes close to being a proof. To encourage and assist that effort is the main purpose of this book.

A Check-up Quiz Some of the following passages are arguments. What is the conclusion, and what is the logical indicator, in each?

1. Since the speaker has refused his support, the supporters of the bill will probably not succeed in getting it on the floor of the House.
2. I don't think that a national health-insurance program would necessarily be financially ruinous, because the United States already pays a higher percentage of its gross national income for medical care than either England or Sweden, though the average health is lower.
3. There is no chance that he can escape a fine this time. It is his fourth arrest for speeding.
4. There is a slight chance that he can escape a fine this time. But in any case he will no doubt be arrested again for the same offense.

5. In the light of available evidence of discrimination by the voting registrars, it seems obvious that the officeholders are not truly representative.
6. Since he finished his freshman year at college, he has become aggressively skeptical.
7. The town declined into poverty because the remaining ore was so low-grade that it was no longer profitable to mine it.
8. If it is true that the proposed highway will destroy irreplaceable historic buildings, then it should not be built.
9. Fly now! We will bill you later.
10. He bought the gun. He must have intended to kill.

For Further Study Stephen F. Barker, *The Elements of Logic,* pp. 7–15. New York: McGraw-Hill Book Company, 1965. Richard B. Angell, *Reasoning and Logic,* Ch. 1. New York: Appleton-Century-Crofts, Inc., 1964.

§3. getting the point

When we recognize that a discourse is an argument and wish to look into it further from a logical point of view, the next step is to discover what it is arguing *for* and what it is arguing *from.* In a complex argument, some statements will be used to support other statements, and at the same time will themselves be supported by still other statements. The logical structure of the argument consists of a network of these relationships. And when the structure is either too complex to be immediately apparent or else is obscured by poor writing, it can be made clear by diagramming the argument.

Consider, for example the following passage that might appear in a college newspaper (and no doubt would elicit some equally decided disagreement):

> Do college students have the right to academic freedom, like their teachers? We believe they do. For freedom to learn is the necessary counterpart to freedom to teach. Consequently, students must have the right to join voluntary associations; they must be permitted to

> invite any speakers they wish to visit the campus; and they must be allowed to express their views on controversial matters just like any other citizen. Without freedom to learn, the whole purpose of an institution of higher education is frustrated.

This argument, as it stands, is comparatively simple, and most thoughtful readers would be impatient to get on with the task of weighing its soundness—either to point out gaps and weaknesses in the argument, or to come to its defense with further support. But let us hold that critical spirit in abeyance for the moment, and make quite sure that we know exactly what the argument is.

First, we want to know what is the *point of the argument.* Unless the argument happens to go around in a circle—a possibility that we shall consider in the following chapter—there will be at least one assertion that is supported by reasons but is not itself used as a reason to support any others. These assertions are the *final conclusions,* and they are the point of the argument. On the other hand, there will be at least one assertion that is presented as a reason, but is not itself a conclusion from any other reasons. These assertions are the *basic reasons* in the argument—the foundation on which it rests.

When we look over the little argument for student academic freedom, we do not encounter many difficulties in grasping its structure. But a few questions arise, and they are worth some consideration, for they are not atypical.

We may begin by looking for the logical indicators, to see how much they tell us explicitly about the logical structure. There are two: "for" and "consequently." Next we must get clearly in mind the actual ingredients of the argument—the individual assertions that make it up. There are five sentences, of which the fourth is a compound one with three separable parts. Sentences 1 and 2 obviously go together; together they amount to a single assertion, that students have the right to academic freedom. Let us call this Assertion 1. Sentence 3 is introduced by "for," and thus is offered as a reason for Assertion 1. Let us call it Assertion 2.

If the argument consisted only of these three sentences, it could be very simply diagrammed, for there would be one reason and one conclusion. We would first prepare the text, separating the individual assertions by brackets, numbering them, and underlining or italicizing the logical indicators.

> ① [Do college students have the right to academic freedom, like their teachers? We believe they do.] *For* ② [freedom to learn is the necessary counterpart to freedom to teach.]

And, using an arrow to mean "therefore," we could diagram this argument this way:

Now let us look at the rest of the argument. Sentence 4 can be separated into Assertions 3, 4, and 5. Sentence 5 is Assertion 6.

> ① [Do college students have the right to academic freedom, like their teachers? We believe they do.] *For,* ② [freedom to learn is the necessary counterpart to freedom to teach.] *Consequently,* ③ [students must have the right to join voluntary associations;] ④ [they must be permitted to invite any speakers they wish to visit the campus;] and ⑤ [they must be allowed to express their views on controversial matters just like any other citizen.] ⑥ [Without freedom to learn, the whole purpose of an institution of higher education is frustrated.]

One thing might puzzle us at once—what is the relationship between the two logical indicators? The "for" shows that Assertion 1 is a conclusion from Assertion 2. The "consequently" shows that Assertion 2 is a reason for Assertions 3, 4, and 5. What, then, is the relationship between Assertion 1 and Assertions 3, 4, and 5?

The fourth sentence seems to spell out in more detail what the writer conceives student academic freedom to be; it says again what the first two sentences say, but adds further specifications. It seems best to regard Assertions 3, 4, and 5 as a consequence of Assertion 1 —even though they are so close in meaning that this inference doesn't go far.

Another question arises about Assertion 6. It evidently fits into the scheme, but there is no logical indicator to tell us where. We have to stop and think about its meaning, in relation to the other assertions, and especially to note that it picks up a phrase ("freedom to learn") from Sentence 3. It is best understood as a (somewhat tardy) support of Assertion 2: without freedom to learn, the purpose of higher education would be frustrated; *therefore,* freedom to learn is the necessary counterpart to freedom to teach. Of course this inference rests on several assumptions that would have to be made explicit and carefully examined in order to make sure that the argument is a really good one. But that is not our job now—before we can see what the argument lacks, and needs, we must see what it has.

Having sorted out the elements of the argument, and discerned its structure, we can diagram it in this way:

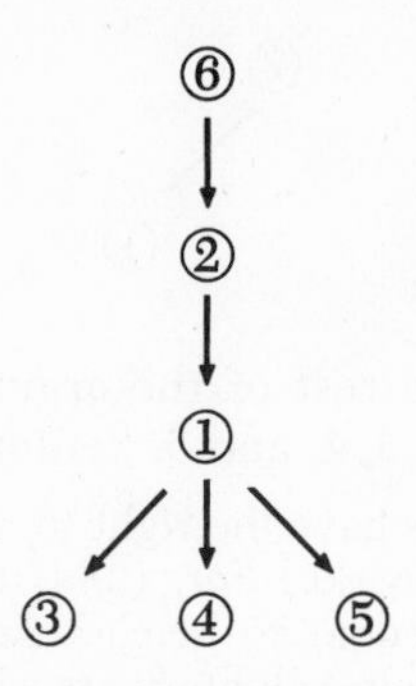

There is one basic reason and there are three final conclusions.

It is certainly not necessary to diagram every argument you meet. The diagram method is something to fall back on when you have to make an effort to see how an argument hangs together. Some practice with the method should help to sharpen your ability to grasp the structure of an argument quickly and clearly. And it may also help you to give your own arguments a firmer and solider structure, and to make their structure clearer when you write them out.

Consider the following paragraph, which might turn up in a variety of circumstances:

> Despite all the fancy pseudoscientific science-fiction talk about taking vacations on the moon and Mars, and colonizing and mining them, a realistic consideration of the actual situation leads to the conclusion that the exploration of space is futile, as far as any benefit it may confer upon earthlings is concerned. And it is also wasteful of resources that could be put to better use on Earth, since the five billion dollars or more that it will take to put a man on the moon for a few hours could go a long way to eliminate slums, conquer disease, and raise the standard of living in underdeveloped countries. We won't succeed in getting our excess population to live on the moon until there is overcrowding on the Himalayan Mountains and at the South Pole—which are far more comfortable places to live than the moon is. And there are no minerals on the moon that we could ship to Earth cheaply enough to make it worthwhile—which bears out my earlier point. Finally, how can any scientific advantage be obtained from space exploration? As Dr. Vannevar Bush has said, a man "can do no more than an instrument; in fact he can do less."

It's easy to see that this is an argument, and that it has a point;

but there is something confused and confusing about the way the argument develops. Can we make it clearer and more perspicuous? Let us begin by diagramming the relationships among its various assertions.

There are a few questions to answer, and decisions to make, before we can put the argument in condition for diagramming. First, where does it begin? Even if a discourse contains an argument, it may be that not all of its clauses and sentences are part of the argument. The argument consists only of those assertions that are reasons or conclusions or both. Now the first twenty-seven words of this passage are preliminary, introductory—clarifying and useful, no doubt, but not necessary to the argument. The next phrase "leads to the conclusion that" is a logical indicator. Second, the last clause in the fourth sentence, "which bears out my earlier point," is another logical indicator, which is rather indefinite; but the "point" referred to seems to be the first one, that "the exploration of space is futile." Third, the question in the fifth sentence seems to be rhetorical, and therefore amounts to a negative assertion. Fourth—and most surprisingly—the actual conclusion of this argument seems to be implicit, rather than explicit, and perhaps we should supply it in parentheses, just to make the structure complete. For the drive of the whole passage is evidently to dissuade us from spending huge sums to explore space, and the conclusion strongly suggested is something like, "The government should not undertake large-scale space exploration."

Bearing in mind these considerations, we may set up the argument as follows:

> . . . *the conclusion* [*is*] *that:* ① [the exploration of space is futile, as far as any benefit to earthlings is concerned.] And ② [it is also wasteful of resources that could be put to better use on Earth,] *because* ③ [the five billion dollars or more that it will take to put a man on the moon for a few hours could go a long way to eliminate slums, conquer disease, and raise the standard of living in underdeveloped countries.] ④ [We won't succeed in getting our excess population to live on the moon until there is overcrowding on the Himalayan Mountains and at the South Pole—] ⑤ [which are far more comfortable places to live than the moon is.] And ⑥ [there are no minerals on the moon that we could ship to Earth cheaply enough to make it worthwhile]—*which bears out my earlier point.* Finally, ⑦ [how can any scientific advantage be obtained from space exploration?] ⑧ [As Dr. Vannevar Bush has said, a man "can do no more than an instrument; in fact he can do less."] ⑨ [(The government should not undertake large-scale space exploration.)]

When an argument is somewhat complicated, and the relationships within it are not wholly explicit, there may be some room for dispute about what the structure actually is. But this argument probably lines up in this fashion—with two main branches leading to the implicit conclusion:

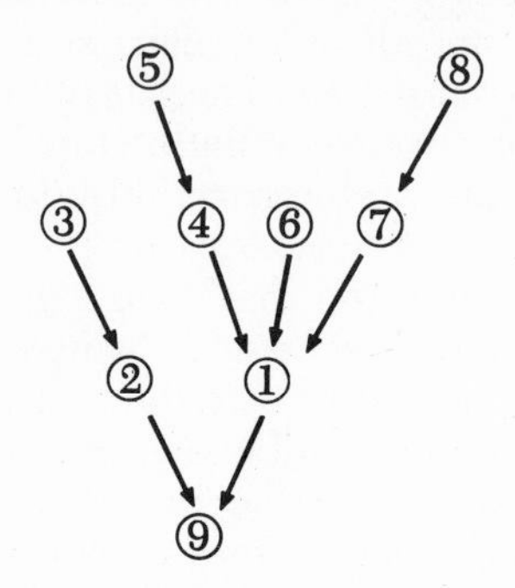

If this is the way the argument shapes up, the diagram gives us valuable guidance in rewriting the argument to present it more clearly. The writer's main problem, in formulating an argument, is to insure as far as he can that the order and syntax of his prose reflect and emphasize the logical relationships of the argument. And there are two rules that ought to be kept in mind.

The first is the *Rule of Grouping*. When you have to present several reasons for the same conclusion, they should be kept as close together as possible, and their similar logical status should be conveyed by a parallel grammatical position. The logical force of the reasons will be dissipated if they are scattered about, with other, irrelevant matters in between. It may not matter (or if it does, it will matter because of other considerations) whether the reasons come before or after the conclusion, but they should all go in a body, and they should go as close to the conclusion as possible. By separating Assertion 1 from Assertions 4, 6, and 7, and by separating Assertion 4 from Assertions 6 and 7, the passage on space exploration violates this rule.

The second is the *Rule of Direction*. When you have a series of assertions, one being a reason for the next, and the next for the next, and so forth, then the argument should move in a single direction. Again, it may not matter (or not much) whether you bring them forth in the order one-two-three or the order three-two-one, but keep the argument moving in the same direction. Otherwise, you may send your reader off on a wild-goose chase and discourage him before he manages to figure out what is the real logical order disguised behind the rhetorical order. By leaving us to draw the conclusion (Assertion 9) ourselves, at the end, and putting the two reasons for it early in the passage (Assertions 1 and 2), the passage above violates this rule, though in general it moves from conclusions back to reasons (from 2 to 3, from 1 to 4 to 5, and so forth).

If the passage is rewritten in accordance with these two rules, it is almost certain to be improved. Of course there are several ways of doing this, and when I suggest one of them I do not mean it to be taken as the only model, or even as the best possible version. Because of the general polemical tone of the passage, and in order to preserve the quite strong beginning, it seems best to retain the general direction of the thought, while tidying up the relationships between reasons and conclusions. Some writers would consider it a kind of last resort to introduce numbers to mark main points. But when you have, as in this example, two main reasons for the conclusion, and they must be separated to some extent because of the number of subordinate reasons related to each, it is permissible to tag the main reasons for the reader. Sometimes this is almost unavoidable if you want to be clear. Here is a possible version, then:

> Despite all the fancy pseudoscientific science-fiction talk about taking vacations on the moon and Mars, and colonizing and mining them, anyone who considers the problem realistically will conclude that the government should not undertake large-scale space exploration. In the first place, it cannot confer much benefit on earthlings. Its economic value is doubtful, for two reasons. We won't succeed in getting our excess population to live on the moon until there is overcrowding on the Himalayan Mountains and at the South Pole—which are far more comfortable places to live than the moon is. And there are no minerals on the moon that we could ship to Earth cheaply enough to make it worthwhile. Even its scientific value is insignificant, for, as Dr. Vannevar Bush has said, in space exploration a man "can do no more than an instrument; in fact he can do less." In the second place, the attempt to send men up in space is wasteful of resources that could be put to better use on Earth, since the five billion dollars or more that it will take to put a man on the moon for a few hours could go a long way to

eliminate slums, conquer disease, and raise the standard of living in underdeveloped countries.

A Check-up Quiz What is the point of each of the following arguments? If the point is not explicitly stated, put it in your own words.

1. When we know that the automobile has killed more Americans than all the wars we have ever fought in, isn't it obvious that safety devices—such as seat belts and padded dashboards—should be required equipment on all new cars?
2. John Dewey says, truly, that "As long as art is the beauty parlor of civilization, neither art nor civilization is secure." The liberation of energies, the refinement of perception, the nurture of creative imagination, that works of art produce when they deal with basic human experience, are indispensable to the highest development of the human spirit.
3. In view of the author's well-known commitment to pacifist causes, and notwithstanding his present popularity with left-wing groups, his views on the present crisis are not worthy of acceptance, and consequently (there being, it should also be observed, considerable evidence of his lack of information) he should not be invited to take part in the discussion, even if (as I agree it should be) the point of view should be represented.
4. Only those who are in the poverty group themselves can really know what it's like to be poor. Unless the Antipoverty Steering Committee contains some people who know this, how can it be effective in carrying out the programs supported by the Office of Economic Opportunity?
5. You have asked for a letter of recommendation supporting Mr. Dash for the position. Though he has been reasonably faithful in performing his duties here, he has not been an outstanding success. Some inward block seems to prevent him from carrying projects through to a final stage, and his general lack of originality and inability to think clearly and to the point have been some handicap to him in his work. Likeable though he is as a person, he tends to bog down unless his supervisor prods him and gives him frequent help.

For Further Study Richard B. Angell, *Reasoning and Logic*, Ch. 5. New York: Appleton-Century-Crofts, Inc., 1964.

§4. induction and deduction

Whether or not an argument is a good one depends ultimately on its structure. Consequently, before you can judge an argument accurately you must discover what that structure is, or, in other words, what kind of argument you have to deal with.

There are several ways of classifying arguments, and these classifications yield many varieties—for example, arguments involving definition, or causality, or comparison and contrast, or an appeal to authority. But the most fundamental classification is that which divides all arguments into two jointly exhaustive, and mutually exclusive, categories: inductive and deductive.

There are a number of complications in this distinction that a more advanced treatment of logic would have to introduce and discuss, but for our purposes they can be set aside. The essential thing about an argument, as has been said, is that it aims to get someone to accept a certain assertion as true, and that it does this by providing some support for that assertion—that is, some other assertion on the basis of which a reasonable person would be inclined, at least to some extent, to accept the conclusion. There are two possibilities here. Either the argument gives a *conclusive* reason for the conclusion—a reason so strong that anyone who accepts it is bound to accept the conclusion—or it gives a reason that falls short of conclusiveness, though lending some degree of support to the conclusion. This is the difference that is required for the distinction between the two basic kinds of argument.

To understand what is special about a deductive argument, we must grasp the nature of **logical implication** (or, as it is sometimes called, *logical entailment*). Consider the following brief argument:

> *A* has the right to walk on *B*'s sidewalk;
> *Therefore, B* has a duty not to interfere with *A*'s walking on his sidewalk.

We are not concerned with the question whether or not these two statements are true, but only with the relation between them. If the first statement is true, then the second *must* be true, for it follows necessarily from the first. To put it another way, it is logically impossible for the first statement to be true and the second one false: *A*'s right with respect to *B* is inherently connected with *B*'s duty with respect to *A*. In that case, let us say that the first statement implies, or entails, the second.

Contrast this argument with another that has the same reason, but a different conclusion:

> *A* has the right to walk on *B*'s sidewalk;
> *Therefore, B* has the right to walk on *A*'s sidewalk.

Here, as we can see after a little thought, the conclusion does not follow necessarily from the reason. Of course the reason has some force, and if this is all we know of the situation we must say that the reason (assuming it to be true) lends a degree of likelihood, or probability, to the conclusion. But suppose *A*'s sidewalk has just been repaired, and the cement is still wet; then *A* might have the right to walk on *B*'s sidewalk, without *B*'s having the right to walk on *A*'s sidewalk. Of course, if we add further statements to the reason, specifying that *A* and *B* are both residents of the same block, and their sidewalks are in the same condition, and no court has enjoined *B* from using *A*'s sidewalk, and so forth, then this second argument will take on the character of a necessary inference. That is, the reason will come to imply the conclusion. But as it stands, this is not quite the case.

When an argument moves from reason to conclusion with logical necessity, it is a deductive argument. And it is said to be **valid.** But even if an argument does not succeed in being valid, it may still be a deductive argument if it *claims* to be valid. For example, suppose the store clerk says:

> You have purchased two pairs of socks, and they are on sale, three for $1.69. $1.15, please.

He claims to be doing arithmetic, and reaching his result by calculation. If the result were correct, the argument would be valid (like any correct piece of mathematical reasoning). Thus, though he has made a mistake in his calculation, we can say that the argument implicitly claims to be valid, and therefore that the argument is deductive (but unsound).

A **deductive argument,** then, is an argument that either is one, or claims to be one, whose conclusion follows necessarily from the reason. All arguments that are not deductive are **inductive.** Every single reason that is given for every single conclusion in an argument can be considered to be an argument in its own right, and every reason is either a deductive or an inductive reason for its particular conclusion.

In a deductive argument, the statements that make up the reason are called the **premises** of the argument. Two premises that go closely together and depend on each other for help in supporting the conclusion are considered to constitute a single reason. For example, if someone argues:

> Unions are a good thing, *and*
> The closed shop promotes unions,
> *Therefore it must be the case that* the closed shop is a good thing,

he seems clearly to be claiming that his conclusion follows necessarily from the premises, and the two premises together evidently are inseparable parts of the same reason.

It is not always obvious that an argument is deductive, since the claim to validity may not be put forward very firmly. Certain words, such as "necessarily," "it follows that," "consequently," "implies," generally make a strong claim for the argument, and may signal that it is deductive. Sometimes the form of the argument can be recognized as deductive—for example, if it moves from general statements down to more limited ones (from an assumption about unions in general to a conclusion about this union, or from an assumption about unions in general to a conclusion about unions in closed shops). As you study deduction further in the following chapter, you will become more adept at recognizing certain common deductive forms. And in any case, whenever you wish, you can treat an argument as deductive, tentatively—that is, you can look to see whether in fact it is valid. If it is, it is deductive—and that is an important thing to know about it. If it falls short of validity, you can always turn to the next inquiry, which is to see how much inductive support it gives its conclusion.

In an inductive argument, the statements that make up the reason are called the **evidence.** They are alleged to be facts from which the conclusion is *induced.* A typical inductive argument marshals its evidence—whatever it has—this way:

> In what part of the earth did mankind originate? Until recently, it was universally believed to be Asia. But startling discoveries, and bold theorizing, have given us another, and more probable, answer: Africa. First there was Raymond Dart's discovery in the Transvaal (1924) of a creature midway between man and ape, with human teeth but an apelike brain—*Australopithecus africanus* (South African ape). The huge numbers of pieces of bone that Dart turned up in the great Makapan cave in the northern Transvaal give the important clue. For they are deliberately flaked and fashioned into sharp tools. The prehuman creatures of the Makapan cave must have been the first to use tools, and in using them their hands developed the parts of their brain

> that control dexterity. This was what brought man—*Homo sapiens*—into being. It made him walk upright so that he was free to use the tools, and it gave him higher intelligence.

The logical indicator does not always make clear that the argument is inductive, nor does it always show exactly what degree of strength is claimed for the argument. Phrases like "probably," "most likely," "very probably," "almost certainly," and "apparently," mark an argument as inductive, and give a rough indication of how much is being claimed. The strength of an inductive argument is a matter of degree—not, like validity, an either/or matter. As we shall see more clearly and fully in Chapter 3, it is a question of both the quantity and the quality of the evidence, which may merely lend a slight degree of acceptability to the conclusion or may place it beyond a reasonable doubt.

As will become clear in the course of the next two chapters, the difference between success and failure in reasoning hinges on the relationship between the reason and the conclusion. If the reason is to lend some support to the conclusion, there must be a logical connection between them that justifies or warrants the inference. The business of the logician is to study such connections and to reduce them as far as possible to rules. These are **rules of inference.** With the help of such rules we can say whether a particular argument succeeds or fails because it obeys or disobeys the relevant rule. An argument is a good one only if it can justify itself by a rule of inference. If it gets some plausibility by seeming to conform to some rule of inference, but actually violates that rule, then it is said to be fallacious, or to commit a **fallacy.**

In the course of this book we shall encounter a number of fallacies, and they are important to notice, if we want to escape the temptation to fall into many common traps of reasoning. But of course we are not only interested in what might be called the pathology of reasoning—the ways in which it may go astray. The purpose of studying, and mastering, the main rules of correct reasoning is to recognize good reasons when we meet them, and to require of ourselves that we have good reasons for what we want to say.

A Check-up Quiz Which of the following arguments are deductive, and which are inductive?

1. She uses a henna rinse; therefore, she must have some gray hair.

2. The population of the city has grown from 45,000 to 60,000 in the past decade; therefore, there has been an increase of 33⅓ per cent.
3. It rained the last three times we planned to have a picnic; therefore, if we plan a picnic today, it will rain.
4. Johnny developed an itchy rash on his arms and legs the day after he was playing in the woods: therefore, he has poison ivy.
5. Henry is an executive; therefore, Henry's wife is an executive's wife.
6. Mars has two satellites, the Earth only one; therefore, Mars has more satellites than the Earth.
7. From all accounts, he is loyal, hard-working, intelligent, able, cool, judicious, and cooperative; therefore, he will be a success at the job.
8. His fingerprints are on the gun; therefore, he handled the gun.
9. The mayor has promised to see that the stadium is built in the North End; therefore, he will see that it is built in the North End.
10. Sally is older than Susan, and Susan is older than Sadie; therefore, Sally is older than Sadie.

For Further Study Stephen F. Barker, *The Elements of Logic,* Ch. 1. New York: McGraw-Hill Book Company, 1965.

OUTLINE-SUMMARY: chapter one

A sentence, or part of a sentence, that is either true or false is a *statement*. And a statement is an *assertion* when it is uttered in such a way as to evince and invite belief that it is true.

A *discourse* is a sentence, or a series of sentences. When it consists of, or contains, assertions it is an *assertive discourse*. An *argument* is an assertive discourse that contains reasons; all others are *exposition*.

An argument ("Since Miss Jones did not come to work today, she must be ill") contains (1) one or more assertions set forth as *conclusions* ("[Miss Jones] must be ill"), (2) one or more assertions set forth as *reasons* in support of the conclusions ("Miss Jones did not come to work today"), and (3) a claim that the reasons support the conclusions. This claim is generally made by means of a *logical indicator* ("since"), but it may be merely suggested, as may the conclusion itself.

An argument is *deductive* if it claims that its conclusion follows necessarily from its *premises* (whether or not this claim is made good; that is, whether or not the argument is *valid*). It is *inductive* if it claims only that the *evidence* it provides renders the conclusion more or less probable.

In a sound argument the conclusion is drawn according to a logical *rule of inference,* which prescribes that reasons of such-and-such a sort yield conclusions of such-and-such a sort. If an argument has the appearance of conforming to a rule of inference but actually violates it, the argument commits a *fallacy*.

Exercise 1

Read the following paragraphs carefully, and decide whether each one is exposition or argument. If it is an argument, pick out the conclusion, or, if the conclusion is only implicit, supply it in your own words.

1. If it be admitted that a man, possessing absolute power, may misuse that power by wronging his adversaries, why should a majority not be liable to the same reproach? Men are not apt to change their characters by agglomeration; nor does their patience in the presence of obstacles increase with the consciousness of their strength [Alexis de Tocqueville, *Democracy in America*].

2. Facts unwillingly released by the Treasury Department at the insistence of Senator Douglas make interesting reading to conscientious taxpayers. Twenty fat cats whose income last year exceeded one million dollars found enough loopholes in the tax laws so that they got away without paying a penny in federal taxes. A $100-a-week worker with two children must pay an income tax of about $456. Yet five men whose income was 1,000 times as high didn't have to pay a cent. One method is to donate property to charity and write off, not the original cost of the property, but its appraised value. One man got a charitable deduction of 21 million dollars on property that had originally cost him less than $500,000.

3. The Seattle City Council has recently passed an ordinance raising the age limit to 21 for movies classified by a Board of Theáter Supervisors as "adult entertainment." In an application of the 1957 *Roth* criterion of obscenity, the statute prohibits the showing of motion pictures to anyone under 21 years of age (unless accompanied by a parent or guardian) when "the dominant theme of the work when taken as a whole appeals to the prurient interest of the average person

of the age of 18 to 20 years inclusive, applying contemporary community standards." *Irma La Douce* and *Tom Jones* were offered at the hearings as examples of obscene films that no segment of the community should be exposed to. The Washington State ACLU will present a friend-of-the-court brief on behalf of two suits challenging the statute as unconstitutionally vague.

4. When we look about us and see the competitiveness in ownership of goods, the vast differences between rich and poor, young and old, with respect to their political values, sex codes, consumption patterns, and so forth, we become very much aware of the extent to which the United States has become a class-conscious society—a nation of status-seekers. People are greatly concerned with their social position, with the "character" of the neighborhood they live in, with the prestige of their occupations. Even the church on the corner has become the focus of competition for status, with each congregation claiming to include the "best people," and showing inhospitableness to newcomers who belong to different groups.

5. Directed mostly at automobiles and electrical appliances, resentment is running high at slovenly workmanship, careless assembly and inspection, leading to constant costs of repairs and early junking of the machine. Repairs are becoming more expensive—the average family spends an estimated $100 to $150 annually to keep appliances in working order. Moreover, today industrial designers are hired by the thousands to perform annual face-liftings and restyling, to speed up consumption. The white refrigerator becomes old-fashioned when the pink and blue ones are all the rage, then the "square look" retires the others even before they wear out. The scramble for new looks puts a premium on bad design and debases taste. How meaningful is the achievement of a $600-million gross national product when the goods will fall apart or be junked so soon?

Exercise 2

Show the structure of the following arguments by means of a diagram.

1. Our major argument against live televising of criminal trials is that television creates an atmosphere that makes its impossible to conduct a fair trial. This is because the trial judge is forced to devote an unduly large portion of his time and attention to keeping the situation within manageable bounds. In a recent case, for example, the judge made no less than ten separate rulings on television coverage during the trial. Furthermore, the presence of television cameras and

technicians tends to distract and divert witnesses, and can have an unpredictable effect on their testimony.

2. Has it been found that bodies of men act with more rectitude or greater disinterestedness than individuals? The contrary of this has been inferred by all accurate observers of the conduct of mankind; and the inference is founded upon obvious reasons. Regard to reputation has a less active influence, when the infamy of a bad action is to be divided among a number, than when it is to fall singly upon one. A spirit of faction, which is apt to mingle its poison in the deliberation of all bodies of men, will often hurry the persons of whom they are composed into improprieties and excesses, for which they would blush in a private capacity [from *The Federalist Papers*].

3. Intrinsically immoral actions cannot be rendered moral by subservience to a good end. For good intentions are not availing unless accompanied by intelligent foresight of consequences, since all the consequences of an action may have to be taken into account in judging its morality, and moreover we have a duty to take consequences into account in action. It follows that infringements upon individual rights are not a legitimate means of securing evidence for criminal convictions, and therefore evidence obtained in this fashion should not be considered admissible in court.

4. The soul is one thing, the body another; they are often at odds. And the superiority of the former to the latter is evident from its capacity to be moved by ethical obligations, to reason about remote and abstract things, and to direct the course of a person's life. Considering these facts about the soul, plus its apparent inner unity and consequent indestructibility, our belief in the immortality of the soul could not be more securely based. And this is a cause of satisfaction, since the justification for moral behavior rests upon that belief.

5. In recommending the use of hallucinogenic drugs (such as LSD and mescaline), the speaker was completely mistaken, as well as performing a disservice to the community. Those who experimented with X rays in the early days did not find out until years afterward that they had started permanent bodily damage—evidently it can be dangerous to experiment with things whose effects are not yet well known. (Remember thalidomide—nobody had the slightest suspicion that it would deform unborn babies.) Then there is the fact that hallucinations are a symptom of severe mental disorder, a temporary psychosis, which it can hardly be a good thing to produce in a normal, healthy mind, for however short a period. Finally, taking these drugs

is against the law, and therefore to recommend their use is to urge people to break the law, and to patronize and encourage the underworld.

Exercise 3

In each of the following arguments, the logical connections between the statements are somewhat obscured by the order in which they are presented. Rewrite each argument to make it as brief and orderly as you can. It may be helpful to diagram the arguments before rewriting.

1. The importance of beautifying our highways, eliminating auto graveyards, dumps, and unsightly billboards that block our view of greenery can be seen from a few of the basic facts about the situation (and bear in mind that if we undertake this beautification we will have to be prepared to exert strong federal power and we will also have to spend a considerable sum of money). The United States has about a mile of roads and streets for every square mile of land, so that it matters what those roads look like; moreover the average American spends two months or more of each year behind the steering wheel of his car. Beauty is important to man, and it is also politically appealing; and the only people who are really against making our highways not only safe but delightful to drive on, are those who care more about money than anything else—while the importance of beauty to man is supported by expert psychological testimony in its favor.

2. It is safe to say that the critics of the "oil-depletion allowance" written into our federal income-tax law have never mucked in oil field mud or spent sleepless nights wondering if their money would hold out until their drill struck oil. This principle of depletion is largely responsible for the fact that, in war or peace, we have never been hamstrung for want of oil. This tax provision—which simply gives the producers of oil the right to deduct the approximate value of their depleted capital in computing their income tax—is attacked as a "special privilege" for the "oil interests." They do not seem to know that the same provision applies (in different amounts) to all producers of exhaustible natural resources—coal, tin, zinc, marble, clamshells, and so forth—and now even well-water, apparently. That's one thing that makes it fair—and there is also Article V of the Bill of Rights, which requires just compensation for taking private property. The sale price of oil after it has been brought to the surface includes some value representing the capital worth of the oil in its original condition; so it is only just and right that the producer be permitted to write off 27½

per cent of his net taxable income, representing the value of the oil that he has forever lost by selling it. It must also be remembered that oil producers take more chances than others, since thousands of wells run dry each year and have to be replaced, while thousands of the new wells dug each year—at an estimated average cost of $40,000 per well—turn out to be dry.

3. The Assembly has again refused to pass a meaningful law setting up standards of professional ethics for assemblymen. One more unfortunate bit of evidence that political ethics is on the decline, if not on the skids. A few weeks ago it was the disclosure that Assemblyman Dirk's son was part owner of the same race track for which Dirk's special bill was designed to secure special treatment. Before that, you recall, the governor had to veto another bill that would have sold a large tract of state land for a song to a mining company whose solicitor happens—just happens—to be the speaker of the assembly! These examples show that without a law spelling out the objectionable conflicts of interest, there is going to be increasing hanky-panky, and therefore a law must be drawn up and passed without delay. Which is not going to be done until the public wises up to its own interest and starts pressing for the law, as it should immediately. Perhaps the most crucial argument is that there seems to be increasing cynicism about the morality of legislators: one was quoted as saying, "What's all the fuss about? Everybody is in it for himself, and we get very little out of it, considering the work we do." Certainly he should be impeached for saying that.

Exercise 4

Say whether each of the following arguments is deductive or inductive, and give your reasons for saying so.

1. When Jeane Dixon was only eight years old, her mother took her to see a gypsy woman camped on the nearby estate of Luther Burbank. The gypsy looked at her palm and gasped. "Here is a Star of David, with a double headline leading from it; moreover, there is a tremendous star reaching out in all directions, a headline that completely crosses the palm and wraps around the hand, with a half-moon on its outer cuff. This child is blessed with the gift of prophecy," she said solemnly, "for only those with the gift of prophecy have these rare markings."

2. The Republicans have strongly intimated that what they call "crime in the streets" is largely due to Negroes and is encouraged by

civil-rights demonstrations. But in Washington, D.C., where Negroes make up 54 per cent of the population, the crime rate is only three-fourths of what it is in the candidate's own home town of Phoenix, Arizona, which is 95 per cent white. And a city such as New York, which has had a great many civil-rights demonstrations, has a lower crime rate than Los Angeles, which has had fewer demonstrations. Washington, which has been so often attacked, is actually thirteenth among American cities in its crime rate.

3. To the Editor: Mr. Ogburn has written a witty plea for linguistic purism. But when he laments the deterioration of *presently* to the meaning of *now,* and the relegation of *now* to the dustbin of *eftsoons,* he should remember that Lear was still sane when he cried:

> Go tell the Duke and's wife I'd speak with them,
> Now, presently!

For *presently* once meant *now,* not what it means now. And *presently* will probably mean *now* once again presently.

4. No free community ever existed without morals; and, as I observed in the former part of this work, morals are the work of woman. Consequently, whatever affects the condition of women, their habits and their opinions, has great political importance in my eyes [Alexis de Tocqueville, *Democracy in America*].

5. It was high time that the principles of morality were upheld and the Board of Regents prevented the paintings of nudes from being shown at the University Union Building. If the Lord wanted the unadorned body exhibited in public, would he have taught us how to make clothes?

chapter two | VALID DEDUCTION

Imagine a small-business manager who is asked for a comparative rating of two of his employees. He writes, "Well, I guess Able is better than nobody, and certainly nobody is better than Baker; therefore, Able must be better than Baker." This piece of reasoning is hardly likely to fool anyone—though even if you see immediately that it won't do, you may not be able to say immediately why it won't do. But what if an editorial writer argues this way:

> Only those who are in need of legal aid are assigned to a public defender, and therefore it cannot be maintained that everyone who needs that aid does in fact receive adequate counsel, since not all of those who are assigned to public defenders actually receive adequate counsel.

It might take a little thought to break through the surface of this argument and get to the heart of it. When we do, we find that it is a fairly straightforward deductive argument, and we are ready to ask whether it is a *good* one.

In order to decide whether or not a deductive argument is a good one, we must ask two distinct questions: (1) Is the argument valid? and (2) Are the premises true? A deductive argument cannot legitimately claim to establish its conclusion if it fails by either of these tests. If the argument is invalid, then it doesn't matter whether the premises are true or not, since the alleged conclusion doesn't follow from them anyway. On the other hand, if the premises are not true—if even one of the premises is not true—then it doesn't matter whether the argument is valid or invalid, since the premises, taken as a whole, are no support for the conclusion. The argument has no foundation—or at least no foundation on which this particular structure can be built (other logical consequences may, of course, follow from those premises). If all the premises are false, then even if the argument is valid, we still don't know whether the conclusion is true or false, for false premises may imply a true conclusion:

All babies have tails.
All dogs are babies.
Therefore, all dogs have tails.

Though truth and validity are very different things (remember that only statements or assertions can be true, while only arguments can be valid), there is a relationship between them. When an argument is valid, the premises and conclusion can all be true, or they can all be false, or the premises can be false and the conclusion true. But a valid argument cannot combine true premises with a false conclusion. For this is precisely what validity is—a guarantee that *if* all the premises are true, *then* the conclusion must be true. When an argument is invalid, then, of course, anything goes.

Thus the two questions to be asked of a deductive argument (concerning the truth of the premises and the validity of the argument) must be separated, though they are both pertinent. To discover whether the premises are true we see whether we can test them out in our own experience or support them by evidence, or perhaps deduce them as conclusions from other known premises. The problems involved in supporting them by evidence will be considered in the following chapter. If we deduce these premises from others, then that only pushes the problem one step back. Sooner or later, in any case, we will have to ask the second question: whether the argument is valid. And this is the topic on which we shall concentrate our attention in this chapter. What makes an argument valid? And how do we know whether an argument is valid or invalid?

§5. molecular arguments

To clarify our understanding of what is involved in deductive reasoning, let us begin with some sample forms of argument that are both simple and familiar. Indeed, they may be so simple and familiar that it requires a little effort to stop and scrutinize them; you may find yourself gliding so smoothly from premises to conclusion that you don't even realize that you are reasoning.

From a logical point of view, we may say that statements are the units, or atoms, of assertive discourse: each statement carries its individual message, either true or false. This suggests a convenient way of dividing up deductive arguments. In some arguments, statements are broken up, and their parts are shifted about and recombined: there is fission and fusion, as in atomic processes. Let us call these **subatomic arguments**, since to understand them we shall have to analyze the statements into their constituent subatomic parts in order to see how they are related. In other arguments, statements are not broken up, but are shifted about as wholes, combined and recombined in the course of the argument. Let us call these **molecular arguments,** since they are like chemical processes rather than nuclear or electronic ones.

The simplest deductive arguments of all are molecular ones, and more particularly those involving three fundamental logical words, "if," "and," and "or." These are also the most familiar. For example:

> *If* Congress passes the Blunker Act next week, *then* the decline of our gold reserves will cease.
>
> Congress will pass the Blunker Act next week.
>
> *Therefore,* the decline of our gold reserves will cease.

There are some points to note about this deductive argument—besides the fact that it *is* a deductive argument, in which the conclusion does follow from the two premises.

First, note that the first premise of the argument is a compound one. It is really made up of two independent statements, put together in the construction "if . . . then —." An "if . . . then —" statement is called a **conditional,** or hypothetical, **statement.** Within it, the statement preceded by the "if" is called the **antecedent** of the conditional, and the statement preceded by the "then" is called the **consequent.** These elementary statements can stand by themselves, as indeed they do in the second premise and conclusion—except for one slight change. The antecedent would not sound quite idiomatic by itself, removed from its context—"Congress passes the Blunker Act next week." Since the passage of the bill is predicted for next week, the tense should be future—"Congress will pass the Blunker Act next week."

Second, note that the second premise is the same as the antecedent of the first premise (after the tense has been adjusted), and that the conclusion is the same as the consequent of the first premise. Since the argument is valid, there must be some deductive rule of inference that it obeys, and that rule might be put this way:

> Whenever a conditional statement can be asserted, and its antecedent can be asserted, then its consequent can also be asserted.

In any deductive argument we can distinguish a *form* and a *content.* For example, in the argument just examined, we can say that its content consists of two statements, "Congress passes (will pass) the Blunker Act next week" and "The decline of our gold reserves will cease," each of which appears twice in the course of the argument. Whenever we remove the content, what is left is the form:

> If . . . then —.
>
> . . . .
>
> *Therefore,* —.

We must leave spaces here to replace the statements that have been left out, but we must also label the spaces by means of dots and dashes, or some other device, to mark the original location of the deleted statements. If we were to put them back in the wrong places, we would get a different argument, and not a good one. For example,

> If Congress passes the Blunker Act next week, then the decline of our gold reserves will cease.
>
> The decline of our gold reserves will cease.
>
> *Therefore,* Congress will pass the Blunker Act next week.

This argument, which has the form:

> If . . . then —.
>
> —.
>
> *Therefore,* . . . ,

is evidently not valid. For even if the premises are true, the conclusion is not necessarily true. Granted that if Congress passes the bill, the decline will cease. But suppose Americans tire of foreign travel or there is deflation or American troops stationed abroad are withdrawn—these events may cause the decline of our gold reserves to cease, even if Congress doesn't pass the bill. In that case, both premises could be true, but the conclusion false—so the argument can't be valid.

Another, and more convenient, way of representing the form of a

conditional argument (that is, an argument with one conditional premise and one atomic premise) is to use *variables,* say *P, Q,* and *R,* to stand for statements:

If *P,* then *Q.*
P.
Therefore, Q.

Remember that this is not an argument, but only the skeleton of one; it needs to be filled in with statements in order to become an actual argument. But no matter what statements you put in—provided you put in the same one for both *P*'s and the same one for both *Q*'s—the argument you get will be valid. It will be valid even if the resulting statements are false or ridiculous:

If babies love vinegar, then the Hoover Dam leaks.
Babies love vinegar.
Therefore, the Hoover Dam leaks.

The great thing about deduction is that you don't have to know whether the statements are true or false, or even sensible, to know that the argument is valid. For its validity depends on its form alone —that is, on the rule of inference that governs that form.

Since any statement can be either affirmed or denied—that is, we can either assert that it is true or assert that it is false—there are four possible forms of the conditional argument. The first premise is always a conditional statement. But the second premise can either affirm or deny either the antecedent or the consequent of the first premise.

Two of these forms have already been illustrated. Given the conditional premise, "If Congress passes the Blunker Act next week, then the decline of our gold reserves will cease," (1) we can affirm the antecedent, as in the first example above. Then we are permitted to draw the conclusion that the consequent is true. Or (2) we can affirm the consequent, as in the second example above. Then we are not permitted to draw any conclusion; and if we try to draw the conclusion that the antecedent is true, we commit the **fallacy of affirming the consequent.**

The other two forms are parallel to the first two, one valid and one invalid. The valid one (3) consists in denying the consequent and concluding that the antecedent is false:

If Congress passed the Blunker Act last month, then the decline of our gold reserves has ceased.

The decline of our gold reserves has *not* ceased.

Therefore, Congress did not pass the Blunker Act last month.

(I chose a somewhat different conditional premise this time, to make a more natural argument, but that does not affect the principle involved.) The invalid one (4) consists in denying the antecedent and concluding that the consequent is false:

If Congress passed the Blunker Act last month, then the decline of our gold reserves has ceased.

Congress did *not* pass the Blunker Act last month.

Therefore, the decline of our gold reserves has not ceased.

This argument commits the **fallacy of denying the antecedent.**

While we are considering arguments in which conditional statements play a part, there is one other common form that we should take notice of. This is the **conditional chain argument.**

If P then Q

If Q then R

If R then S

Therefore, if P then S.

This chain has three links, but evidently it could have any number. And in fact some fairly remote inferences can be obtained in this way. When, in January 1960, Jacques Piccard and Lt. Donald Walsh, in the bathyscape *Trieste,* descended off the coast of Guam, seven miles below sea level, into the deepest known hole in the oceans, they saw a fish. And they reasoned as follows:

If there is a fish at this depth, then there is oxygen.

If there is oxygen, then there are currents coming down from above (where the water has oxygen in it).

If there are currents coming down from above, then there are currents going up.

If there are currents going up, then any radioactive "garbage" (the waste-material from atom-powered plants) dropped here would have its radioactivity carried to the surface.

If any radioactive "garbage" dropped here would have its radioactivity carried to the surface, then it would not be safe to drop it here.

Therefore, if there is a fish at this depth, it would not be safe to drop radioactive waste here.

That is quite a deduction—and its conclusion may prove to be momentous.

The conditional statements that we have looked at so far have all been in what may be called *standard logical form.* There are various ways of stating a conditional:

> If you don't go, then I won't go.
> I won't go if you don't go.
> I won't go unless you go.
> I won't go except on condition that you go.
> I will go only if you go.
> I will go, provided you don't stay home.

I do not say that all of these statements have exactly the same meaning. But they all share a core meaning, and the differences in meaning are mostly of a different sort—a sort which we shall deal with in Chapter 5. The first statement in the list seems to convey the core meaning most plainly and explicitly, and with the least additional suggestiveness. Thus it is favored by logicians, and it is chosen as the standard logical form for all conditional statements.

When you encounter a conditional statement you need not, of course, insist on recasting it in standard form. But if you want to make its core meaning very clear, and especially if it is part of an argument that you wish to test, you may find it helpful to begin by transforming the statement—without losing sight of those subtle meanings that you may be, for the moment, setting aside. Thus suppose you should be puzzled by an argument such as this:

> It will be impossible for the United States to avoid making costly errors in its foreign policy unless the government realizes that it cannot commit itself in all parts of the globe at once. But the commission of such errors will be sufficient to unseat the administration. It follows that the administration cannot expect to remain in office if it does not realize the necessity of limiting its global commitments.

Perhaps the validity of this argument is perfectly and immediately clear to you. If not, it may be well to recast it in its standard logical form for a more careful look:

> If the United States does not realize that it cannot commit itself in all parts of the globe at once, then it will make costly errors in its foreign policy.
>
> If the United States makes costly errors in its foreign policy, then the administration will lose the next election.
>
> *Therefore,* if the United States does not realize that it cannot commit itself in all parts of the globe at once, then the administration will lose the next election.

This is a conditional chain argument, and it seems to hold together.

There are two other basic ways in which atomic statements can be combined to produce molecular ones. (I say "basic ways" because, of course, molecular statements themselves can be further combined, without limit, to any conceivable degree of complexity.) These require two of the most valuable and yet unobtrusive words in our language, "and" and "or."

For our purpose here, there is not much that needs to be said about "and." Its use is to combine separate assertions into compound ones. If *P* is true and if *Q* is true, then the molecular **conjunctive statement** (or **conjunction**) "*P* and *Q*" is true. If you are willing to assert that your cat is yellow, and if you are also willing to assert that your cat is long-haired, then you must be willing to assert that your cat is both yellow and long-haired. ("The cat is yellow *and* long-haired" is short for "The cat is yellow *and* the cat is long-haired.") This is not a very surprising inference, nor is the inference in the opposite direction:

Henry is a scholar and a gentleman.
Therefore, Henry is a scholar.

So readily do we perform these inferences in everyday talk and thought that we are not conscious that we are reasoning at all. Thus it is not very useful to dwell on these statements involving "and," except that they provide a further illustration of the distinction made a moment ago between core meaning and suggested meaning. The standard logical form "*P* and *Q*" is common to many English expressions:

He went to the party *and* I went to the party.
He went to the party *but* I went to the party.
He went to the party *although* I went to the party.
He went to the party, *despite the fact that* I went to the party.
He went to the party; *then* I went to the party.
He went to the party *because* I went to the party.

It is apparent that these statements mean very different things. But part of what is meant by all of them is what the first one says—they are all, in basic logical form, conjunctions, even though some of them add to the conjunction the notion that one event is surprising in view of the other, or that one event is later than another, or that one event is a cause of the other.

The other logical word, "or," is capable of generating arguments that are somewhat more noteworthy than the conjunctive ones. These are the arguments in which the first premise is a **disjunctive statement,** or **disjunction,** and the second premise an atomic statement:

Either cars will be required to be equipped with exhaust filters or air pollution will increase to a dangerous degree.
Cars will *not* be required to be equipped with exhaust filters.
Therefore, air pollution will increase to a dangerous degree.

This is the standard logical form of the **disjunctive argument.** The first premise contains two atomic statements, linked together by "either . . . or —"; the two statements inside it are called the *disjuncts.* Notice that it doesn't matter about the order of the disjuncts, as far as the whole argument is concerned, since "Either *P* or *Q*" and "Either *Q* or *P*" will yield the same deductive consequences. But the more tidy standard form of the argument reserves second place for the disjunct that is to be preserved as a conclusion. The force of the expression "either . . . or —" must be carefully noted here: the disjunction is taken in its weaker sense. It says that at least one of the two disjuncts is true; it does *not* say that they are not *both* true. "Henry is either a gentleman or a scholar" remains true even if Henry is both a gentleman and a scholar, for if he is both, then he is at least one of them. In ordinary speech, "or" is often exclusive, and that is why one sometimes falls back on "and/or" for the nonexclusive "or."

In the valid form of the disjunctive argument, then, the second premise denies one of the disjuncts. When this disjunct is eliminated, it follows that the remaining disjunct must be true (assuming the first premise to be true), and that is the allowable conclusion. In the corresponding invalid form of the disjunctive argument, the second premise affirms one of the disjuncts, and the conclusion is drawn that the other disjunct must be false:

Either cars will be required to be equipped with exhaust filters or air pollution will increase to a dangerous degree.
Cars will be required to be equipped with exhaust filters.
Therefore, air pollution will *not* increase to a dangerous degree.

Taking "either . . . or —" in the weaker sense, this conclusion does not follow. For the premises by themselves give us no guarantee that the atmosphere will not be poisoned by industrial smoke, nuclear bomb tests, or invaders from outer space. Not that the last of these is very likely—the point is that as long as it remains logically possible, in view of the premises given, the conclusion cannot be said to follow necessarily from those premises. This argument commits the **fallacy of affirming a disjunct.**

A Check-up Quiz Which of the following arguments commit the fallacy of affirming the consequent? denying the antecedent? affirming a disjunct?

1. If most doctors are opposed to Medicare, then it must be a bad policy. Most doctors apparently *are* opposed. Therefore, it is a bad policy.
2. I grant you that if most of the people growing up in our big cities acquire a sense of purpose and meaningfulness, then ours is a healthy society. But it is not true that most of them acquire this sense, and that's why I say that our society is not healthy.
3. Either our school district conforms to the federal regulations, or its federal funds will be withheld. It will not conform; therefore, its federal funds will be withheld.
4. If capitalism is the most productive economic system, then Western Germany is very prosperous. Western Germany *is* very prosperous, which proves that capitalism is the most productive economic system.
5. If communism is the best form of government for human beings, then civil liberties are not important to human beings. But civil liberties *are* important; therefore, communism is not the best form of government.
6. Either the bridge will be built at Chester or Chester's industry will decline further. The bridge will (unfortunately) not be built. Therefore, Chester's industry will decline further.
7. If the Piltdown Man is genuine, the bones have not been treated with potassium bichromate and iron salt, which they have; consequently, it is a fraud.
8. The refugee situation will be relieved, provided that the Immigration Act is repealed, but it won't be; it follows that the situation will not be relieved.
9. Either the tensions of modern life are normal or tranquilizer drugs are good for you. They are indeed normal, so the drugs are not good.

10. In the event that the government helps farms in the drought area, beef prices will be kept down. The government will help; therefore prices will be kept down.

For Further Study Max Black, *Critical Thinking,* rev. ed., Chs. 4–6. Englewood Cliffs, N.J.: Prentice-Hall, Inc., 1952. Richard B. Angell, *Reasoning and Logic,* pp. 141–62. New York: Appleton-Century-Crofts, Inc., 1964.

§6. basic logical connections

The logical connections that can hold between one statement or set of statements and another determine the ways in which the truth or falsity of one affects the truth or falsity of the other. One of the two most fundamental logical connections, implication, we have already become acquainted with. When *P* logically implies *Q,* as we have seen, then the truth of *Q* is guaranteed by the truth of *P*.

Two statements that imply each other are **logically equivalent.** "Martha Washington is an ancestor of Mrs. Pilkington Adams" is logically equivalent to "Mrs. Pilkington Adams is a descendant of Martha Washington." If either of these statements is true, then the other is true; and if either of them is false, then the other is false. Again, "If the painting sells for less than one million dollars, the museum will buy it," is equivalent to "If the museum does not buy the painting, then it costs at least one million dollars."

When the truth of one statement implies the falsity of another, then those two statements are said to be **logically incompatible.** They cannot both be true. Consequently, anyone who asserts them both must be asserting at least one false statement—and we can be sure of this even if we do not know which of his statements is false. Thus "Beverley is Allen's uncle" is incompatible with "Beverley is George's sister," for one statement implies that Beverley is a male and the other that she is a female.

When a discourse contains at least one pair of logically incompatible statements it is said to be **inconsistent.** There is something futile about it, for it fights against itself, taking away with one hand what its gives with the other.

Because of its self-defeating character, we must be on guard against inconsistency whenever we consider a discourse from a logical point of view—whether our own or someone else's. It is not always easy to be certain, without careful thought, whether an apparent inconsistency is real. For example, it was found in one city that a majority of the citizens wanted gambling to be illegal, and also that a majority of the citizens wanted to gamble. Were some of the citizens inconsistent? Perhaps they simply wanted an opportunity to gamble without allowing everyone else to. This may be morally objectionable, but it is not logically inconsistent. Again, William Blake wrote a famous note in the margin of Joshua Reynold's *Discourses:* "To Generalize is to be an Idiot." This mean that all generalizers are idiots—which is itself a generalization. Is this inconsistent? It is self-incriminating, since it implies that Blake himself is an idiot, but it is not logically incompatible with itself. (If we assume that the idiocy of generalizing is due to all generalizations' being untrue, there is an inconsistency.) On the other hand, when in a short story by Peter Ustinov it is said of a character that "His father had been a professor of music, underpaid and deservedly so," this does seem to exhibit inconsistency, or to verge upon it. Perhaps to be underpaid is to be paid less than the going rate. But if to be underpaid is to be paid less than you deserve, then you can't be deservedly underpaid.

It is only fair for me to confess here that in the previous edition of this book there was an instructive mistake about inconsistency. I said that "Enid is Edward's aunt" and "Edward is Enid's uncle" were incompatible. But a sharp-eyed student at California Western University, with Mark Twain ingenuity (you may recall Mark Twain's story about the man who was his own grandfather), proved to me in a welcome letter that Enid could be Edward's aunt and also his niece—even without incest. She could marry the brother of Edward's father, while Edward married the sister of Enid's father. As he had it worked out, with names and ages of the six people involved, Enid would be 22 and Edward 30. Let it be a lesson to you.

The most interesting and difficult cases of genuine inconsistency are those that occur in longer passages, where they can be partially disguised by separating the incompatible statements.

> Gentleman, I rise to plead with you, in this final hour before the vote is taken, that you cast your ballot for the bill abolishing capital punishment (in most cases). It has been proved over and over again, and the testimony has established this, that capital punishment is no deterrent to the killer. The person who kills in a moment of passion (and most murders are of this sort) does not stop to think of the con-

> sequences; and the hardened professional criminal, in his warped sense of reality, easily convinces himself that he will not be caught. . . .
>
> But let me remind you of another excellent feature of this bill, namely, that it retains the death penalty for those who kill policemen. We must protect the guardians of the law. We must bend every effort to put the fear of the law into those who would be tempted to kill a policeman in the performance of his duty, and that is why we propose to maintain capital punishment of this type of homicide.

Now, of course, it would be possible to argue consistently that only the killing of a policeman should be punished by death. But the arguer in this passage bases his criticism of capital punishment on the premise that the death penalty does not deter homicide, and then he turns around and says it *will* deter homicide in certain cases. This inconsistency is of a familiar sort, known as **special pleading:** it consists in laying down a general principle to defeat an opponent, and then abandoning that principle in supporting one's own conclusion.

Unless you can draw a person out, or unless he is in an expansive mood, you may not be able to tell whether his thinking involves special pleading or not. One way of finding out is to try the form of argument known as **reduction to absurdity.** Its framework is this:

> If you accept such-and-such a general principle (in defending your position), then you are logically committed to such-and-such a consequence.
>
> This consequence is absurd, and therefore unacceptable to you.
>
> *Therefore,* you had better not accept the general principle.

The form of the argument is, of course, denying the consequent. The strength of it lies in convincing the other person that his principles entail a conclusion that is not only unacceptable to others, but even to him, once its absurdity is revealed. Thus the angry opponent of "right-to-work" laws writes to the newspaper:

> All right, suppose (for the sake of argument) that a right-to-work law for labor is justified. That means that the nonunion man gets all the benefits of the union men without any of the duties: he is a free-rider in the shop. Then by the same token, doctors should be free to practice anywhere without belonging to the American Medical Association, and lawyers without paying dues to the bar association. Businessmen should be allowed to use all the facilities of the Chamber of Commerce and the Retailers' Association without paying fees or giving any support. And I should be allowed to live in the city without paying taxes. It's the same principle exactly.

The question is always, of course, whether it *is* the "same principle exactly." This argument charges that anyone who defends the right-to-work law *without* accepting these consequences is guilty of special pleading, and hence of inconsistency. And the defender of right-to-work laws must either withdraw his general principle or show that he is not inconsistent. The reduction-to-absurdity argument is very often abused, because it is not hard to make two distinct principles seem to be the same when they are presented briefly and emotionally. Thus another writer replies to a reduction-to-absurdity argument this way:

> Some assert that fluoridation involves the same principle as does chlorination of the water supply. But I say that chlorination is designed to control communicable diseases through enhancing the purity of the water, whereas fluoridation does absolutely nothing to increase water purity but is mass medication against noncontagious tooth decay.

This at least shows that a distinction *can* be drawn. Suppose *A* objects to fluoridation, and *B* says that *A* is committed to the absurd consequence that chlorination is wrong. *A* can reply that his underlying principle is that "Forced medication against noncontagious ills is wrong," and this principle does not require him to condemn chlorination. It is only if his underlying principle is something like "Forced improvement of the water supply is wrong" that he is committed to that absurdity.

When two statements are incompatible, and their denials are also incompatible, then they are said to be **contradictories.** To put this another way, suppose the truth of *P* implies the falsity of *Q* and the falsity of *P* implies the truth of *Q*. Then one and only one of the pair is true, and they contradict each other. The most clear-cut contradictories are those we form by placing "not" in the right place: "The sea is salt" vs. "The sea is not salt." There are more complex ones: "Henry is both a scholar and a gentleman" contradicts "Henry is either a nonscholar or a nongentleman."

When two statements are logically incompatible, but are not contradictories, they are said to be **contraries** of each other. Contrary statements cannot both be true, though they can both be false. Compare: "The water is hot" and "The water is cold"; at least one of these must be false (assuming that it is the same water we are speaking of), and it is logically possible that both are false (the water may be lukewarm). And compare: "He is both a scholar and a gentleman" and "He is neither a scholar nor a gentleman."

Logical implication (whether one-way or two-way—as in equivalence) and logical incompatibility (whether contrariety or strict contradiction) are the two basic logical connections. When two statements are not connected in either of these ways, they are said to be **logically independent.** This means that nothing follows necessarily about the truth or falsity of either of them from the truth or falsity of the other.

It will help to sharpen our perception of these logical relationships, as well as to prepare the way for our examination of another sort of deductive argument, if we now consider some statements of a very numerous and important kind. Their essential features are exemplified by the statement "All people with scurvy are people with vitamin-C deficiency." There are two things to note about this statement, from a logical point of view. First, the phrases that occur in it refer to two groups, or classes, of people: *people with scurvy* and *people with vitamin-C deficiency.* These phrases are called the **terms** of the statement; they are its content. Second, these two terms are linked together by the construction "All . . . are ——," which claims a certain relationship between the classes referred to by the two terms—namely, that every member of one of the classes is a member of the other. To put it another way, the class of people referred to by the **subject-term** is said to be wholly included in the class of people referred to by the **predicate-term.** When, by the way, I later speak of the subject-term as the "subject" and the predicate-term as the "predicate," I shall be using these words in a technical logical sense; the logical subject and the grammatical subject coincide, but the logical predicate is only part of what is called the grammatical predicate.

The statement about people with scurvy is an **affirmative statement,** because it speaks of class-inclusion. It is also a **universal statement** because it says that *all* the people in the subject-class are included among the people in the predicate-class. If it said merely that "Some people with scurvy are people with vitamin-C deficiency," it would be a **particular statement.** On the other hand, if it spoke of the *exclusion* of one class from another, it would be a **negative statement,** rather than an affirmative one. And again it might be either universal ("No people with scurvy are people with vitamin-C deficiency") or particular ("Some people with scurvy are not people with vitamin-C deficiency").

Given any two classes of things, of whatever sort—that is, given the terms that name those classes—you can construct these four kinds of **two-term statement.** Let us review them once more, paying closer attention to their meaning. And let us use diagrams to bring out the force of each kind of statement. Given any class we can think of, except perhaps the class of *things in general*, we can refer either to members of the class or to nonmembers of the class—that is, to things that do not belong to that class. The class of *credit-card holders*, and the class of *nonholders of credit cards* are **complementary classes,** since each excludes the other. And the terms "holders of credit cards" and "nonholders of credit cards" are **negatives** of each other, though one ("holders of credit cards") is a positive term and the other ("nonholders of credit cards") is a negative term.

Both of these complementary classes lie within a larger, more inclusive class, as we discover when we ask what to put in the class of nonholders of credit cards. Socrates certainly belongs there, and St. Francis, and perhaps your next-door neighbor. But what about Lassie, Pike's Peak, and the Missouri River? It doesn't seem to make much sense to speak of dogs, mountains, and rivers as either holding or *not* holding credit cards. It is *people* we are talking about; this is the general class, or **universe of discourse,** within which we are distinguishing credit-card holders from credit-card nonholders. We can represent this distinction simply by placing a circle inside a rectangle.

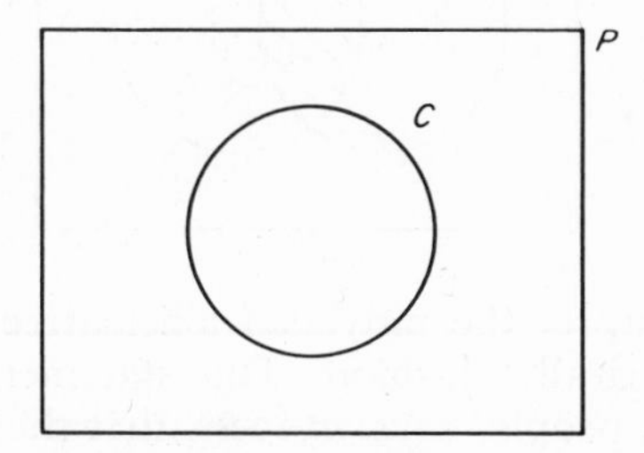

The rectangle includes all people, past, present, and future. Inside the *C* circle (we can imagine) are the credit-card holders, and outside the circle—but within the rectangle—the nonholders.

To diagram a two-term statement, we need only introduce two circles, overlapped so that all possible combinations are presented: (a) those who hold credit cards but are not honest, (b) those who hold credit cards and *are* honest, (c) those who do not hold credit cards but are honest, and (d) those who neither hold credit cards nor are honest.

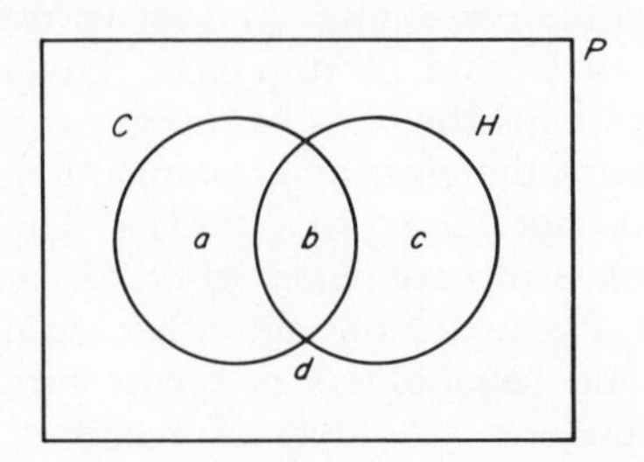

To show that a certain subclass in this universe of discourse is empty, or has no members, we shall shade it out. And to show that a certain subclass does have members, we shall put an asterisk in that part of the diagram.

Consider, to begin with, the **universal negative statement,** or *UN* statement, "No credit-card holders are honest people." This simply says that the area where our two circles overlap—the area where the credit-card holders that *are* honest would go, if there were any—has nobody in it.

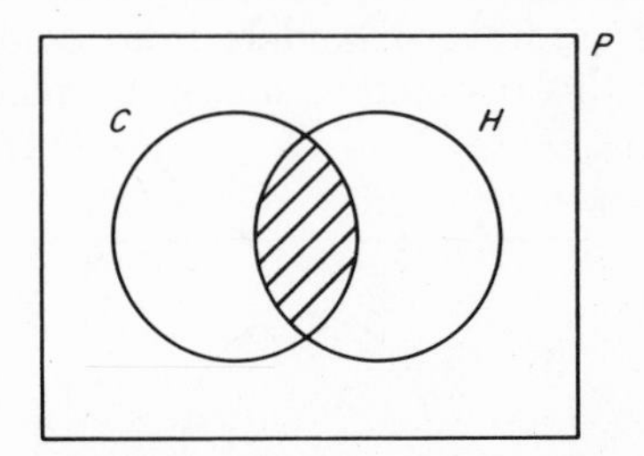

And we shall interpret the **universal affirmative statement,** or *UA* statement, in a parallel fashion. The statement "All credit-card holders are honest people" says, *at least,* that there are no dishonest credit-card holders, in other words, that the part of the *C* circle outside the *H* circle is empty.

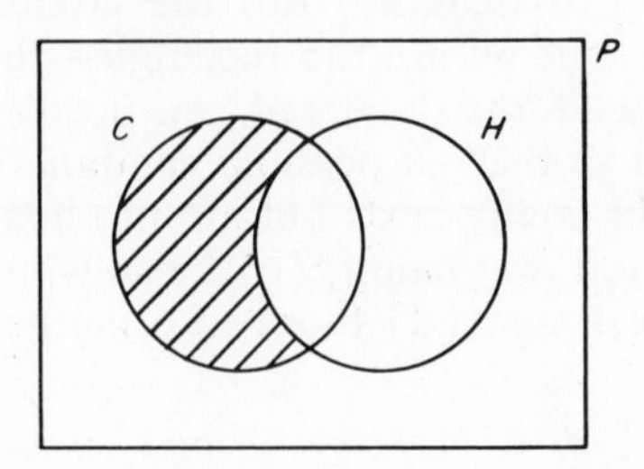

Perhaps sometimes a *UA* statement says more than this, and we must take that into account. But even when it says no more than this, it certainly says no less. So let us interpret universal statements in a conditional way: "All honest people are admirable people" means "If there are (or have been) any honest people, then they are (have been) admirable people."

When we turn to particular statements, however, we find that a quite different interpretation is required. The **particular affirmative statement** or *PA* statement, "Some credit-card holders are honest people," says that the subclass where *C* and *H* overlap is *not* empty of people:

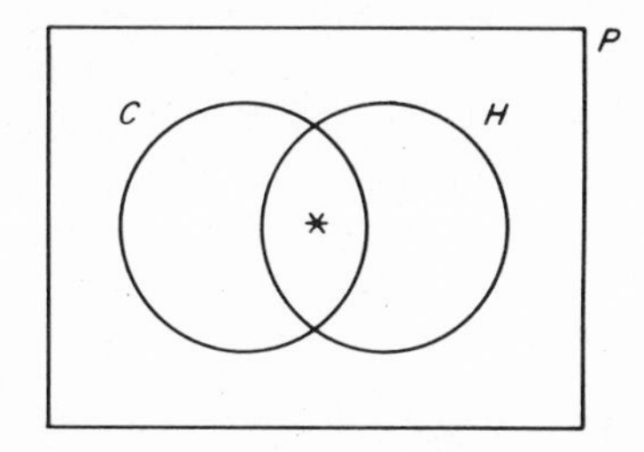

How many people are there in this area? The statement doesn't say. At least one, maybe more. In ordinary speech, "some" often means—or at least suggests—more than one, but here we shall take it in the weakest possible way. "Some" means "at least one." The same holds true for the **particular negative statement**, or *PN* statement, "Some credit-card holders are not honest people":

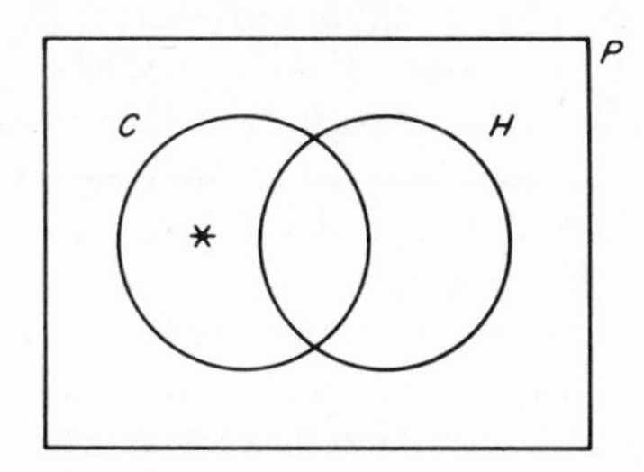

One other kind of statement can be assimilated to this scheme. For more fundamental logical study, its peculiar characteristics would have to be emphasized and explored, but for our purposes we can treat it like the ones just considered. Take "John is an honest person" (affirmative) and "John is not an honest person"

(negative). Since John is not a class, but an individual, these are not strictly two-class statements but class-membership statements. One says that John is a member of the class of honest persons; the other says he is not a member. But for ordinary logical purposes, we can speak, not of John, but of the class whose only member is John. Every individual thing is in *some* class by itself—for example, John may be the only person in the world who was born in St. Vincent's hospital in Bridgeport at one minute after midnight on January 1, 1927, weighing 7 lbs. 2½ oz. So let us adopt this convenient interpretation of "John is an honest person": it says, in effect, "The class whose only member is John is included in the class of honest persons." But since, as you recall from Chapter 1, the statement about John cannot be either true or false unless there *is* a John for it to refer to, we shall have to say that the statement about John not only says that a certain class is contained in another class, but also presupposes that there is a member of that class:

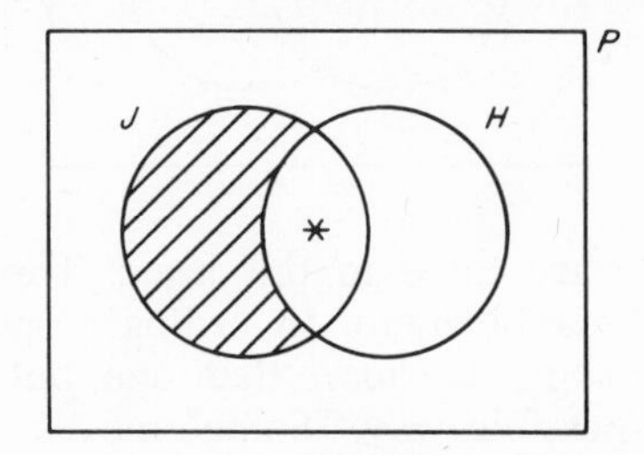

Let us now turn to the basic logical connections that hold among two-term statements. The diagrams give us clues to them.

Two equivalences are immediately evident from the symmetry of the diagrams. The same diagram will serve for "No *A* are *B*" and for "No *B* are *A*," and the same diagram will serve for "Some *A* are *B*" and for "Some *B* are *A*." These are two pairs of equivalences. Four other equivalences arise because we can have both negative and affirmative statements, and we can have both negative and positive terms. Thus we convey the same information about the relations between the classes *A* and *B* whether we say that all *A* are *B* or that no *A* are non-*B*. The diagrams are the same. And, similarly, "Some eighteenth-century writers are witty" is equivalent to "Some eighteenth-century writers are not nonwitty." Two negatives can cancel each other out—if they are in the right place. The rule for this kind of inference is: Negate the predicate and negate the whole statement, and the resulting statement will be equivalent to the original. The main problem is to make sure that the negatives are properly located. For this purpose, the prefix *non-*, though artificial, is helpful—providing we attach it to the right word. It would not do to say, for example, that "No honest people are credit-card holders" is equivalent to "All honest people are non–credit-card holders"—which seems to imply that they hold some other kind of card.

When we ask what one-way implications hold among two-term statements, we immediately encounter a difficulty that it is just as well to clear up at this point, or it will bother us later. Consider the following deduction:

All chimeras are fire-breathing animals.
Therefore, some chimeras are fire-breathing animals.

You might say that this is not a very natural-sounding inference, since anyone who (presumably) knows that *all A* are *B* is not very likely to want to make the weaker statement that *some A* are *B*. But the question for us is not whether the deduction would probably occur, but whether it would be valid if it did occur. Now, if we compare the diagrams of the two statements (let the universe of discourse be *animals*), it is clear that the inference is not valid.

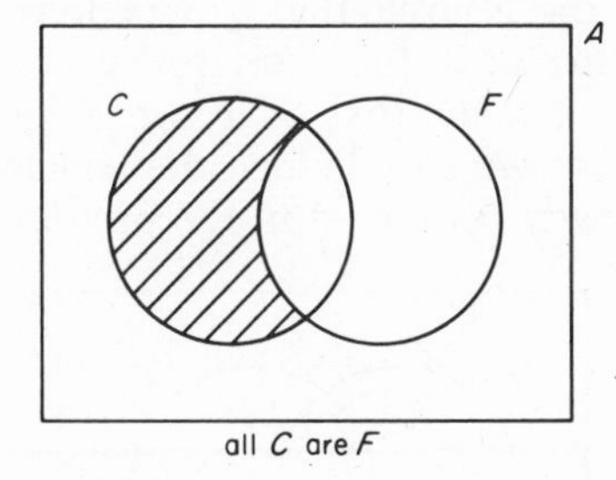

all *C* are *F*

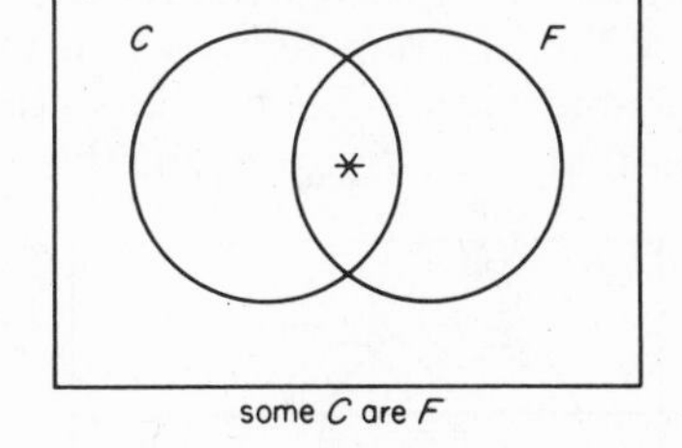

some *C* are *F*

The diagram is a test of the validity of the inference. For the conclusion of the argument cannot follow necessarily from the premise if it contains any information that is not already contained in the premise. In the premise, one area is shaded out; in the conclusion, another area has an asterisk in it. Surely, then, the two statements are completely independent.

And when we turn back to the argument to reconsider it, this judgment seems to be justified. For to say that some chimeras breathe fire is to say that there actually are chimeras. But chimeras are mythical beasts; they don't exist, and never have existed, so that the deduction really is fallacious. It is true that if anything *were* a chimera, it would breathe fire from one of its three throats (premise); it is false that there are some chimeras that actually breathe fire.

But now consider the following deduction:

All firemen are fire-extinguishing people.
Therefore, some firemen are fire-extinguishing people.

Here we may find ourselves making a different decision. Surely if something is true of *all* firemen, then it must be true of *some* of them. How can it be true of all, unless it is true of some? The argument seems to be valid. How, then, can we resolve this apparent discrepancy in our treatment of the two small arguments?

There is one and only one difference between the two arguments, from a logical point of view (which is not concerned with the topic of an argument, whether chimeras or firemen): chimeras don't exist, but firemen do. Assuming that there are such things as firemen, we can make the second deduction valid. And we can even show this by the diagram, if we add this further assumption to it. First put two asterisks in the *F* circle, connecting them by a bar—because we are making the assumption that somewhere in this circle there are actually existing things, though we don't know where. Second, shade out the part of the *F* circle that is outside the *E* circle. This leaves the remaining asterisk in the overlapping part. Now the diagram tells us two things, namely, that all *F* are *E* and that some *F* are *E*. It is no wonder that we can deduce the conclusion that some *F* are *E*, for this is already contained in the premise:

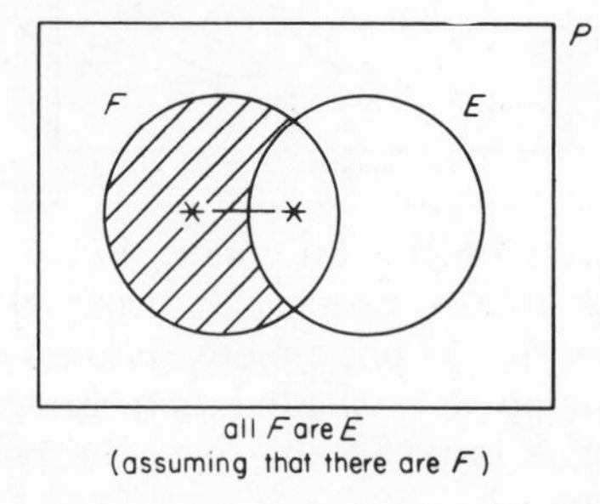

all *F* are *E*
(assuming that there are *F*)

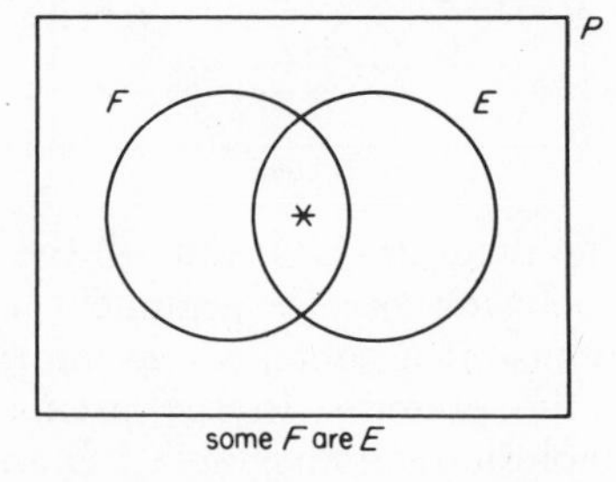

some *F* are *E*

A universal statement by itself, then (whether affirmative or negative), leaves open the question whether its subject-class has members. When the statement occurs in certain contexts, we can make the *existence assumption,* and then certain things follow that wouldn't follow otherwise. When can we make the existence assumption? Sometimes it is clear, when a writer asserts "All *A* are *B*," that he believes that there are *A*. For example, an elaborate recipe on how to make chicken stew, with directions for selecting, cutting, boiling, seasoning, and serving the chicken, certainly reveals the assumption that there are such things as chickens. Or it may be well known that *A* exist, and therefore the writer has the right to assume that there are *A*. In that case, when he says "All dogs have fleas; *therefore,* some dogs have fleas," you can give him the benefit of the existence assumption and agree that (on the assumption that dogs exist) his inference is valid.

The existence assumption also plays a role when we ask about the logical incompatibilities among two-term statements. Some of these are straightforward. The *UN* statement and the *PA* statement are contradictories: "No *A* are *B*" and "Some *A* are *B*." And the *UA* statement and the *PN* statement are contradictories: "All *A* are *B*" and "Some *A* are not *B*." But what is the connection between the *UA* statement and the *UN* statement? And what is the connection between the *PA* statement and the *PN* statement?

Let us consider the second question first. Compare "Some planets are inhabitable places" and "Some planets are not inhabitable places." Now obviously these are not incompatible with each other; they could both be true (and doubtless are). But could they both be false? If there are such things as planets, they can't both be false, for even if there is only one planet, it must either be inhabitable or uninhabitable. On the other hand, if there were no planets, there would be no inhabitable ones, and there would be no uninhabitable ones, so both of the statements would be false.

Two statements are said to be **subcontraries** if at least one of them must be true and they are not incompatible with each other. Since the *PA* statement "Some *A* are *B*" implies that *A* exist, and the *PN* statement "Some *A* are not *B*" also implies that *A* exist, they will both be false if in fact no *A* do exist. But if we can make the existence assumption that some *A* exist (as we probably can do for most of the things we ordinarily reason about), then the *PA* statement and the *PN* statement are subcontraries. The same reasoning applies to the two forms of universal statement, "All *A* are *B*" and "No *A* are *B*." If there are no *A*, then these statements can both be true. But if there are *A*, they cannot. So on the existence assumption, the *UA* statement and the *UN* statement are contraries.

These relationships are commonly shown by what is called a *Table of Opposition.*

TABLE OF OPPOSITION
(Making the Existence Assumption)

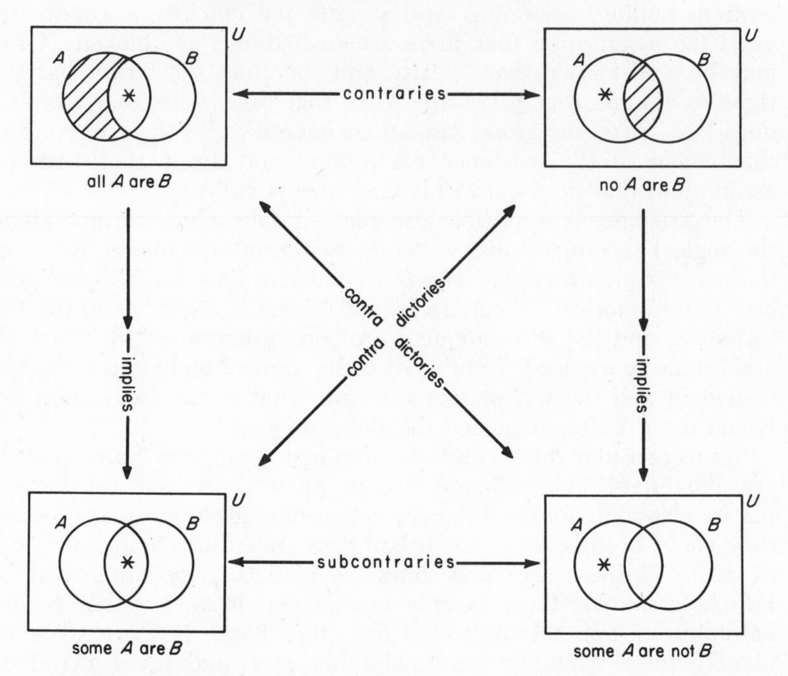

A Check-up Quiz Say whether the two statements in each of the following pairs are equivalent, incompatible, or neither (on the existence assumption).

1. (a) The butter is on the table.
   (b) The butter is under the table.
2. (a) It seems that he has neither decided to call off the campaign nor reconciled himself to its inevitable failure.
   (b) He has not reconciled himself to the inevitable failure of the campaign, and he has not yet decided to call it off.
3. (a) Mrs. Jones' children have bought a rabbit.
   (b) Mrs. Jones' children have bought an animal.
4. (a) Male turtles are lonely without female turtles.
   (b) Female turtles are lonely without male turtles.
5. (a) Some members of the club who did not get elected to the

Executive Committee are not members who are protesting the election procedures.
(b) Some members of the club who are protesting the election procedures are not members who did not get elected to the Executive Committee.

6. (a) The governor has resigned and he intends to run for the Senate.
(b) The governor has not resigned and he does not intend to run for the Senate.

7. (a) If the conductor is open-minded about contemporary music, he will put compositions by Boulez and Stockhausen on the program.
(b) If the conductor does not put compositions by either Boulez or Stockhausen on the program, then he is not open-minded about contemporary music.

8. (a) He is the oldest senator.
(b) No other senator is as old as he.

9. (a) People of Polish descent have never been admitted to the country club.
(b) The membership of the country club has never included any people of Polish descent.

10. (a) Few who have been abroad are provincial people.
(b) Few provincial people are people who have been abroad.

For Further Study Stephen F. Barker, *The Elements of Logic,* pp. 34–61. New York: McGraw-Hill Book Company, 1965. Irving M. Copi, *Introduction to Logic,* 2nd ed., Ch. 5. New York: The Macmillan Company, 1961.

§7. syllogistic arguments

There is, of course, a vast variety of deductive arguments—even if we ignore their content (what they are about) and pay attention solely to their logical form. But most of those that we encounter in the ordinary affairs of life are combinations of a fairly small set of quite simple and familiar forms. Some of these we have already studied in §5 above—those are the ones I have called "molecular arguments" because their validity depends on the way atomic statements are put together into molecular statements with the help of words like "and," "or," and "if . . . then ——." Let us turn now to those deductive arguments I called "subatomic arguments," because their validity depends on internal connections among the constituent statements, that is, on the way in which part of one statement is connected with part of another.

The form of argument we shall now consider is the **syllogism.** It is easily defined. A syllogism (1) consists of exactly three two-term statements: two premises and one conclusion; and it (2) contains exactly three terms, of which one appears in both premises, and each of the others appears in one premise and in the conclusion. Here is an example (the horizontal line has the meaning of "therefore"):

No orderly minds are creative minds.
Some philosophers' minds are creative minds.
___
Some philosophers' minds are not orderly minds.

Taking the universe of discourse to be *minds* in general, the term that appears in both premises (the middle term) is "creative minds"; the terms that appear both in a premise and in the conclusion (the end terms) are "orderly minds" and "philosophers' minds." The syllogism is in standard form (for syllogisms): the conclusion is carefully separated from the premises, and the forms of the three statements are clearly marked—the premises are evidently a *UN* statement and a *PA* statement, and the conclusion is a *PN* statement.

It is not hard to see that this syllogism is a valid one, that if the premises are true, then so is the conclusion. But the class of syllogisms, as I have marked it out, includes both valid and invalid ones. The following argument is just as much a syllogism as the first one, though it is fallacious:

No orderly minds are creative minds.
Some philosophers' minds are not creative minds.
___
Some philosophers' minds are orderly minds.

You may be prepared to accept the conclusion, in the light of some of your own reading in that field; but you will have to find some other reason to base it on, for these premises are incapable of providing deductive support.

The valid syllogisms can be clearly and decisively distinguished from the invalid ones by means of a small set of rules. They are worth keeping in the back of your mind, to apply when common sense fails you or when a dispute arises that can only be settled by an impersonal appeal to principles. I will state the rules first, then explain and illustrate them.

Rule 1. The middle term must be distributed exactly once.

Rule 2. No end term may be distributed only once.

Rule 3. The number of negative premises must equal the number of negative conclusions.[1]

The one technical concept here that is still unfamiliar to us is that of distribution. Each of the terms in a two-term statement is either **distributed** or **undistributed.** And this depends entirely on its position. For example, whatever term you put in as the subject of a *UA* statement is automatically distributed in that position; if you put the same term in as the predicate of another *UA* statement, it will be undistributed in that position. The distribution of terms in the four types of two-term statement can be simply stated:

In a *UA* statement, the subject is distributed but the predicate is not.
In a *PA* statement, neither the subject nor the predicate is distributed.
In a *UN* statement, both the subject and the predicate are distributed.
In a *PN* statement, the subject is not distributed but the predicate is.

If you are satisfied to take these four principles as they stand, without pressing further, you need get into no trouble in applying the three rules. "Term *T* is distributed" can be taken as shorthand for "Term *T* appears either as the subject of a universal statement or as the predicate of a negative statement." Instead of speaking of "distribution," we could speak of "the preferred positions" and rewrite Rule 2, for example, as: "No end term may appear in a preferred position exactly once"—that is, it must either appear in a preferred position twice or not at all.

However, a further explanation can be given, and it may as well be included here for those who demand it.[2] A term is distributed in a certain kind of statement when we can say the following: that if the statement is true of the class of things referred to by the term, then it is true of every subclass of that class. For example, suppose it is true that "All philosophers' minds are orderly minds." Then it is necessarily true that all German philosophers' minds are

---

[1] I have borrowed this formulation of the rules from Wesley C. Salmon, *Logic* (Foundations of Philosophy Series) (Englewood Cliffs, N.J.: Prentice-Hall, Inc., 1963), p. 40.

[2] I borrow this explanation of distribution from Stephen F. Barker, *The Elements of Logic* (New York: McGraw-Hill Book Company, 1965), pp. 43–46.

orderly minds, and all existentialist philosophers' minds are orderly minds, and all gloomy philosophers' minds are orderly minds, and so forth—in short, that whatever group of philosophers we select, the statement will apply to them just as it applies to the whole class of philosophers' minds. Therefore the term "philosophers' minds" is distributed as the subject of this *UA* statement. But—still granting that all philosophers' minds are orderly minds—what follows about the subclasses of the class of orderly minds? Does it follow that all philosophers' minds are deep orderly minds, or witty orderly minds, or compassionate orderly minds? No, none of these follows. Therefore the term "orderly minds" is not distributed in this statement.

The same test can be applied to the other three kinds of two-term statement. It will show that in a universal statement (since the statement is about its whole subject-class), the subject is always distributed; and that in a negative statement (since the subject-class is excluded from the whole predicate-class), the predicate is always distributed.

Now we are equipped to examine the three syllogistic rules a little more closely.

Rule 1 says that the middle term must be distributed exactly once—at least once, and at most once.

> Some socially justifiable actions are violations of civil liberties.
>
> All cases of house-searching without a warrant are violations of civil liberties.
>
> ---
>
> Some cases of house-searching without a warrant are socially justifiable actions.

The middle term is "violations of civil liberties," and since in both of its appearances it turns up as the predicate of an affirmative statement, it is not distributed in either location. Therefore this syllogism is invalid; it commits the **fallacy of maldistributed middle.**

The same syllogism will also serve to illustrate Rule 2. There are two ways of violating this rule: (1) one way is for an end term to move from an undistributed position to a distributed one; (2) the other is for it to move from a distributed position to an undistributed one. In either case the syllogism commits the **fallacy of uneven distribution.** In the example at hand, one of the end terms is "cases of house-searching without a warrant"; it is distributed in the second premise, as the subject of a universal statement; and it is undistributed in the conclusion, as the subject of a particular statement. Therefore, the syllogism is invalid on two counts (but one is enough to disqualify it).

The third rule is needed to make the set complete, but it is not likely to be of frequent practical application, for the syllogisms it serves to disqualify are rather wayward ones whose invalidity is pretty hard to disguise. It eliminates all syllogisms with two negative premises (such as the second one given in this section). And it eliminates syllogisms having the following form (which would probably not fool anyone):

All *A* are *B*
All *B* are *C*
___
Some *C* are not *A*

A syllogism of this form does not violate either Rule 1 or Rule 2, but because it has one negative conclusion and no negative premises it is invalid according to Rule 3. Let us say that it commits the **fallacy of unequal negation.**

At some point while you are trying out these rules, you may run across a few syllogisms that seem to run counter to the claim that I made a little earlier: namely, that all syllogisms that violate one or more of these rules are invalid. For example, suppose you encountered the following argument:

All philosophers' minds are orderly minds.
All philosophers' minds are profound minds.
___
Some profound minds are orderly minds.

This syllogism violates Rule 1, since the middle term is distributed twice. Yet if you stop to think about it, you may want to protest that, after all, the conclusion *does* follow. If we put all the philosophers' minds inside the class of orderly minds, and also inside the class of profound minds, surely the classes of orderly and profound minds must overlap, and there must be some minds that belong to both.

The difficulty here is the one that already turned up in the previous section when we were discussing the square of opposition: it is the existence assumption. When you say that this syllogism is valid, you are assuming (quite properly, of course) that philosophers do have minds, and that there are (or have been) philosophers. Now, when we begin adding existence assumptions to a syllogism, then of course we will be able to draw more conclusions than we could without them. For example, if we are allowed to assume that all three classes in the syllogism have members—and even more, if we are allowed to assume that their complementary classes have members—we will have a good deal of information to work with. But it is better to set up the minimal rules of the syllogism without taking all these things for granted. And if you wish to validate the syllogism above, that can be done by methods already provided in this chapter. You begin with the first premise, "All philosophers' minds are orderly minds." As we saw in the previous section, if we can assume that philosophers' minds exist, then we can directly infer the corresponding *PA* statement: "Some philosophers' minds are orderly minds." Then this statement can be combined with the second premise to construct a syllogism that is perfectly valid by our rules:

Some philosophers' minds are orderly minds.
All philosophers' minds are profound minds.

Some profound minds are orderly minds.

The most important application of the diagram introduced in the previous section can now be explained. You can test the validity of any syllogism by the rules. But in some cases you may be able to make even more clear to yourself or others that a syllogism does or does not hold up, by diagramming it—and the diagram will tell you not only whether the proposed conclusion follows, but whether any other conclusion (of a syllogistic sort) can be drawn.

Since a syllogism involves three classes, the diagram will have three circles, overlapped in such a way that every possible combination is included:

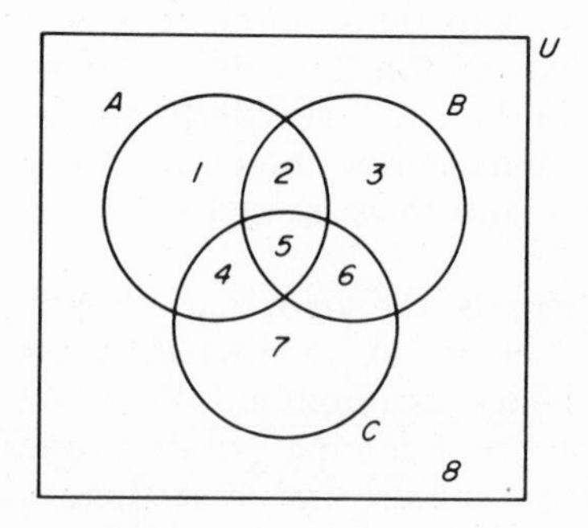

Here the subclasses are numbered for reference as we go along.

Now, for the purpose of diagramming, we can divide all syllogisms into two groups—those that contain only universal premises, and those that do not. And it is simpler to consider the wholly universal ones first.

The principle of diagramming a syllogism is this: The conclusion of a syllogism follows necessarily from the premises because the information it presents is already contained implicitly in the premises. So if we diagram the premises together, we ought to be able to read off the conclusion from the diagram. Consider, for example, this simple syllogistic form—using only letters for the moment, to concentrate on our immediate task.

All *B* are *C*.
All *A* are *B*.
―――――――
All *A* are *C*.

To diagram the first premise, we shade out the part of *B* that is outside *C* (subclasses 2 and 3). To diagram the second premise, we shade out the part of *A* that is outside *B* (subclasses 1 and 4). Then we try to read the conclusion off the diagram. Now the conclusion says that that part of *A* that is outside *C* (subclasses 1 and 2) should be shaded out. And it is. Therefore the conclusion follows, and the syllogism is valid.

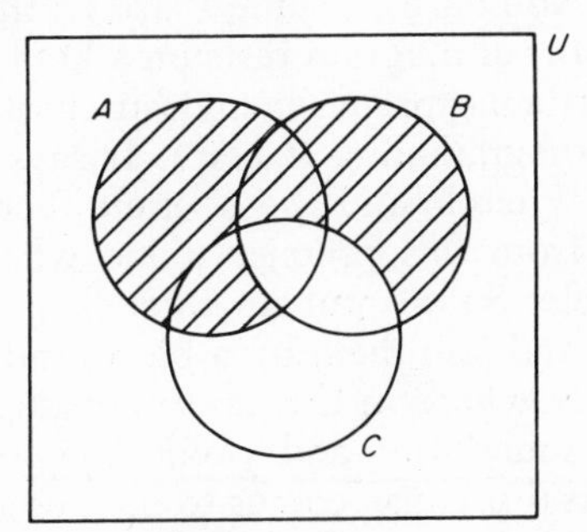

For an example of a syllogism that is invalid, let us turn to the one discussed above in connection with the existence assumption: "All philosophers' minds are orderly minds; all philosophers' minds are profound minds; *therefore,* some profound minds are orderly minds." We can see at once that *this* conclusion does not follow from the premises, because the conclusion would call for an asterisk in the diagram, but the premises will not provide any asterisk. Still, perhaps some other conclusion might follow; we can't be certain until we inquire. When we diagram the two premises, however, we find that they do not give us as much information as the pair of premises just considered, for they shade out only three subclasses, not four. (I have pointed this up by making my shading go in two different directions, but that is not necessary once you are used to the diagrams.)

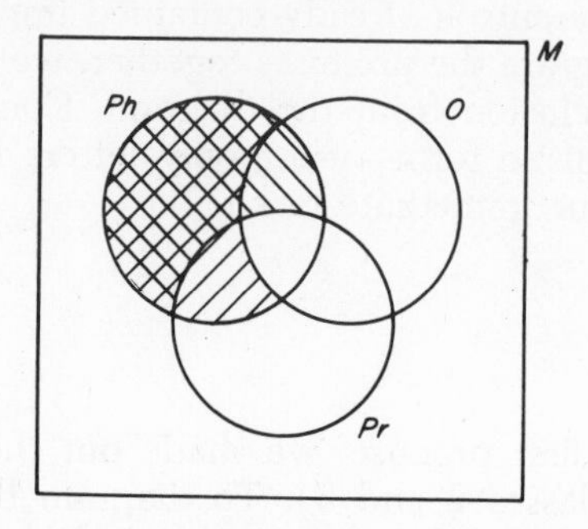

From so meager a pair of premises, no syllogistic conclusion can be drawn.

The second type of diagram is illustrated by the first syllogism displayed in this section; using appropriate letters, it may be outlined as follows: "No *O* are *C;* some *P* are *C;* therefore, some *P* are not *O.*" Now this sort of diagram rests on a kind of disjunctive argument. Take the particular premise (and for clarity it is best to follow the procedure of diagramming it first). It says that somewhere in the overlap of the *P* circle and the *C* circle there is something; but we do not know from this premise alone whether it is inside or outside the *O* circle. So we put an asterisk in each of these subclasses (5 and 6), and join them by a bar to indicate that we are in doubt about exactly where in this area the asterisk ought to go. If the syllogism is a sound one, and yields a conclusion, that will be because the universal premise comes to our rescue, and tells us that

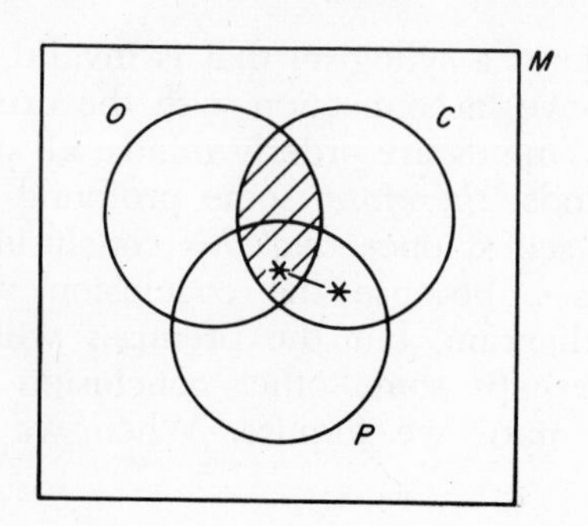

the asterisk does *not* belong in one of the subclasses—from which we can infer that it belongs in the other. The universal premise pushes the asterisk out of one area into another. The diagram tells us that some *P* are not *O*.

It is obvious from this analysis that two particular premises will not get us anywhere—because at least one universal premise is needed to resolve the doubt about where the asterisk goes. It is also plain that if the area shaded out by the universal premise doesn't touch either of the asterisks, no conclusion can be drawn from the premises. This is the case, for example, with the syllogism used above to illustrate Rules 1 and 2. In capsule form, the argument went: "Some *S* are *V*; all *H* are *V*; therefore, some *H* are *S*." The diagram:

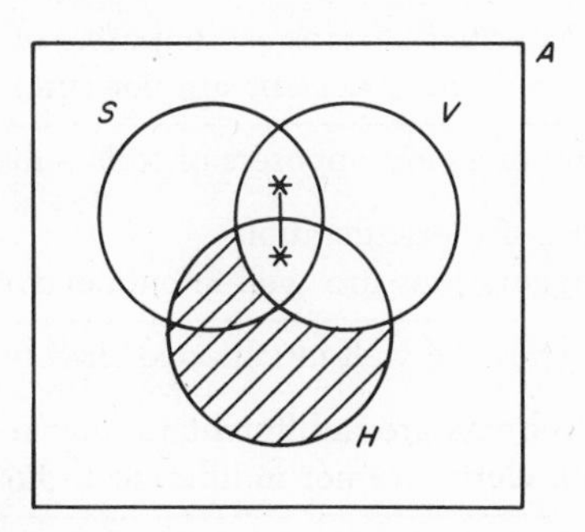

The premises simply don't connect.

A Check-up Quiz Which fallacies (maldistributed middle, uneven distribution, or unequal negation), if any, are committed by each of the following syllogisms?

1. All night clubs are expensive places.
   All night clubs are exclusive places.

   All exclusive places are expensive places.

2. All newspaper stories are pieces that are written in a rush.
   All pieces that are written in a rush are inaccurate reports.

   All newspaper stories are inaccurate reports.

3. No great men are heroes to their valets.
   Gideon Parzifal is not a hero to his valet.

   Gideon Parzifal is a great man.

4. All spring water is water that is beneficial to drink.
   Some spring water is polluted water.
   ___
   Some polluted water is beneficial to drink.

5. All people who are unlucky at cards are people who are lucky in love.
   Some misogynists are people who are not unlucky at cards.
   ___
   Some misogynists are people who are not lucky in love.

6. Some surfers are bachelors.
   No bachelors are people without pride.
   ___
   Some people without pride are not surfers.

7. No public-spirited persons are opposers of train subsidies.
   Some public-spirited persons are not commuters.
   ___
   Some commuters are opposers of train subsidies.

8. All eulogies are exaggerations.
   Some exaggerations are well-intentioned discourses.
   ___
   Some eulogies are well-intentioned discourses.

9. No bank robbers are indifferent to financial gain.
   Some bank clerks are not indifferent to financial gain.
   ___
   Some bank clerks are bank robbers.

10. Some subjects worthy of study are boring subjects.
    Some of the humanities are not boring subjects.
    ___
    Some of the humanities are not worthy of study.

For Further Study Henry W. Johnstone, Jr., *Elementary Deductive Logic,* Chs. 12–15. New York: Thomas Y. Crowell Co., 1954. Max Black, *Critical Thinking,* 2nd ed., Chs. 3, 8. Englewood Cliffs, N.J.: Prentice-Hall, Inc., 1952.

§8. sizing up a syllogism

The syllogisms we have dealt with so far have all come to us in a tidy condition, ready for testing by rule and diagram. But those we usually encounter in ordinary life present us with some difficulties that have to be overcome before we get to the stage of testing, for they are couched in the casual, elliptical, and sometimes careless language of journalism, or (more troubling) in the intense, emotional, and often confusing language of persuasion. We need an orderly procedure by which syllogistic arguments in their natural state, so to speak, can be processed or prepared for logical appraisal.

I will outline seven steps for sizing up a syllogism. Not all of them are called for in every case, but a great many arguments require a little attention to some of these points if we are to be quite sure that we know exactly what the argument *is* before we try to judge its validity.

Step 1. Read it carefully (of course).

> Your accusation that I admit the existence of truly religious people who take no part in the struggle for social justice is false, because my philosophy is against the principle that only irreligious people are excluded from the company of those who live up to their moral obligations, and my philosophy also holds that it is one's duty to join the struggle for social justice.

This example bristles with more than the average number of difficulties, and it will serve to illustrate several points.

Step 2. Separate premises from conclusion.

In our present example, this is not hard to do, because the first statement seems quite definitely, even aggressively, presented as a thesis, and the logical indicator "because" clearly marks the other two statements as premises. So it is not hard to sort out the two main parts of the argument. And it is not even necessary (as it often is) to eliminate pronouns that refer back to previous terms, and to replace them with their antecedents.

> My philosophy is against the principle that only irreligious people are excluded from the company of those who live up to their moral obligations.
>
> My philosophy holds that it is one's duty to join the struggle for social justice.
>
> ---
>
> Your accusation that I admit the existence of truly religious people who take no part in the struggle for social justice is false.

Step 3. Identify the universe of discourse and its three classes.

A syllogism connects three classes with each other, and to follow it we must understand exactly what the classes are, and within which universe of discourse they lie. One problem is that if we take each statement separately, we can readily find a universe of discourse appropriate to it; but if the syllogism is to be valid, and if we are to escape confusions about negative terms, there must be a single universe of discourse for the whole syllogism. This must be broad enough to contain all of the three classes.

In the first premise and the conclusion, the universe is quite evidently *people.* The second premise, taken by itself, is a statement about a kind of *action,* namely, joining the struggle for social justice. But to treat this argument as a syllogistic inference, we must find a way of reinterpreting the second premise so that it, too, deals with the relationship of two classes within the universe of people. Can this be done?

If it is one's duty (*anyone*'s duty) to join the struggle for social justice, then anyone who does his duty is someone who has joined that struggle. This revised version of the second premise does not pretend to mean exactly the same thing; it merely selects from the second premise that part of its information that is needed if this argument is to be an effective syllogism. Of course the argument, after some scrutiny, may turn out not to be a syllogism at all—or even if it is, it may not be a good one. But it is superficially enough like a syllogism to invite us to consider it as one—to see whether it can be justified by the syllogistic rules of inference.

If we understand the second premise, then, as connecting the two classes, *people who do their duty* and *people who join the struggle for social justice,* we find the following terms in the argument:

irreligious people
people who live up to their moral obligations
people who do their duty
people who join the struggle for social justice
truly religious people
people who take no part in the struggle for social justice

These six terms are far too many for a syllogism, of course—they are enough for two syllogisms. To get them into one syllogism, we have to reduce them to three. And this can be done in two ways.

In the first place, if two terms are sufficiently close in meaning, we may take them as synonymous for the purposes of the argument at hand. Again, we must not lose sight of subtle distinctions (this point will be emphasized in later chapters of this book). But if the two terms mark out the same class of things (in this case, people), they can be considered the same term in the syllogism. We have, for example, "people who do their duty" and "people who live up to their moral obligations," and the arguer in this example seems to treat these as interchangeable. Again, we have "people who join the struggle for social justice" and "people who take . . . part in the struggle for social justice," and these seem to be close enough in meaning to be regarded as the same term. It is best to select one member of each pair and let that do the work of both.

In the second place, if two terms are negatives of each other, then we may be able to eliminate one of them by changing the whole statement to an equivalent one. We have, for example, "irreligious people" (or "nonreligious people") and "truly religious people," and we don't need both. But this procedure is best postponed until after the statements have been put in standard form. We now have the following set of terms:

people who do their (moral) duty
religious people (*vs.* nonreligious people)
people who join the struggle for social justice (*vs.* people who do not join the struggle for social justice)

Step 4. Analyze the logical structure of the three statements, and make this explicit by putting them in standard form.

In our present example, it seems as though the arguer has gone out of his way to make his assertions in a roundabout fashion. The second premise, now that we have gotten clear about its universe and its classes, raises no difficulties; it is evidently a *UA* statement: "All / people who do their duty / are / people who join the struggle for social justice." (When the terms are rather complex, as in this example, it is a help to separate them by slanted lines or some other device.) The first premise states a "principle" and then asserts its denial, so there are two steps in getting it straight. The principle is that "Only nonreligious people / are / people who do not do their duty." The construction "Only *A* are *B*" says, in effect, that you must be an *A* if you are a *B*, or that all *B* are *A*. So the "principle" in the first premise is "All / people who do not do their duty / are / nonreligious people." But what the arguer is asserting is the contradictory of this, namely: "Some / people who do not do their duty / are not / nonreligious people."

The conclusion, again, is a denial of a statement. The "accusation" is that the arguer admits the existence of people who both (a) are religious and (b) do not join the struggle for social justice. The "accusation" is then a *PA* statement: "Some / religious people / are / people who do not join the struggle for social justice." But to say that the "accusation" is false is to assert its contradictory; so the conclusion really is the *UN* statement, "No / religious people / are / people who do not join the struggle for social justice."

These examples raise a few of the many questions that can arise in putting ordinary English sentences into standard logical form. We cannot review them all here, but the main idioms should be mentioned. "All *A* are *B* except *C*" can be recast as "All the *A* that are not *C* are *B*" (in this case *A* is probably the universe of discourse). "*A* are never *B*" can be recast as "No *A* are *B*." "There are *A* that are *B*" can be recast as "Some *A* are *B*." And "Not all *A* are *B*" can be recast as "Some *A* are not *B*." Sentences like "All *A* are not *B*" are to be avoided, though they are all too common. Depending on what has just been said, the remark that "All bail-bondsmen are not poor people" might mean that some of them are not poor, or that none of them is poor.

As a result of our analysis, we can put the whole argument together this way:

> Some / people who do not do their duty / are not / nonreligious people.
>
> All / people who do their duty / are / people who join the struggle for social justice.
>
> ---
>
> No / religious people / are / people who do not join the struggle for social justice.

Step 5. Put the whole syllogism into standard form.

Even though the individual statements are in good shape, we still have too many terms to make a syllogism. We must now try to reduce them to the required number. It may turn out that we cannot reduce them to three; in that case the argument, strictly speaking, is not a syllogism (some would call it a "four-term syllogism"), and it cannot be valid by the syllogistic rules—though it might be valid by some other rules.

When we undertake to reduce the number of terms by substituting equivalent statements for some of those above, several choices may be open to us. Providing we are correct in our substitutions, it doesn't matter how we do it. We may wind up with a different syllogism, which may commit a different fallacy, but we can be sure of one thing: if a syllogism commits a fallacy, then any syllogism made from it by substituting equivalent statements will also commit some fallacy.

We can transform the second premise by turning it around and negating the terms. If all duty-doers are struggle-joiners, then all non–struggle-joiners are non–duty-doers. We also have to change the first premise from a *PA* statement to an equivalent *PN* statement, in order to change "nonreligious people" to "religious people." If some non–duty-doers are not nonreligious, then they *are* religious. The result:

Some / people who do not do their duty / are / religious people.
All / people who do not join the struggle for social justice / are / people who do not do their duty.

No / religious people / are / people who do not join the struggle for social justice.

Step 6. Test the syllogism by the rules.

To apply the first rule, we seek out the middle term, "people who do not do their duty." As the subject of a particular statement in the first premise, and as the predicate of an affirmative statement in the second premise, it is not distributed in either location. So the syllogism commits the fallacy of maldistributed middle.

To apply the second rule, we look for end terms that are distributed in one location but not in the other. "Religious people" is distributed in the conclusion as the subject of a universal statement, but it is undistributed in the first premise as the predicate of an affirmative statement. Second fallacy: uneven distribution of end term.

To apply the third rule, we try to match the negative conclusion with a negative premise. But both premises are affirmative. Third fallacy: unequal negation.

In fact, a clean sweep.

Step 7. Check by means of a diagram.

When you are dealing with negative terms, it is important to choose letters with care. Indeed, it seems best to let the letters and circles stand for positive terms.

Let *D* be "people who do their duty."
Let *R* be "religious people."
Let *J* be "people who join the struggle for social justice."

Remember, then, that the non-*D* are the people *outside* the *D* circle, and the non-*J* are the people *outside* the *J* circle.

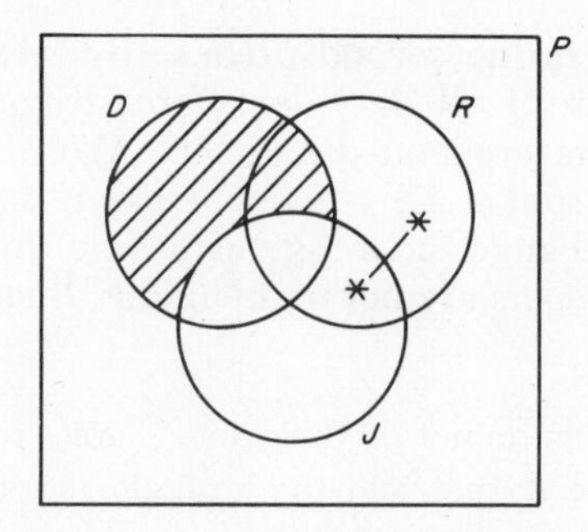

It is hardly necessary in this case to assure ourselves by a diagram that the syllogism is defective.

So far we have been looking at syllogisms from one point of view: given a pair of premises, can you or can you not derive this or that conclusion from them? But we can also look at the situation from the other end: given a conclusion, what would be required to prove it? Any conclusion can be deduced from an indefinitely large number of pairs of premises—though not from that many true ones. But suppose we are given one of the premises; then we can always find the other, by reasoning backward according to the syllogistic rules.

> Reducing taxes will inevitably stimulate a rise in business because it will increase purchasing power.

This is typical of many of the arguments we encounter in daily life. It is two-thirds of a syllogism, and since it claims (apparently) to be a deductive inference, the question is whether the inference is justified. One of the premises has been left out—it is taken for granted. And unstated premises are among the most dangerous; we must be especially careful to see exactly what they are, before we are ready to accept the conclusion.

In this case, we are not testing the validity of the syllogism. Our task is to supply the missing premise that will make it valid by the syllogistic rules. We begin by putting it into standard form, as far as it goes:

All / acts of reducing taxes / are / acts that increase purchasing power.

All / acts of reducing taxes / are / acts that stimulate a rise in business.

It is easy enough to see what the missing premise is, once we set out the argument formally. Since the conclusion is affirmative, the other premise must be affirmative; and since the conclusion is universal, the other premise must be universal. Therefore it is a *UA* statement. The order of terms is easy to figure out, and the premise is:

[All / acts that increase purchasing power / are / acts that stimulate a rise in business.]

The statement is put in brackets to indicate that it is understood, not expressed. Of course the arguer, when confronted with his missing premise, may disavow it. But he has a hard choice: either he must confess that he is committed to the premise (and be prepared to stand by it) or else he must abandon his argument, for without that premise the conclusion does not follow.

Single syllogisms do not take you very far in reasoning, but when several syllogisms are combined, the final conclusion may be somewhat unexpected. A **syllogism chain** is a series of syllogisms so linked that the conclusion of one syllogism is a premise of the next. The principle of the syllogism chain can be illustrated by this somewhat artificial exercise: what conclusion can be derived (syllogistically) from the following set of premises?

1. All major social reforms are carried through against determined opposition.
2. When bitterness is created by a reform, wholehearted cooperation is not obtained.
3. Financial reforms are always major ones.
4. Without cooperation, a reform cannot succeed.
5. No reforms carried through against determined opposition fail to create bitterness.

The task is to select two of these statements with a common term that can serve as the middle term in a syllogism, and to derive from them a valid conclusion, which can be combined with another statement to derive a further conclusion, and so on, until the premises are used up. It does not matter where you begin—the end result will be the same, if you proceed correctly. For example, we might begin with 1 and 5, and from them derive the conclusion: "No major social reforms fail to create bitterness." This can be combined with 2, and their conclusion with 4, and that conclusion with 3. Result? "No financial reforms can succeed."

A complicated argument, involving an elaborate syllogism chain intermingled with other forms of inference, may give us some trouble in tracking down all the premises, including those tacitly assumed. But this trouble is fully worth it in cases where an argument falls into one of the most fundamental fallacies of deductive reasoning. The fallacies we have dealt with so far are breakdowns in the course of reasoning—points at which the argument, though claiming to take us somewhere, fails to make good because there is a missing connection, like the airplane that arrives in Chicago just too late for you to catch the plane to Denver. But there is another way in which (if I may press the analogy) a plane ride can be futile—and that is when the plane leaves the ground, flies off, turns around, and lands again at the same airport where you boarded it. A deductive argument may be perfectly valid, and its premises may even all be true, but if the conclusion it purports to prove is already to be found among its own premises (perhaps in different words), it is surely futile. It is a **circular argument.** It commits the error of assuming what it sets out to prove, the **fallacy of begging the question.**

It is naturally not easy to find or construct a brief example of a circular argument that has much plausibility. The secret of success in circular reasoning is to keep the premises far enough away from the conclusion, and if possible to suppress some premises, so that the failure of the argument can be concealed.

> I am sure that none of our really responsible citizens are opposed to the City Council's plan to build a gigantic new municipal sports stadium over the Pennsylvania railroad tracks. Obviously the health of our citizens is a prime consideration, which any responsible citizen supports, and sports mean health. If we attract a major franchise, it will also bring money to the city. I realize that some will question my argument, and cite the names of various people who have expressed disagreement with the City Council's position, but that does not refute my claim. For if they are opposed to so excellent a plan, then by the same token they must be lacking in responsibility.

This is perhaps not one of the tightest examples, but it illustrates some of the factors involved in circularity. One way of exposing the circularity is to take the first statement, "no responsible citizens are opposed to the plan," as the conclusion. This is supported by a rather shaky syllogism, but let that pass. The speaker seems to be aware that further support would not be amiss, and so he tries a second approach: suppose, he says, that someone is cited as opposed to the plan; since they are opposed, it follows that they are not responsible. This does follow, if we assume, as a suppressed premise, that no one who is opposed is responsible. But this is the very conclusion to be reached.

Another way of analyzing the argument (for a circle can be broken into at any point) is to take the final conclusion to be "The plan is an excellent one." The reason is that the plan is supported by responsible citizens, and opposed by irresponsible ones. How do we know which are which? Well, anyone who is opposed to good things is somewhat irresponsible (the speaker says in effect), and *since the plan is good,* those who oppose it are irresponsible. The circle is a little larger in this interpretation, but it is no less complete.

The word "really" in the very first sentence should put us on our guard. Not that it is always a sign that a question is being begged, but when a writer or speaker qualifies a general statement with "essentially" or "genuinely" or "truly" or "at heart," there is a strong possibility that something odd is taking place. "I always welcome really *constructive* criticism," says the boss, with a slight emphasis on "constructive." Then we may take warning that any criticism he doesn't want to hear will be dismissed as not "constructive." The freewheeling generalizer (whose acquaintance we shall make in the following chapter) may hope to get away with some loose statement about "all Republicans" or "all Democrats" by one of these little question-beggars. We reply, "But so-and-so is Republican, and your generalization doesn't apply to him"—and rather than withdraw it, he will try to show that so-and-so is not "really" or "essentially" a Republican, so the counter-evidence doesn't count. These words have important uses, but when they are used to escape criticism by this maneuver—which defends an assertion by tacitly assuming it is true—they are *weasel-words.* Another serious, and at the same time subtle, way of making an argument in a circle is a technique that we shall discuss in Chapter 6—the question-begging definition.

Our only protection against circularity is to keep a firm grip on the logical structure—what is asserted as the conclusion, what is asserted as a premise, and by what steps the argument moves from one to the other.

A Check-up Quiz Put the following sentences into standard logical form.

1. What people don't know won't hurt their feelings.
2. Only *mental* anguish can be caused by insults.
3. It isn't every husband who's got a wife that can play the zither.

4. Non-Catholics are not all Protestants.
5. Not only the horses are tired.
6. The members were all present, except the officers.
7. Inflation is never dangerous unless it continues a long time.
8. The show was witty in spots.
9. Denying a rumor does not necessarily squelch it.
10. Unheard-of things are not unheard of.
11. "There is no excellent beauty that hath not some strangeness in the proportions" [Francis Bacon].
12. The building contained more fire-extinguishers than working fire-extinguishers.
13. "In other words, just from wondering whether the wedding is on or off, a person can develop a cough."
14. To appreciate the music of Monteverdi, one must enjoy hearing augmented fifths.
15. "There isn't a person here who didn't buy his house after the tract was zoned commercial," he said.

For Further Study Monroe C. Beardsley, *Practical Logic,* Ch. 8 and Ch. 10, §50. Englewood Cliffs, N.J.: Prentice-Hall, Inc., 1950.

OUTLINE-SUMMARY: chapter two

Deductive arguments may be divided into (1) molecular arguments, in which whole statements are combined and recombined in various ways, and (2) subatomic arguments, in which parts of statements (namely, terms) are rearranged in the course of the reasoning.

Two forms of molecular argument are very common and fundamental: (1) In the valid form of the *disjunctive argument,* the first premise is a disjunctive statement ("Either the window was closed or it rained in"), the second premise denies one of the two disjuncts ("The window was not closed"), and the conclusion asserts the other disjunct ("Therefore, it rained in"). In the invalid form of the disjunctive argument, the second premise affirms one of the two disjuncts ("The window was closed"), and the conclusion denies the other disjunct ("Therefore, it did not rain in"); this commits the *fallacy of affirming a disjunct.* (2) In the *condi-*

tional argument, the first premise is a conditional statement ("If the pitcher is dropped, then it will break"); in one valid form, the second premise affirms the antecedent of this conditional premise ("The pitcher will be dropped"), and the conclusion affirms the consequent ("Therefore, the pitcher will break"); in the other valid form, the second premise denies the consequent ("The pitcher will not break"), and the conclusion denies the antecedent ("Therefore, the pitcher will not be dropped"). In one of the invalid forms, the second premise affirms the consequent, and the conclusion affirms the antecedent (this commits the *fallacy of affirming the consequent*); in the other invalid form, the second premise denies the antecedent, and the conclusion denies the consequent (the *fallacy of denying the antecedent*).

A *conditional chain argument* is a series of conditional premises linked in such a way that the antecedent of the first one and the consequent of the last one can be combined in a conditional statement that is a valid conclusion.

One statement *implies* a second one if the second necessarily follows from the first, and two statements that imply each other are *logically equivalent.* When one statement implies the falsity of a second statement, they are *logically incompatible;* if their denials are also incompatible with each other, then they are *contradictories;* if they are incompatible without being contradictories, they are *contraries;* if they themselves are not incompatible, but their denials are, then they are *subcontraries.*

Four types of two-term statement can be distinguished: the universal affirmative ("All *A* are *B*"), the particular affirmative ("Some *A* are *B*"), the universal negative ("No *A* are *B*"), and the particular negative ("Some *A* are not *B*"). The *UA* statement and the *PN* statement are contradictories; the *UN* statement and the *PA* statement are contradictories. If we make the *existence assumption* (that is, assume that there actually are members of the class *A*), then the *UA* statement and the *UN* statement are contraries, and the *PA* statement and the *PN* statement are subcontraries.

The most common type of subatomic argument is the *syllogism,* which involves (1) three two-term statements, of which two are premises and one the conclusion, and (2) three terms, of which one (the middle term) appears in both premises and each of the others (the end terms) appears in the conclusion and in one of the premises. A syllogism is valid if and only if it satisfies the following three rules: (1) The middle term must be distributed (that is, it must be either the subject of a universal statement or the predicate of a negative statement) exactly once; (2) No end term may be distributed only once; and (3) The number of negative premises must equal the number of negative conclusions. A syllogism that violates Rule 1 commits the *fallacy of maldistributed middle;* Rule 2, the *fallacy of uneven distribution;* Rule 3, the *fallacy of unequal negation.*

When the conclusion of a deductive argument appears as one of its own premises, whether tacit or explicit (perhaps in other words), the argument is *circular* and commits the *fallacy of begging the question.*

Exercise 5

What fallacies, if any, are committed by the following molecular arguments?

1. If the President's nominee for the federal judgeship is a man who defied the federal courts when he was governor (and he did), then his nomination should be rejected by the Judiciary Committee.

2. Either the Municipal Art Commission will accept the gift of works by Henry Moore and Archipenko, or it is wholly lacking in appreciation of modern sculpture. We know from past experience that the Commission does not appreciate modern sculpture; obviously, they will reject the gift.

3. Either Project Self-Help will succeed in bringing new hope to the poverty-affected groups in the city or there is little chance that the antipoverty program will get to the roots of the problem. Project Self-Help apparently is not equipped to bring hope to the poor people, and consequently the antipoverty program will not get to the roots of the problem.

4. If we live in a democracy, then decisions about important matters should be made by the majority. If decisions should be made by the majority, then television stations should cancel all programs that have a low Nielsen rating. Therefore, if we live in a democracy, only popular television programs should be shown.

5. The choice that lies before us is to continue on an increasingly risky and unpredictable course or to find a way to negotiate a peace. We shall never negotiate. Therefore we can only continue as we have.

6. If 27 million voters who voted for one candidate can't be wrong, then 43 million voters who voted for the other candidate can't be wrong. But if the 43 million voters are right, then the 27 million voters *must* be wrong. Therefore, if 27 million voters can't be wrong, then they must be wrong.

7. If the Mariner spacecraft's signals were not seriously diminished in passing through the atmosphere of Mars, then the atmosphere is

very thin. If the atmosphere is very thin, it will not support an ordinary parachute. If it will not support an ordinary parachute, astronauts will have to use retrorockets to land there. Therefore, if the signals were not seriously diminished, retrorockets will be necessary for landing.

8. If the value of a product were determined by the amount of labor put into it, then mud pies would cost as much as mince pies. But they don't—which is enough to refute the labor theory of value.

9. "This must be the context of our thinking—the context of human interdependence in the face of the vast new dimensions of our science and our discovery," said Adlai Stevenson. What to most of us appear as mighty confrontations of power, he could see as the "squabbling" of nations "before the awful majesty of outer space." . . . To attain such a view a man must be either a supreme cynic or imbued with a faith that escapes the comprehension of men of more modest capacity. Cynicism, however, is not impressed by "the vast dimensions of our science and our discovery." This leaves faith as the only explanation of the power of Adlai Stevenson [from *The New Republic*].

10. It is idle to expect any great advancement in science from the superinducing and engrafting of new things upon old. We must begin anew from the very foundations, unless we would revolve for ever in a circle with mean and contemptible progress [Francis Bacon, *Novum Organum*].

Exercise 6

Examine the following pairs of statements and determine in each case whether one of the statements implies the other, or whether they are equivalent, contrary, subcontrary, contradictory, or independent.

1. (a) A majority of those who voted for the Republican candidate are middle-class people.
   (b) A majority of those who voted for the Democratic candidate are middle-class people.

2. (a) Only rash people take unreasonable risks.
   (b) Only those who take unreasonable risks are rash.

3. (a) Bills passed by a considerable majority are never vetoed by by the governor.
   (b) Bills passed by a considerable majority are seldom vetoed by the governor.

4. (a) Anyone who is a friend of Charlie is the friend of a racketeer.
   (b) Charlie is a racketeer.

5. (a) The banquet will be held next Friday.
   (b) The banquet will be held next Saturday.

6. (a) Not all the members of the Liquor Control Board are teetotallers.
   (b) Not all the members of the Liquor Control Board are non-teetotallers.

7. (a) All games of chance publicly played for the purpose of gambling are illegal in this state unless they are managed by churches or fire companies.
   (b) No public gambling in games of chance that are not managed by fire companies or churches are legally permitted in this state.

8. (a) Aggressor nations should be curbed by the U.N. if it is agreed that the aggression is unprovoked.
   (b) No aggression that should not be curbed by the U.N. is the unprovoked aggression of aggressor nations.

9. (a) All power corrupts.
   (b) Absolute power corrupts absolutely.

10. REPLY BY EMILY POST: Since a baked potato is never served at a formal dinner, any dinner at which it is served is an informal dinner so you may do as you like.

Exercise 7

Analyze the following syllogisms and determine whether they are valid or invalid, and if invalid, what fallacies they commit.

1. Without charity, just actions are ineffectual, but with intelligence they are effectual; therefore, just actions cannot be both charitable and intelligent.

2. Among the Bushongo there will not be found any women who have been admitted by initiation to the rank of magic-maker, and all those who tend the river-cows are similarly among the uninitiated. It follows that only women tend the river-cows.

3. Some readers of the *Lit* are certainly unfamiliar with the writings of Alistair Cooke, for they are not subscribers to the *Phoenix*, but subscribers to the *Phoenix* are all familiar with his writings.

4. Marry in haste, repent at leisure, but long engagements mean unhasty marriages; therefore, long engagements mean no repenting at leisure.

5. Some translations of Russian poetry are very faithful to the original, but translations that are not faithful to the original are never highly poetic; therefore not all highly poetic translations are of Russian poetry.

6. Candidates for the presidential nomination who are fearful of not winning always announce their intention early, and therefore have a good chance to win, since only those who announce their intentions early have a good chance to win.

7. In the absence of an administration that is not budget-conscious, we cannot expect to be leaders in space exploration, for without a firmly supported missile program no country can be a leader in this field, and budget-conscious administrations never give firm support to such programs.

8. Not every theological work in the library is written in Dutch, and none of the Dutch books are written by Unamuno; from which it follows that some of the books by Unamuno are theological works.

9. To the Editor: Goldwater's statement that discrimination is morally wrong but constitutionally right ineluctably implies that our Constitution is immoral.

10. Our state has a Democratic governor and a Republican legislature. Since, as Disraeli said, "No government can be long secure without a formidable opposition," it follows that our state government is secure indeed.

11. Every citizen who, by reason of old age, is incapable of self-support should clearly receive social-security payments. Hence some women between the ages of 62 and 65 should not receive such payments, since they are not incapable of self-support.

12. We know that some Democrats voted for him in the primary this time, but no Democrats voted in the primary for him last time. Therefore, some who voted for him last time did not vote for him this time.

13. Religion always provides a basis for ethics; consequently our schools must teach religion if they are to be sound schools, since only schools that provide a basis for ethics can be sound.

14. If a person is never happy unless he's well fed, but always happy unless he's poor, it follows that he's never well fed when he's poor.

15. Oriental rulers should not be judged according to our moral standards, but according to theirs; they live in a different culture, and it is not fair to judge people in a different culture by any standards but their own.

16. First of all, let us agree that there are really no great paintings that are insincere. Second, you will concede, I think, that there are some great paintings that are not strictly beautiful (though they may be powerful, sublime, and moving). Therefore, there are some beautiful paintings that are sincere.

17. The leaders of Russia can come to understand and respect the United States only if they see it at first hand; consequently, visits by them ought to be encouraged, since it is highly desirable that the Russian leaders understand and respect the United States.

18. Farmers who participate in the soil-bank plan will inevitably find themselves bossed around by Washington bureaucrats, because they will have to accept certain marketing quotas, which in turn require federal supervision, and that leads to bureaucratic bossing.

19. No permanent solution of the farm problem can be fair to everyone concerned, for no solution will immediately raise farm income, while any solution that raises farm income will bring it closer to that of factory workers, and this is a fair thing to do.

20. No one ought to be condemned in a security case without knowing who is his accuser. For if he does not know who his accuser is, he cannot confront him, and, deprived of this opportunity, he is in no position to secure evidence concerning the reliability of the accuser as a witness, which is a necessary condition of his being able to conduct a fair defense.

Exercise 8

Cast the following syllogistic arguments into standard form, and test their validity (a) by the syllogistic rules and (b) by a diagram.

1. Solicitor General Archibald Cox Before the United States Supreme Court: The major premise of our argument is the familiar rule that the powers delegated to Congress by the commerce and necessary-and-proper clauses authorize Congress to regulate local activities, at least activities that are local but separately considered,

even though they are not themselves interstate commerce, if they have such a close and substantial relation to commerce that their regulation may be deemed appropriate or useful to foster or promote such commerce, or to relieve it of burdens and obstructions.

The minor premise of our argument is that Congress, to which the economic question thus raised is primarily committed, had ample basis upon which to find that racial discrimination does in fact constitute a source of burden or obstruction to interstate commerce. And, of course, from those premises the conclusion would follow that this is a legitimate exercise of the power under the commerce clause.

2. If, then, in a creature endowed with the faculties of foresight and reason, the social affections could not have unfolded themselves uncountenanced by the faith that Man is an immortal being; and if, consequently, neither could the individual dying have had a desire to survive in the remembrance of his fellows, nor on their side could they have felt a wish to preserve for future times vestiges of the departed; it follows, as a final inference, that, without the belief in immortality, wherein these several desires originate, neither monuments nor epitaphs, in affectionate or laudatory commemoration of the deceased, could have existed in the world [William Wordsworth, "Upon Epitaphs"].

3. Millions of words have been spoken and written about juvenile delinquency. . . . How can I dogmatically assume to know the answer? . . . Open your Bible to Proverbs 22:6 and read. . . . Psalm 119:9 says, "Wherewithal shall a young man cleanse his way? By taking heed thereto according to thy word."

What word? The Word of God!

Already I can sense many turning away, perhaps on the basis that this is narrow-minded thinking. However, the truth is always narrow, as any scientist can testify. Two plus two always equals four, whether we like it or not. And yet, in our homes, in our schools, in our churches, in our government, and in our businesses, we have all too often subscribed to the modern belief that there are shades of right and wrong in practically every area of life [from an article on "The Cure for Juvenile Delinquency"].

4. The history of liberty is a history of the limitation of governmental power, not the increase of it. When we resist, therefore, the concentration of power, we are resisting the processes of death, because concentration of power is what always precedes the destruction of human liberties [Woodrow Wilson].

5. Some maintain that no law, however bad, ought to be disobeyed by an individual citizen; that his opposition to it, if shown at all, should only be shown in endeavoring to get it altered by competent authority. This opinion (which condemns many of the most illustrious benefactors of mankind, and would often protect pernicious institutions against the only weapons which, in the state of things existing at the time, have any chance of succeeding against them) is defended, by those who hold it, on grounds of expediency; principally on that of the importance, to the common interest of mankind, of maintaining inviolate the sentiment of submission to law. . . . But again, some say that all laws which are inexpedient are unjust; since every law imposes some restriction on the natural liberty of mankind, which restriction is an injustice, unless legitimated by tending to their good [John Stuart Mill].

Exercise 9

Supply, in standard form, the premise that is missing from each of the following syllogistic arguments.

1. The proposed federal monetary policy will slow up the school construction program, for it will raise interest rates to the point where cities cannot afford to borrow.

2. Since to encourage the exploitation of natural resources is of benefit to the public, natural-gas producers should be freed from federal control.

3. Parents who help their children with their homework are laying the foundations of juvenile delinquency, for it inevitably weakens one's sense of responsibility to be excused from doing one's duty.

4. There is no need for the country to follow the sheepskin parade and send so many young people to college; we got along well enough a hundred years ago, when only a small percentage had college degrees.

5. Our enormous economic and military aid to foreign nations has not succeeded in making them love us; consequently, it should be written off as a failure and discontinued at once.

6. Unfortunately, my opponent's argument has a hidden premise which he has not explicitly stated; therefore, the conclusion is not acceptable.

7. He will undoubtedly succeed in developing his project, the

Chester Home Improvement Program, into a valuable community organization, for he believes wholeheartedly in what he is doing.

8. Without confidence in our ultimate triumph over totalitarianism, we in the democracies have no hope of winning; hence it is necessary for our great mass media to play up good news and play down or suppress bad news.

9. Some of the accused members of the State Highway Commission must have been guilty of taking bribes. Otherwise, why would they have resigned when the investigation got started?

10. To sustain the individual freedom of action contemplated by the Constitution is not to strike down the common good, but to exalt it; for surely the good of society as a whole cannot be better served than by the preservation against arbitrary restraint of the liberties of its constituent members [Justice George Sutherland].

Exercise 10

Explain all inconsistencies and circularities of reasoning in the following passages.

1. Asked if he believed that President Johnson and Senator Humphrey were personally "soft on communism," as Senator Goldwater charged this week in Ohio, Mr. Miller replied: "I think the policies which they seem to be following, in my judgment, would indicate to me that this allegation could be justifiably made in the campaign, just as they try to make an issue of the fact that Senator Goldwater is 'trigger-happy,' which we know, as former President Eisenhower said, is poppycock" [*New York Times,* October 3, 1964].

2. Senator Jackson, in an address at the National Press Club, stated a few commonplaces and then moved on to the ambiguous and the contradictory. He said that the United Nations "should continue to be an important avenue of American foreign policy," yet wondered whether "the involvement of the U.N. in our policy making has not at times hampered the wise definition of our national interest. . . ." He stated that "the maintainance of peace depends . . . on the strength and will of its [U.N.'s] members to uphold the charter," but later amended this by insisting that "peace depends on the power and unity of the Atlantic Community and on the skill of our secret diplomacy." He questioned the value of "U.N. presences to halt infiltration of guerillas across frontiers," leaving his audience to wonder whether he thought United States military forces might more efficiently

police the peace in the Congo or the Sinai peninsula. Then, having advocated that the U.N. make fewer decisions, and talk more, he said that "Everyone talks too much. . . . Sometimes it seems that the appropriate legend to place above the portals of the U.N. might be: 'Through these doors pass the most articulate men and women in the world' " [*The Reporter*].

3. There are many ways of responding to a work of art, including burning it up, but not all these responses are strictly aesthetic responses. As has been pointed out by several aestheticians, an aesthetic response is a response to the *essentially artistic* elements of the work. For example, you listen to the melodies in the music, rather than daydreaming about the composer's love affairs, and you pay attention to the design of the painting rather than to its religious message. In short, to tell whether a response is legitimately aesthetic, you must see what it is a response *to*. . . . .

It is also necessary to tackle a further question: What are the essentially artistic elements in a work of art? And how are they to be distinguished from the nonessential or peripheral ones? To some extent there is agreement on these—the biography of a composer, for example, is not a part of his music. On other matters there is disagreement—for example, concerning the relevance of knowledge about the symbolic meaning of objects in a painting to appreciation of its artistic merit. So the best way of discovering whether a particular element is essentially artistic is to ask what sort of response it can give rise to: if it evokes a strictly aesthetic response, then we know that it is an essentially artistic element. If not, then not. This is the only useful and conclusive test.

4. Gentlemen, as an automobile manufacturer, I am glad of this opportunity to appear before the General Services Administration and explain why we are opposed to the proposal to require numerous safety devices installed on 60,000 cars which the United States government will be buying this year. I have said before, and I repeat, that no one really knows what causes automobile accidents. The wise and sensible course is not to jump to conclusions, and blame it on this, that or the other thing, but to undertake a program of research to discover the true causes. I am proud to announce that General Motors is making a grant of one million dollars to M.I.T. to undertake this study. Let us not be emotional; let us be reasonable. My position, to put it bluntly, is that all this emphasis on safety gadgets, special steering wheels and so on, is beside the real point. They are only a drop in the bucket. A study made a while back by the National Safety

Council showed that 90 per cent of all accidents are the fault of the driver, and this is not going to be helped by making the cars safer.

5. It should be stressed again in this connection that commonly the people putting forth these [ideological] propositions are perfectly sincere. The moral effort to lie deliberately is beyond most people. It is much easier to deceive oneself. It is, therefore, important to keep the concept of ideology distinct from notions of lying, deception, propaganda, or legerdemain. The liar, by definition, knows that he is lying. The ideologist does not [from an introduction to sociology].

6. Big spending has frequently been used as a weapon against conservatives. A well-known example was the experience of Senator Carter Glass—the staunchly anti-New Deal senator from Virginia.

Glass was a bitter opponent of Rooseveltian spending—including WPA. Thus, whenever he sponsored an application for a WPA project by a Virginia community, he was subjected to a torrent of abuse by "liberals" in press and government. "The nerve of the man," they screamed. "He lambastes big spending as an evil, then he sneaks around to the back door to get his share."

Asked to explain the alleged inconsistency, Glass replied: "If taxes to pay for government projects were levied geographically according to the votes for or against by members of Congress, then the 'liberals' would have a right to complain. But once a spending bill that I oppose becomes law, Virginia must pay its share of the costs and Virginia is therefore entitled to its share of the benefits."

7. Why are so many people shocked when they hear the freedom philosophy spelled out? It is reasonable. It is logical. It is just. But when it is brought down from the general to the particular, there is immediate objection.

To illustrate: Question the propriety of government education, the characteristics of which are compulsory attendance, government-dictated curricula, and the forcible collection of the wherewithal to pay the bills. You will literally stun your listeners, for the position runs counter to accepted practices, to our *mores*.

Now, for an experiment, take the principles which are presently supported in education and extend them to a related field. Advocate that there be compulsory attendance at churches, sermons according to state prescription, and all citizens taxed to pay the church bills. Again, you will literally stun your listeners, for your position runs counter to accepted practices, to our *mores*.

Such persons, twice stunned, cannot successfully argue that the Ten Commandments, the Golden Rule, and moral behavior are less important than the government schools' "life-sharing" periods, "evaluation," lessons in democracy, or even reading, writing, and arithmetic. Yet their inconsistency in reasoning does not bother them at all [adapted from *Notes from FEE,* The Foundation for Economic Education, September 1959].

8. Parents are understandably disturbed about the decline of public education in the hands of the progressivists and the educators' unions. Despite all the attempts to get around it, the *real* facts (not just a lot of statistics) prove that education is less effective today than fifty or seventy-five years ago. There's no getting around it. An article I read the other day said that in Springfield, Massachusetts, some old examination papers, originally used in 1856, were found in an attic, and given to the same grade in the schools of 1924, and that the pupils of 1924 did uniformly better on the test than those of 1856. But what kind of a test was that? If the test was incapable of revealing the decline of educational methods in the Springfield schools, it could not have been a very well-designed test and we need not put any stock in it.

9. Most of the parents who are working up a hue and cry about the decline of our schools are drawing fallacious conclusions from rosily distorted assumptions about what the schools used to be. I have heard a parent argue, "We had no classes in remedial reading when I went to school. The fact that we have them today shows that reading instruction is less effective than it was in my day." But if we're going to argue this way, we might as well say that heart clinics today prove that doctors know less about how to treat heart disease and are less effective in their therapy than they used to be. But the clinic, of course, shows that we have a better recognition of the problem and greater capacity to do something about it.

10. Dear Sir: As a civic leader and responsible citizen, you have been selected, along with others, to help the Legislative Committee of our State Bar Association deal with a growing civil-liberties problem, namely, the invasion of privacy. We believe that this has gone too far in our modern society, and technological progress is making it even worse, and our plan is to draft legislation to curb this development. When we speak of invasion of privacy, we mean a wide range of encroachments upon the individual's right to speak without being overheard by wiretaps, to write without having his mail opened by Post Office snoops, to sit in quiet without being interrupted by the telephone and solicited to buy a graveyard plot before it is too late, to be free from unsolicited letters that various groups write to him, enclos-

ing questionnaires or posing various questions he is supposed to answer about the state of the world, the problems of society, his choice of deodorants, and the rest. What we would like from you is a detailed statement of your opinion about the forms of invasion of privacy that bother you, and what you think might be done to stop them.

chapter three | WEIGHING THE EVIDENCE

One of the continuing problems of a democratic society is how to modify traditional procedures in police investigation and in the criminal courts so as to keep individual liberties alive under changed conditions, and if possible, to enlarge those liberties without danger to the social order. For example, there is the antiquated bail system under which the bondsman charges ten per cent of the bail, no matter how short the period before trial; though if the defendant does not appear, the police or the FBI do the work of bringing him back. At this rate of interest, it is not surprising that bondsmen grow rich, while many poor people accused of crimes remain in jail for weeks and months and cannot look for witnesses or help in preparing their own defense. The result: a study of first offenders a few years ago showed that 59 per cent of those unable to make bail are found guilty and sentenced to jail, whereas only 10 per cent of those on bond receive jail terms.

Consider another example. Most people do not realize that they may be stopped by the police some rainy night and arrested on suspicion of fleeing from a crime. So they become indignant when the courts free a defendant because he was held for a long period before being allowed to consult counsel, or was forced or frightened or tricked into signing a confession. Newspapers often editorialize about police being hamstrung by this absurd fussiness about constitutional protections for the accused—even though another study has shown that only 12 per cent of those charged with crime actually go to trial, and only a fraction of them are freed on constitutional grounds.

As with all really important social problems that are publicly discussed, this one is bound to arouse emotions on both sides, and as soon as the complexities and dimensions of the problem begin to emerge, many people will become impatient for quick and easy solutions. They will damn the police or the magistrates or permissive parents or progressive educators or liberal-arts colleges or some other handy group. And as they warm to their subject, they will become far more interested in pinning the blame on someone else than in finding out what the trouble really is, and why.

But in a calmer and more objective mood, we can all see that there is only one rational way to go at the problem. First, we must get solid information about what is going on—specific information about what happened in this case or that. From these facts we must extract general knowledge about how the system is actually working, in terms of percentages of cases handled in various ways, the incidence of the third-degree and other extralegal police methods, and so forth. In short, we must undertake some careful inductions in order to acquire the knowledge on which to base our judgments about which parts of the system deserve to be retained, and which parts should be improved or abandoned.

The foundation on which an inductive argument rests is the body of evidence we are given to begin with: these facts are the *data* of the argument. They may themselves be conclusions of earlier inductive arguments. But in any particular process of inductive reasoning, it is essential to distinguish clearly between the statements we are taking as established and those we are claiming (or hoping) to prove as a result of the argument—what we *sup*pose and what we *pro*pose.

Our main concern in this chapter is with the procedures by which we move from acceptance of the data to acceptance of the inductive conclusion. But before we come to that, it is well to note a few points about the data themselves. They may come from *direct observation:* seeing the arrow of the fuel gauge pointing to "Empty," hearing the clock strike, smelling the thick exhaust of the diesel bus—or even counting, like that enterprising man in Belgrade a few years ago who spent 74 days satisfying his curiosity about the number of hairs on a friend's head (total: 334,560). When an observation is made under controlled conditions, it is an *experi-*

ment. To test the socket by trying another bulb, to vary the cake recipe in one chosen particular, to simulate a long space voyage by having a team of men live underground for weeks—these are ways of deliberately manipulating the environment for the purpose of observing the consequences. When we are not ourselves in a position to observe, we must rely on the *testimonial evidence* provided by others. And here, of course (if we are willing to take reasonable precautions), we look for witnesses who are equipped to observe what they claim to observe, who are capable of reporting their observations accurately, with the least admixture of their own speculations, and who are known to be truthful.

Needless to say, we are sometimes disappointed by all these sources of evidence—and not least by the testimony of others. It is well known that even if we see something with our own eyes, it may not be so. The history of boxing has never been the same since the celebrated heavyweight bout in May 1965, when the experts who saw Sonny Liston knocked out came up with amazingly different descriptions: Cassius Clay himself said his blow was "a twisting righthand punch"; the referee (Jersey Joe Walcott) said it was "a left to the jaw"; and various sportswriters said it was "a perfect punch," "a tiny shot," and that "no blow was landed." Experiments, when they are painstakingly prepared and are repeated by a number of independent and impartial observers, yield the best results—but even there, we may overlook some factor we thought we had under control, when it wasn't. And as for testimony. . . . Obviously, we would be hopelessly lost in modern society if we could not depend, more often than not, on the expert—the dentist, the druggist, the bus driver. But there are many others who claim to be experts—to have seen, to have studied, to have investigated—and yet give us the wrong data for our inductions.

It was only a few years ago that the founder and leader of the John Birch Society estimated that one-half of one per cent of the Catholic clergy in the United States are Communist sympathizers—or "Comsymps," as they are called by the experts. *The Pilot*, official publication of the Boston archdiocese, asked him how he had learned this figure. "It was a complete guess," he explained, "simply pulled out of a hat." And in 1963, there was considerable dissatisfaction and skepticism about the reliability of the television program ratings that meant life and death for those programs. The officials of the most famous rating firm defended their exact statistical methods and their careful choice of typical people as a basis for their percentages—but it turned out that they had not yet gotten around to using the 1960 census figures.

When we must consider the strength of an inductive argument, then, we will always want to ask: What are the data? Where did they come from? Do we have sufficient reason to regard them as reliable? For if they let us down, we have no hope of getting any more ambitious conclusion out of them. Now let us suppose that the data are reliable; then the other questions arise—about the relation between the data and the conclusion. Induction is a matter of weighing evidence—not as we weigh meat upon a scale, expecting an exact answer, but as we heft a stone and roughly estimate its weight, or heft two stones and judge one to be much heavier than the other.

In all successful inductive arguments, the data **confirm** the conclusion to some degree—they render it more or less probable or acceptable. But there are two quite different ways in which this is done, and two correspondingly different kinds of inductive conclusion: generalizations and hypotheses. We shall deal with each in turn.

§9. dependable generalizations

A *general statement* is a statement about the distribution of some characteristic among the members of a certain class: "All grasshoppers are incapable of hearing the low notes of a bass singer" (this was discovered at Princeton University); "In nearly every Presidential election in this century, the taller candidate has won"; "More suicides occur on Wednesday night, and fewer on Saturday night, than on any other night of the week"; "Approximately 6 per cent of Americans who have reached a drinking age are alcoholics." Unlike *singular statements,* which refer to individual persons, places, or things ("The city of Denver has an elevation of 5,280 feet"), general statements are answers to questions about what is true of all the members of a group or of some portion or of the average member.

When a general statement is accepted as the conclusion of an inductive argument, it is a **generalization.** What makes an argument inductive, as we have seen in Chapter 1, is that the conclusion takes a leap beyond the data supporting it, and cannot follow necessarily from those data. To generalize is always to go from information about some members of a class to an inference about more members of the class. Therein lie the risks, and the benefits, of generalizing.

The essential ingredients of a generalization argument, then, are three. Take this simple example:

> This grasshopper is insensitive to bass notes.
> That other grasshopper is insensitive to bass notes.
> The grasshopper tested by Professor Jones is insensitive to bass notes.
>
> .
> .
> .
>
> -
> All grasshoppers are insentitive to bass notes.

The broken line here means "therefore," as the unbroken line did in the deductive arguments of the preceding chapter, but it embodies a weaker claim: not "therefore, necessarily," but "therefore, probably." First, in a generalization argument there is always the **population under investigation**—the things (in this case *grasshoppers*) we are trying to find out about, or trying to prove something about. Second, there is the **characteristic in question** (in this case, *insensitivity to bass notes*), whose occurrence in members of the class is what we are inquiring after—that is, we are interested in knowing, or showing, that it is to be found in all or no members of the class, in most or few, in nine out of ten, or whatever. And third, within the population under investigation, there is the subclass that contains those individuals who have actually been observed, examined, or tested, and who provide the evidence on which the generalization is based. This subclass (in our example, the class of grasshoppers whose insensitivity has been put to experimental test) is a **sample** of the population under investigation.

From a practical point of view, there are two directions in which inductive reasoning may go. The cannery inspector, for example, is under orders to produce a generalization about the probable quality of the canned tunafish that is coming off the conveyor belt to be shipped. His task, then, is to choose the right sort of sample that will justify him in judging, for example, that all of the cans are of high quality. He can choose how much evidence to get for his generalization. He doesn't open all the cans, of course, because then they would only have to be done over again; but if they have been processed under highly controlled and exactly similar conditions, an occasional check will be sufficient. On the other hand, a meteorologist who receives the weather reports day after day and tries to discover regular patterns among the various factors reported on—wind direction and velocity, barometric pressure, humidity, temperature at various heights, and so forth—has the opposite task. For he cannot control the amount of data, but must decide how far he can generalize, and with what degree of assurance, from the data he is given.

But the logical problem is the same in both cases, for both inferences can be set forth as inductive arguments supporting a generalization. And the basic need is to know what generalization is warranted by what data—or what sample would warrant what generalization. It is easy to say what we are looking for in a sample: we want it to be *representative*. Suppose we select certain grasshoppers to test, for example; every one of them that turns out to be insensitive to bass notes is an **instance** of the generalization "All grasshoppers are insensitive to bass notes." (It is also an instance of many other generalizations, of course—for example, "Most grasshoppers are insensitive to bass notes" and "All creatures insensitive to bass notes are insects.") A sample doesn't give us any evidence at all for a given generalization unless at least some of its members are instances of that generalization. Now the ideal sample would be one in which the proportion of members having the characteristic in question is exactly the same as the proportion in the entire population under investigation. The generalizer tries to base his generalization on a sample that is chosen in such a way as to provide a good indication of the rest of the population. If every tested grasshopper turns out to be insensitive to bass notes, then he wants to be justified in concluding that *every* grasshopper (not only the tested ones) is insensitive to bass notes. And if his study of suicides gives him a sample in which the percentage of Wednesday suicides is greater than the percentage of Saturday suicides, then he wants to be justified in concluding that approximately this ratio will (probably) hold for all suicides—including those that have not yet happened.

What can we do to make a sample representative? Fortunately even a rough answer to that question can be of use to all of us, for to give a precise answer would take us into the mathematics of sampling theory. Since we are not concerned with technical problems such as would engage a statistician employed in industry or government, we must be content with a qualitative, or nonnumerical, answer.

The first principle in sampling is the one that we commonly turn to in ordinary life when we want to make sure that something happens without having been deliberately arranged by anyone with an axe to grind or an overriding desire to promote his own welfare. To get a fair deal in bridge, we shuffle the cards; to give everyone an equal chance to win a new car in the hospital lottery, we shake up the ticket stubs in a large drum. Then the bridge hand and the winner of the lottery are decided by *chance,* that is, by processes independent of any human will. When a sample of a population is chosen by chance, it is said to be a **random sample,** and such a sample evidently is in a good position to be a fair, or representative, one. It *may* not be representative—even a well-shuffled deck may produce a hand consisting of all spades. But it is more likely to be representative than one that has been purposefully selected.

In order to obtain a random sample, it may be necessary to give much thought to eliminating possible biases. One temptation to which we are all prone is to think we have a fair sample when we don't. The fact that the grasshoppers we selected for our experiment were the first ones that happened to hop along doesn't mean that they are a random sample. To make sure that the sample is really random (if we want to generalize about the whole class of grasshoppers), we must take pains to include Northern as well as Southern ones, Australian as well as Indian, old and young, green and brown, and so forth.

When, as with grasshoppers, there is quite a variety of subclasses within the population under investigation, it is clear that in order to be really random, our sample must be of a certain size. It must be large enough so that it *can* be representative of the group, in all its variety. And, generally speaking, up to certain limits, the larger the sample, the more reason to believe the generalization. Anyone who generalized about all grasshoppers (or even all the grasshoppers in a given autumn field) after catching and examining one or two would be jumping to conclusions. At least, the conclusion could be strengthened by further data. After he caught fifty, and found them all to have a certain characteristic, with no exceptions, he might well conclude that this is almost certainly true of the entire *local* population.

Again, without a rigorous mathematical treatment we can speak only in these loose terms. To accept a generalization on the basis of a sample that is not really random or not sufficiently large to be representative is to commit the **fallacy of hasty generalization.** It is a common enough mistake. We all know of people who make universal medical recommendations to their friends, on the ground that if wheat-germ or blackstrap molasses (as they think) remade *their* lives, it should work for everyone. Even more unfortunate are those widespread myths about important social problems that begin with someone's careless observation of a few instances in his immediate experience and then are perpetuated by confident repetition. The wealthy and highly educated Eastern suburbanite, for example, observes that several of his friends are divorced, and he concludes from this sample that wealthy people, educated people, and Easterners have higher divorce rates than their complementary classes. And his belief is strengthened by the avid publicity given to the divorces of those who are wealthy and prominent. It is hard to shake him loose from this even when the sociologists or social researchers discover, on the basis of larger and fairer samples, that business and professional groups have the lowest divorce rates and working-class people the highest; and that the divorce rate in Western states is about four times as high as in Northeastern states. (One of the difficulties about this subject is that the United States government does not officially record divorce statistics, which are not as well kept or as widely available in this country as in others.)

When you must make up your mind whether or not to be convinced by a generalization argument, there are certain tests to apply. If you are satisfied on these counts, then you can put some trust in the conclusion. You can't avoid taking some risk, when you believe it and act upon it, and of course the greater the evils that would follow from making a mistake, the stronger the evidence you should require (for example, if a mistake would mean putting an innocent man in jail or sinking a ship or ruining someone's career). But you can say that the generalization has some *dependability*, that is, a reasonable person would be justified in accepting it and being guided by it in the conduct of his affairs.

The questions to raise about any generalization argument can be illustrated by the following one:

> Dr. Brill and Dr. Malzberg studied the records of over 5,000 people who had been released from mental hospitals. Comparing these cases with an equal number of people who had never been admitted to a mental hospital, and who were divided into similar groups by age, sex, previous arrest records, and socioeconomic status, they found that arrests for sex crimes among the general population are 50 per cent higher than among former mental-hospital patients, and that arrests for rape are 1,000 per cent higher. They concluded that former mental-hospital patients are generally more law-abiding than other citizens.

The first question is whether the class under investigation is clearly defined, so that we know exactly what group we are generalizing about. In this example, there is no uncertainty, for the class of former mental-hospital patients is definitely enough determinable. If the generalization had been, say, about "mentally ill people," further qualifications might have been required to make it reasonably clear who is assumed to belong to this group, and who not.

The second question is whether the *scope* of the generalization is sufficiently clear—that is, whether the conclusion is supposed to be true of some, all, or most, or some specific fraction of the class under investigation. In the example at hand, we do not have a generalization about the incidence of crime in either of the two classes compared, but we have a statement about the ratio of these two incidences: that the number of rapes—say, per thousand—is ten times as high in one group as in another. It is clear enough what is being claimed, though we are not given all the information. The trouble arises when generalizations have no quantifiers—"Americans are materialistic" (*What* Americans? All? Some? Most?)—or when abstract terms avoid any plain commitment—as in statements about "Science" (meaning scientists?) or "*the* Negro" or "Campus, U.S.A."

The third question is whether the characteristic in question is clearly enough defined so that we can tell whether it is present or absent in a given case. In the present example there is an interesting ambivalence. The conclusion speaks of *law-abidingness* in general, though the evidence refers to *sexual law-abidingness*. But, aside from the possibility of a fallacy on that point, we can say that *law-abidingness* is subject to pretty objective determination, as the passage indicates, since crimes are a matter of record. But there is some room for maneuver here, and an opportunity for trickery. For example, the figures cited are *arrests,* rather than convictions. Are they, we may question, a good index of law-abidingness? Suppose fewer former patients are arrested than non-patients, but more are actually convicted? Wouldn't they be less law-abiding? (This may be unlikely.) Then again, perhaps not—probably if equal numbers from both groups were brought to trial, more of the former patients would be convicted, even if they were all innocent (juries being what they are). On the other hand, former patients known to be in the vicinity are more likely to be picked up by the police when a sex crime is committed, just on general principles. So probably the proposed criterion of law-abidingness is not biased in favor of the conclusion.

The fourth question is whether the sample is likely to be representative. Here we must check the generalization against our own experience, and general knowledge of matters of the sort under discussion. Is there any reason to believe that the sample is not typical of the class under investigation? Is there any reason to suspect that it is too small to be dependable? In the present example, a sample of 5,000 seems, offhand, a fairly considerable one. And we have no particular grounds for suspecting that the doctors intentionally or unintentionally selected the sample so that the results were distorted. Still, before we accept the conclusion (if it matters to us), we should stop and think. Would the doctors be more likely to select patients with good records, rather than bad ones—because these would be easier to find or more accessible? It doesn't seem so. How were the non-mental-patients selected? There is a possibility of error there—though the doctors seem to have made an effort to avoid it by making sure that the second group was comparable in various respects to the first one.

One form of generalization that is especially important is the *causal generalization.* This is a statement not merely about the distribution of a characteristic in a group (*insensitivity to bass notes* among grasshoppers) or about the comparative distribution of a characteristic in two groups (*law-abidingness* among former mental patients and non-patients), but about the causal connection between two characteristics or events. It may be a simple and direct one, as when we say that long exposure to the sun will cause sunburn (though even this is not as simple as it seems, because to make it strictly true we would have to add a number of careful qualifications about the atmosphere, the kind of skin involved, the absence of suntan lotion, and so forth). Or it may be a more modest one, as when we say that having O-type blood makes one much more susceptible to peptic ulcers than having other types of blood, or that heavy smoking is a factor in producing lung cancer in many people.

There has been a great deal of dispute, of course, about the correct way of putting this last claim. Some have objected to the requirement that a health warning be put on every pack of cigarettes, on the ground (as an M.D., a Professor of Public Health, wrote to *The New York Times*) that "no evidence exists that the the smoking of that one pack will threaten the health of anyone." When the American Cancer Society presented one of its reports on cigarette smoking in June 1957, the Tobacco Industry Research Committee commented that the statistics (showing, for example, that the death rates among cigarette smokers are far higher than among nonsmokers) "do not prove cause-and-effect relationship." The report of the Public Health Service (January 1964) stated that while "no simple cause-and-effect relationship is likely to exist between a complex product like tobacco smoke and a specific disease in the variable human organism," the relative importance of cigarette smoking as a "causative factor" in diseases of the lungs and bronchial tubes, for example, is "much greater" than that of other things, such as air pollution. Statements about causal connections, then, vary in the intimacy of the connection ascribed to the characteristics or events in a given case.

Causal statements may be either singular or general. We speak of one event (leaving the parked car lights on from 9:00 to 10:00 P.M.) as causing another event, or state of affairs (dead car battery at 10:00 P.M.). But these singular causal judgments, about individual events, involve, and indeed depend upon, generalizations. We hear thunder, and sneeze. One event follows the other, but we don't say that the thunder *causes* the sneeze, because we can't believe there is any connection between them, or any general tendency for thunderclaps to be followed by sneezes. It is a coincidence. When we say that leaving the car light on caused the battery to be dead, we assume that there is a true generalization connecting not just these events, but these *types* of events: *whenever* the lights are left on (assuming certain conditions, such as a normal battery and no one recharging the battery at the time), the battery will be dead.

Therefore it is always an illegitimate inference to suppose that because *B* follows *A* on one occasion, there must be a causal connection between them. This is the **fallacy of *post hoc, ergo propter hoc*** ("after this, therefore because of this"). It amounts to trying to establish a generalization from a single instance. Since, as we have seen, a single case (this thunder followed by this sneeze, this burning light followed by this dead battery) can be an instance of an indefinite variety of generalizations, we cannot begin to know which of the generalizations to choose until we have more instances. The post hoc fallacy is an extreme case of hasty generalization, but it is a not uncommon form of gullibility. We owe to it, quite probably, our major lingering superstitions—such as that thunder causes milk to sour, and that failure to knock on wood after acknowledging good fortune will cause misfortune, and that a sty can be cured by rubbing it nine times with a gold ring.

Perhaps the most successful uses of this time-worn fallacy are made by politicians on the hustings. There must no doubt be some plausibility in the argument, but there need not be much. "When our party came into office, we took a firm stand for Americanism; immediately, it was noted that significant victories were achieved by our side in various parts of the world, from Germany to Southeast Asia." Now there *may* be a causal connection here, though a devious and roundabout one; the point is that to prove this connection would require the establishment of relevant generalizations and a careful application of them to the facts of the present case. But no such effort is made; it is simply taken for granted that if *B* followed *A*, then *A* can be credited (or, if it's the other party, damned) for *B*.

An argument for a causal generalization infers a causal connection from a correlation, or association, of characteristics or events. And so when we face an argument of this sort, we have two sets of questions to ask. The first set we have already reviewed: they bear on the genuineness of the supposed correlation. But granting that the correlation holds, we want to know whether to acknowledge the claim that it is proof of a causal connection. To test this claim, a second set of questions is available.

The first question is whether the correlation is significant—whether it is decisive enough to warrant the inference. Without introducing the mathematical techniques of statistics, no general rules can be given, except to note a few common errors to avoid. That *A* and *B* go together (or that *B* follows *A*) a hundred times, or most times, or even every time, may not be *by itself* sufficient evidence to warrant the causal conclusion—unless we can supply relevant information out of our own experience. One thing that is crucial in making a correlation is to know the negative, or comparative, cases. For example, suppose we are told that so many men who smoke a pack a day die of lung cancer, or that such-and-such a percentage do. This doesn't prove anything about the connection, of course, until we know how the nonsmokers are faring. When the Public Health Service presented its report, it compared rates for various groups (of men)—showing, for example, that the death rate among one-pack-a-day smokers is over twice that for nonsmokers. And this is significant. If there is no comparison with what experimenters call a *control group,* there is no significance. After all, everyone who eats frankfurters eventually dies; does this prove that eating frankfurters is (ultimately) fatal?

Another thing to watch out for in a causal argument is the

degree of care exercised in comparing the two groups. If the men who smoked and the men who did not smoke differed in too many other ways (say, in where they live), it would be hard to be sure that smoking is the most probable cause of their cancer. This is the second question: we ask whether we know of any other factors that might account for the effect, besides the alleged cause. For example, the Public Health Service report pointed out that lung-cancer deaths in the United States increased from 3,000 a year in 1930 to 41,000 in 1962—an increase far exceeding that for cancer of any other site. At the same time the per capita consumption of cigarettes (counting people 15 years or older) rose from 1,365 in 1930 to 3,986 in 1961. This is a striking correlation, but of course by itself it gives only very feeble evidence for a causal connection, since so many other things were increasing at the same time (such as the national debt, the top speed of aircraft, and the number of volumes in the Library of Congress). When two early studies of the problem were reported in 1955, a medical statistician, Dr. Joseph Berkson, criticized them severely along this line. In the American Cancer Society study, volunteers were asked to register and record their smoking habits, if any; then when they died, the cause of death was added to the record. In the first 32 months of the study, 8,105 men died; out of 7,962 death certificates obtained, there were 285 cases of lung cancer. Dr. Berkson claimed that the death rate in the whole group studied was less than that in the general population, and he suggested that people who knew themselves to be ill might not be willing to volunteer for the study. Moreover, the ratio of nonsmokers to smokers was higher in the group studied than in the general population—perhaps, he suggested, because smokers were reluctant to help prove a causal connection between smoking and lung cancer. Whether or not Dr. Berkson's criticisms held up under further investigation, they illustrate an important kind of thinking which is essential to the critical examination of such causal arguments: supposing that the correlation holds, can it be accounted for in terms of factors that have been overlooked, or in terms of a certain unconscious bias in the selection of the evidence?

The third question is whether we know any other facts that make it unreasonable to suppose that the causal connection actually holds. Even if everyone who smoked died of lung cancer, for example, we would not say that the lung cancer was the cause of smoking, because the smoking comes first in time. That is fairly obvious, but more complex problems can arise. In 1957, Dr. Ernest

Wynder of the Sloan-Kettering Institute looked for a group of people similar in every respect to the rest of the population, except for being strict nonsmokers, and he found it in the Seventh-Day Adventist Church—whose 300,000 members included 20,000 living in the polluted air of the Los Angeles area. In all diseases that could not be connected with smoking (or drinking), the rates for this group were exactly as predicted from the rates in the general population. But of the predicted 10 or 11 cases of lung cancer, only one was found—a man who had been a heavy smoker for 25 years before joining the church. In reporting his results, Dr. Wynder noted that those defending tobacco have proposed that there is a "neuro-hormonal" factor which causes lung cancer and also causes people to want to smoke heavily. Certainly this is logically possible—that there is no direct causal connection between smoking and cancer, but that both are effects of something else. Dr. Wynder claimed that his own study made this conclusion unlikely: "They would now have to propose that this neuro-hormonal factor not only predisposes to lung cancer and causes one to smoke, but that it also prevents one from joining the Seventh-Day Adventist Church—a combination of factors virtually impossible to accept." His critics replied that the study did not prove a causal connection, because it overlooked other possibilities—for example, Seventh-Day Adventists eat less meat, drink less coffee and whiskey, and drink more milk than others. These cannot, of course, be ruled out dogmatically, but they cannot cast very serious doubt on the study as long as we have no other evidence to suggest how there could be a causal connection, say, between drinking milk and getting lung cancer.

Any causal generalization argument that passes these three tests—that gives us, in other words, good answers to our questions—is one that it is reasonable to accept, even though its conclusion may be overturned by later experience.

A Check-up Quiz Here are some generalizations and the samples on which they are based. In each case, give a reason why the sample may not be typical of the class under investigation.

1. *Generalization:* The selections performed by this rock-and-roll group tonight are lacking in warmth, vigor, and tension.

   Sample: The first three selections performed by this rock-and-roll group tonight.

2. *Generalization:* Readers of books are twice as interested in social problems as in travel books.

   Sample: A survey of books taken out over the past years from the West Branch of the Public Library.

3. *Generalization:* The urge to escape prison declines steadily after the second month.

   Sample: A study of attempts to escape from the Seagoville (Texas) Correctional Institution, between 1945 and 1960.

4. *Generalization:* A habit of changing jobs frequently causes a tendency to have automobile accidents.

   Sample: An examination of records of people who have had several automobile accidents, showing that a substantial number of these people had changed jobs once or more within the preceding year.

5. *Generalization:* The rich get better medical care than the poor.

   Sample: A comparison of the hospital records of a group of high-income and low-income people, showing that the average number of operations in a year is higher among the first group than among the second.

For Further Study Harold Larrabee, *Reliable Knowledge,* rev. ed., Ch. 12. Boston: Houghton Mifflin Co., 1964. Stephen F. Barker, *The Elements of Logic,* Ch. 6. New York: McGraw-Hill Book Company, 1965.

§10. appraising a hypothesis

We all understand, at least in a superficial way, what it is to give an *explanation* of some event or state of affairs—though a more rigorous philosophical examination of this notion reveals unexpected subtleties and complexities. When we discover that Uncle Joe has been losing money on the harness races recently, we say that explains why he has been behaving so irritably. The presence of arsenic in some strands of hair shaved from Napoleon's head the night after his death on St. Helena in May 1821 can be explained by the supposition that one of his fellow exiles had been secretly poisoning him for some time before his death. Whether or not we are prepared to accept these explanations, we recognize that they *are* explanations; and if we do accept them, they can put an end to the doubt or bafflement that we might have felt earlier, and might have expressed in a question: Why has Uncle Joe been irritable? How did the arsenic get into Napoleon's hair?

When we stop to examine these and other typical examples of explanation, we find that they involve three essential elements, no matter how simple or how complicated they may be. First, there is the event or state of affairs that puzzles us—the irritability, the arsenic. The statement, or set of statements, describing this puzzling situation may be called the **statement to be explained.** Second, there is the **explaining statement**, or set of statements ("Uncle Joe has been losing money on the harness races"; "Someone poisoned Napoleon"). And third, there must be some connection between the events described by the statement to be explained and the explaining statement—a connection that would be described by a true generalization about the *kinds* of events involved. Uncle Joe's losses can explain his irritability only because we know some such generalization as "Whenever a person of a certain temperament under certain conditions loses money gambling, he will be irritable." And the poisoning can explain the arsenic only if we are justified in assuming that whenever a man is fed arsenic under certain conditions, over a long period of time, then hair removed a day after his death will show traces of the poison. (These traces were discovered by a process of irradiation, which transformed the arsenic into a radioactive isotope.)

In an **explanation,** then, an explaining statement is asserted to account for a statement to be explained on the basis of one or more generalizations connecting the events or states of affairs described by the two statements.

There is an important difference between the two examples just given. In the first example we already know from other sources that Uncle Joe has been losing, and we put this information to use in explaining his behavior. In the second example, when the arsenic was discovered in the hair—which was in the possession of a Swiss textile manufacturer—it was not already known that Napoleon had been poisoned. In fact, historians had generally accepted the verdict of the doctors who performed the autopsy, that his death was due to cancer of the stomach. So in this second example a significant inference is made from the observed fact today to the event long ago:

There is arsenic in Napoleon's hair.
- -
Napoleon was poisoned.

As the broken line indicates, this is an inductive inference. The conclusion does not follow necessarily, and indeed no one after a little thought would claim that it did. Poisoning is not the only *possible* way in which the arsenic could have gotten into the hair—even if we can't offhand think of a better way to do it. Still, the statement about the arsenic is certainly *some* reason to think that the conclusion is true; it lends some degree of probability to the conclusion. But notice that it does not do this in the same way as the data in a generalization argument; it does not provide an instance of a generalization, but rather a fact that can be explained by the conclusion. We accept the conclusion (if we do—or at any rate, we incline somewhat toward believing it) because if it is true it would explain how the arsenic got there. It is a hypothesis.

When the evidence in an inductive argument consists of assertions that are explained by the conclusion, and it is claimed that the conclusion is acceptable to some degree because it explains those data, then the conclusion is a **hypothesis.**

The little induction about Napoleon may be misleading in some respects, because we can't generally support a conclusion well without more than one piece of evidence, as will be plain shortly. This example may even look at first like a syllogism with a missing premise. If we were to supply the requisite premise, "All corpses with arsenic in their hair are victims of poisoning," then the conclusion would follow necessarily. But, as I have said, the arguer in this case need make no such dubious assumption. He is merely trying to convince us that the conclusion is probably true. And it is easy to see this when we reflect on a few features of this inference.

For one thing, no matter how strongly convinced we may be that the hypothesis is true, it could always be made at least a little more conclusive by further evidence. We might, for example, exhume Napoleon's remains from their resting place at Les Invalides in Paris, and perform further chemical tests. If these tests also showed the presence of arsenic in large enough quantities to cause death, we would have much stronger evidence. Even then, the hypothesis would not be absolutely certain (though it would be pretty soundly established, no doubt), because with some ingenuity we could think of still further evidence that might turn up to make the hypothesis *less* probable than it was before. For example, suppose we found a statement by a respected divine, whom we have every reason to credit, confessing that he once dug up Napoleon's body and put arsenic in it. That's not very likely, to be sure, but since it could conceivably happen, the argument cannot be deductive.

We can best appreciate the implications of these points if we think of a hypothesis argument as the end of a process of *inquiry*. Its strength is a function of the evidence we have now, which may be different tomorrow as it was different yesterday. And it is to be judged in relation to that evidence. "Inquiry," as I use the word here, is the systematic and persistent attempt to answer a question. A hypothesis is an answer to a question, and the object of inquiry is to discover and establish the hypothesis that gives the best answer obtainable.

Though there is some danger of oversimplifying and overstandardizing the ways in which we go about trying to answer questions —whether as scientists or as ordinary citizens—it is helpful to note that, speaking very generally, an inquiry has four distinguishable steps, some of which may be repeated at different stages. The inquiry begins when someone finds himself confronted with a problem—not necessarily a practical one: the important thing is that he is puzzled in some way. For example, twenty-one people come down with infectious hepatitis in two small Connecticut communities, and a month later there are nine more cases. This raises a practical problem, since we want to stop the epidemic; but even if we could do nothing about it, we might like to understand it.

Step 1 consists in formulating the question we want to answer, as clearly and specifically as we can: What caused this epidemic of hepatitis?

Step 2 consists in looking about in the puzzling situation itself, and using our imagination to come up with a possible explanation. A team rushes to the scene, assembles case records, looks for facts that might suggest a tentative hypothesis. For example, twice as many cases come from Candlewood Shores as from Brookfield. Perhaps there is a difference in the water supplies. Let this be Hypothesis *H:* that the community water supply is contaminated. Step 3 consists in seeing what would follow if this hypothesis is true, so that further relevant evidence can be gathered and used to test the hypothesis. In Step 3, then, consequences are drawn (with the help of available assumptions). For example, if Hypothesis *H* is true, then we will expect all the stricken people to have had access to the same water supply. In Step 4 we go out to make observations to determine whether this consequence is true. And it turns out not to be true: some of the stricken people get their water from the community supply, some from their own independent wells. Since the consequence is false, we must abandon, or at least mend, Hypothesis *H*.

Now we must go back to Step 2 again, and try another hypothesis, *H′*. In this case, the public-health investigators note another suggestive fact—that 20 of the 21 people first stricken are children, and that in fact they all attend the third through sixth grade at the Brookfield Consolidated School. Hypothesis *H′*, then, is this: the water supply of the drinking fountains available to these grades is contaminated. Step 3: we derive the consequence that (if the hypothesis is true) the school drinking fountains must be getting their water from different sources. Step 4: when this is checked, it is found that in fact three different wells feed the school plumbing system. Here is a consequence that turns out to be true, and the fact that it is true gives evidential support to Hypothesis *H′*. But by itself, the support is not strong. So back to Step 3 again, to derive further consequences from the hypothesis: for example, if *H′* is true, then bacterial examination of the water from at least one well will show that it is contaminated. Step 4: we test this; and again the results are positive. At this point the inquiry ends, at least for the time being; the investigators conclude that they have found the source of the epidemic.

From this somewhat abbreviated account (which leaves out other hypotheses that were considered, and other complicating facts), we can see that a hypothesis is always in some degree provisional—resigned to give way to a better one if a better one comes along. It may be the true explanation and may survive all attempts to refute it. Or it may have to be abandoned shortly because of some refractory bit of evidence. There is no way of placing it above the battle; it is always open to further consideration.

It follows from this that the acceptance of a hypothesis is implicitly a choice between it and other possible hypotheses—even if we don't stop to think of them. In the physical sciences, the research worker may be held up at times by inability to formulate any really adequate theory to explain what he wants to explain—for example, exactly how tranquilizers work or what causes the red spot on Jupiter (which seems to be solid and yet drifts like a floating island, and does not rotate with the rest of the planet). But in ordinary affairs of life, as in history, the unsolved mysteries are not due to our lack of ability to imagine hypotheses, but rather to the paucity of evidence for supporting one hypothesis and eliminating others. Who was the woman to whom Beethoven wrote his "Immortal Beloved" letter? How did the elephant and the donkey come to be political party symbols? How did the Olmecs move their 20-ton carved heads through the jungles of Mexico 3,000 years ago, though they did not know about the principle of the wheel? Inquiry into these unanswered questions is held up at Step 4 because we don't know where to go for the decisive evidence.

And similarly, whenever we bring an inquiry to an end—having carried it as far as time or energy or pressing circumstances permit —we are hardly ever left with only one possible hypothesis. No matter how powerful the evidence against the defendant in a criminal case—even if he is caught red-handed, was observed by a parade of witnesses, pleads guilty and signs a voluntary confession —we still have more than one hypothesis: (1) that he was indeed guilty, and (2) that (let us say) he wants to take the blame himself for what someone else did. If we accept the first hypothesis (reasonably enough) it is because it is *better* than the second one—so much better that the second one can be confidently dismissed. We prefer one hypothesis to another because it is the *best* explanation we can think of for the facts we have at hand.

The basic problem, then, in weighing the evidence for a hypothesis, is to discover how good an explanation it really is—to appraise its worth as knowledge. This is a task that faces us innumerable times every day, in matters ranging from the most trivial to the most momentous. It would be convenient if we had exact and easily applied rules by which we could measure the acceptability of a hypothesis in the light of the relevant known data—that is, its degree of probability. One kind of probability we can be precise about—as when we say that the probability of being fairly dealt a bridge hand of 13 spades is about 1 in 635 billion. But when someone says that he thinks it probable that his opponents in a round of the bridge tournament were guilty of cheating, this sort of probability has not been quantified. We can only consider how great, and how strong, is the evidence for this hypothesis, in comparison to other hypotheses that can be proposed. Fortunately, in making these comparisons we have two helpful and important criteria to guide us.

One way in which we can compare different hypotheses for the same statement to be explained is in terms of the **frequency** of the kind of event reported by the hypothesis. For example, here is a car driven by a young woman, weaving in a zig-zag pattern down the street, through a stop sign, and into a pole. Hypothesis 1: The driver is drunk. Hypothesis 2: She is on her way home from her doctor's office; to test his hypothesis that she was allergic to milk, he had had her go without milk for a week, so that the allergy would be "unmasked," and then she had drunk a glass in his office; her driving behavior is the result. Each of these hypotheses fully explains what happened. True, we could easily decide between them with the help of a few more facts: if the police discover that her breath does not smell of liquor or if they check with the doctor or if they learn that she has hypoglycemia, they will accept her story. And until we get more facts, we ought not to make any rash decisions (such as clapping her in a cell for several hours before letting her call an attorney), because neither of the two hypotheses is that much better than the other. Still, one is a little bit better than the other, even if we confine ourselves to this one piece of evidence (namely, the driving behavior). We can ask which of these two kinds of thing happens more often—or more often at this time of day to young women, and so forth. If we already know a generalization that more drivers become intoxicated than suffer strong allergy effects of this sort, then we can say that the first hypothesis has greater frequency than the second. And other things being equal, that makes it more acceptable.

We can still easily go wrong in applying this criterion, of course. I have read about a trio of elderly ladies who like to go camping and who are in the habit of leaving an outsize pair of men's boots in front of their tent when they go to bed. A stranger coming along and seeing those boots would certainly be justified by the principle of frequency in inferring that a man occupied the tent, but he would be wrong. Still, the only way he can be set right is by collecting further data (waiting to see, for example, who emerges in the morning) and using the very same principle, only more carefully. In the case of the hepatitis epidemic, as a matter of fact, water is one of the less common vehicles for transmitting the disease—but the more frequent hypotheses, such as personal contact and infected blood transfusions and milk, were ruled out by various facts. And of course when we think of the frequency of a kind of event, we must make the class as small as possible. If our driver had been a highly respectable elderly lady, we might guess (although statistics are not readily obtainable) that in the group of people to which she belongs any erratic driving is more frequently associated with allergy symptoms than with alcoholic intoxication.

When we have no information, or no very exact information, about the frequency of the explaining event, we cannot use the first criterion for appraising hypotheses. And sometimes even when we can use it, it leaves us in a state of indecision: for the frequency of one hypothesis may (approximately) equal that of another. But we may still be able to make a tentative choice by applying a second criterion, **simplicity.** This is another respect in which we can compare two alternative hypotheses. For example, a science newsletter warns us (very properly) against jumping to conclusions on the basis of superficial evidence. Consider the poor hammerhead shark:

> Hammerheads have picked up an evil reputation as dangerous to man. But the case against them—besides their formidable appearance—rests mainly upon finding the remains of a man, including parts of his clothing, in a shark taken in 1805!

Probably the writer means to warn us against hasty generalization —just because this hammerhead ate someone, don't be prejudiced against the entire species! But he seems to be warning us against taking the evidence as proof that this particular shark killed anyone —a different fallacy, which we shall come to presently.

If we put our minds to it, we could devise a second hypothesis to account for the presence of these miscellaneous items in the shark's stomach. Perhaps the man was drowned before he was ingested, or even foully murdered aboard ship, so the shark was not guilty of his death. Perhaps the shark innocently ran across the remains floating on the water and accidentally swallowed them while gulping greedily for something else. These are *tenable* hypotheses, but they are not as *plausible* as the first one—that the shark killed a human being. Perhaps frequency has some bearing on this case, too, but quite apart from frequency the first hypothesis would be better than its rivals. For the story it tells—the sequence of events it supposes to have happened—is simpler than the alternative ones. It only involves two characters, the shark and the man, whereas the murder hypothesis involves three, the shark, the man, and the murderer. The first hypothesis involves no assumptions about other actions, about ships, about other objects the shark was trying to swallow, and so forth. Simplicity is a difficult thing to characterize briefly, and it cannot be taken here in any strict mathematical sense. But when we compare two hypotheses, including the events and the persons, places, times, and things they include, we can often say that one is more complicated than the other. And other things being equal, the simpler of two alternative hypotheses (hypotheses that explain the same facts) is the more acceptable one.

In the case of the hepatitis epidemic, we could easily have invented more complex hypotheses, but that never became necessary. We could, for example, have speculated on the possibility that twenty-one distinct wells somehow became polluted all at once, and that each of the victims became infected by a different source.

That is quite possible—stranger things have happened. And if, after a long search, we failed to explain all the cases as due to a single source, we would fall back on a double-source or a triple-source hypothesis. The simplicity principle does not guarantee that the explanation will be simple—it only tells us that there is no rational basis for choosing a less simple hypothesis to explain a fact when a more simple one is available. Good thinking in this sort of inductive problem goes from the simpler to the more complex, and aims at the utmost simplicity that is adequate to do the job. This will often lead us astray, no doubt. The detectives who find a thumbprint on the drawer, and cannot connect it with any of the people who could possibly have committed the burglary of the top-secret papers, may finally have to try out the hypothesis that it is not the print of a thumb, after all, but of a big toe. This dodge—which was used by anti-Nazi underground workers to forge identification papers—makes for a slightly more complex hypothesis, because it involves taking off shoes and socks to leave the print. But any mistakes incurred by using the principle of simplicity can be corrected only by applying the same principle to a larger body of evidence.

It is convenient to have a name for the logical error of choosing a hypothesis that is less acceptable, in terms of frequency or simplicity or both, than an available alternative: let us call it the **fallacy of far-fetched hypothesis.** It is not an all-or-none fallacy—a hypothesis is more or less far-fetched depending on how good are the available alternatives that are overlooked. But in making up your mind about any hypothesis argument that comes your way, you must always look around for alternatives, even if none are suggested, and you must think not only about the evidence that is provided but about gaps in the evidence—facts that would be relevant and material, if they could be found. Then you can apply the two criteria, frequency and simplicity, to make a judgment about the degree of confidence to place in the argument's conclusion.

A Check-up Quiz Here are some pairs of statements to be explained and hypotheses. In each case, suggest another hypothesis that would explain the same fact, and suggest another fact that would decide between the two hypotheses.

1. *Statement to be explained:* Johnny is standing on the stove and his hand is inside the cookie jar.

Hypothesis: Johnny is dutifully returning to the jar a cookie recently taken from it by his younger brother.

2. *Statement to be explained:* An empty cash register is stolen from a grocery store and found two weeks later in the bushes with $1.10 in the drawer.

   Hypothesis: The thief used the cash register for two weeks in his own business, after which someone else stole it one night and had to abandon it to escape a police squad car.

3. *Statement to be explained:* Napoleon is usually portrayed with his right hand inside his coat.

   Hypothesis: He suffered from a nervous itch, a perpetual case of shingles, because of his high-strung temperament.

4. *Statement to be explained:* Mrs. Virginia Tighe, under hypnosis, reports, in the first person, detailed and vivid experiences as Bridey Murphy, a resident of Cork, Ireland, in the nineteenth century.

   Hypothesis: Mrs. Tighe is a reincarnation of Bridey Murphy.

5. *Statement to be explained:* Mr. and Mrs. Lewis, a young Negro couple, apply to rent an apartment in an apartment house, and are told after several days that the apartments are all rented and that there is a waiting list; but they learn that a white couple, friends of theirs, who applied the same day they did were given an apartment without question.

   Hypothesis: Mr. and Mrs. Lewis were refused the apartment because of their race.

For Further Study Morris Cohen and Ernest Nagel, *Introduction to Logic and Scientific Method,* Ch. 11. New York: Harcourt, Brace & World, Inc., 1934. Harold A. Larrabee, *Reliable Knowledge,* rev. ed., Chs. 5, 6, 14. Boston: Houghton Mifflin Company, 1964.

§11. classification and analogy

As we have seen in this chapter and in the preceding one, the concept of *class* plays a very fundamental role in much of our thinking, whether inductive or deductive. Grouping things together on account of some characteristic or characteristics which they have in common is a natural and perhaps indispensable way of sorting out our experience and our knowledge to make it readily available for future application. It is hard to imagine what the world would look like to us if it did not present itself, when we become old enough to take a serious interest in its contents, as made up of sorts or kinds of things: male and female, big and small, friendly and unfriendly, edible and inedible.

We have examined two kinds of thinking that involve classes: the syllogism and simple generalization. We must now consider briefly another. It differs from the first two in that it is not a process of reasoning to establish a conclusion but an exploration of relationships between one class and another. It results, when successful, in a new ordering of things, and the clarity and convenience it produces are valuable assets in the task of acquiring new knowledge, though they do not themselves constitute knowledge.

There are three facets, or aspects, of this kind of thinking about classes: *division, subsumption,* and *distinction.*

Given any class, and some predicate that can sensibly be applied to members of that class, we can divide the class into two subclasses. This was, in fact, the method we used in setting up the diagrams for two-term statements. Given the class of musical compositions and the property of tonality, we can divide the class of musical compositions into those that have tonality ("tonal music") and those that do not ("atonal music"). This is a purely logical maneuver, remember: we are not committed to saying that there is any such thing as atonal music—that is a question we can only answer by investigation. The division remains abstract, a set of open logical possibilities.

Given any class, we can look for a larger class that contains it and subsume the first class under the second. Of what more general class, we might ask, is the class of brown cardboard boxes a subclass? Evidently we have a choice; it is part of the class of brown things, of cardboard things, and of boxes in general. All these subsumptions are equally correct, as far as pure logic goes. Whether they are equally to the point depends on what the point may be. I shall return to that later.

Given any two classes, we may need to distinguish them. This involves both subsumption and division, for to make the distinction clear and adequate we will find some general class, or *genus,* of which they are parallel subclasses, or *coordinate species,* and then we will say how they differ from each other. What, for example, is the distinction between horror movies and others? Boris Karloff, who ought to know, suggested some time ago that what should be distinguished are "horror" and "terror" movies: "Horror might be what you see when the door is opened. Terror, on the other hand, is what you experience when you think about what is behind the closed door." Horror, he further amplified, is fright plus being revolted; terror is not revolting. (He claimed that the movies he made were terror movies, not horror movies, by his distinction, though he admitted that in the movie he was then making—his 130th—he ended up as a "mass of fungus.") It seems that his concepts are related in the following way: there is the class of terror movies, which generate fear and suspense and excitement; and the class of horror movies, which also revolt, is a subclass of this class. It is one of the tasks of this kind of logical analysis to get these class relations clear and explicit.

Or, to take a more serious example, what is the distinction between civil rights and civil liberties? These are often opposed to each other, and they certainly are not the same. What is the genus? We might say they are both claims that a person is justified in making. The justifiable claim to equal opportunity in employment, for example, is a civil right but not a civil liberty. The justifiable claim to freedom from government control over one's religion is a civil liberty but not a civil right. But the justifiable claim to equality before the law without regard to race, sex, age, religion, or national origin has been considered both a civil right and a civil liberty. The problem is extremely difficult, and no final answer is to be expected here. But we can see the direction in which thinking must go to clarify this pair of classes. Having agreed upon a genus, we look for significant differences: for example, there are the cases where the government infringes upon an individual's legitimate freedom (to worship as he pleases) and cases where other private individuals infringe upon one's legitimate freedom (employers refuse you a job because you are a Negro). This distinction is surely part of what we are after: a civil liberty is asserted against a government; it is freedom from government control in some respect. Perhaps a civil right, as the term is now generally used, is a right to freedom from discrimination on certain specified grounds. In that case the two classes overlap when it is the state that discriminates.

These examples bring out some of the problems encountered in getting clear about the relationships among classes, whether one is subordinate to the other or they are coordinate with each other—being both subordinate to some third class. In any case, whichever direction our thinking may take, what we end up with is a statement about the subordination relationships or coordination relationships among classes. And such a statement is a **classification.** It does not have to be put in verbal form, but may be exhibited in this familiar pattern:

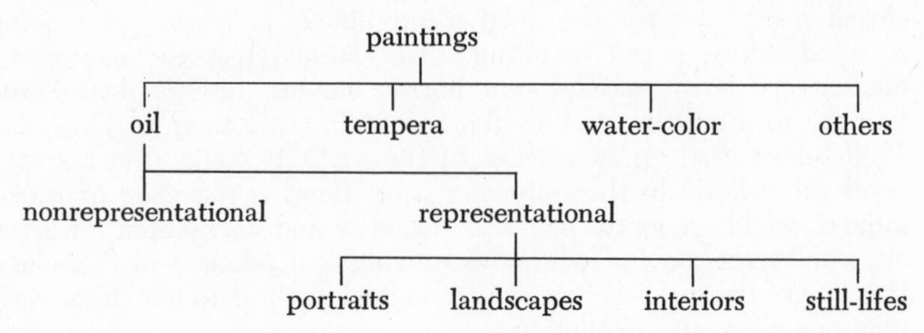

This does not pretend to be a complete classification of paintings, of course—the representational/nonrepresentational distinction could obviously be made for tempera paintings and water-colors as well as for oil paintings. But crude as it is, it will illustrate the essential ingredients of any classification. The classes it contains are called **categories,** to emphasize that they are not necessarily classes with members, but more like pigeonholes, which may or may not turn out, on inquiry, to be occupied. These categories are ordered on various levels, or **ranks,** the more general ranks above the more specific ones. Within each rank, the categories are distinguished by means of a special characteristic, which is the **basis of division.** In the second rank above, for example, the basis of division is *medium,* or physical material used, and the categories are different kinds of physical material. In the fourth rank, the basis of division is *representational content,* or perhaps *dominant representational content,* and of course this could be carried to endless detail (we could wind up with a category of paintings representing an unsmiling male child dressed in blue). There is no convenient name for the basis of division in the third rank, though the distinction is reasonably clear (even if not sharp): we might call it *relationship to real objects,* and say that the categories in this rank are the two possible relationships—sufficient or insufficient similarity to constitute representation.

The two main things to watch for in making a classification or in judging someone else's classification are confusion and triviality.

The rule that guards against confusion is illustrated by the classification just considered: in each rank, the categories are to be distinguished in terms of one and only one basis of division. If *color* is the basis of division, then you have pink, mauve, cerise, tangerine, and so forth. If *size* is the basis of division (among cars) then you have compact, medium, large. But if you divide the cars in a parking lot into the categories of pink cars, sports cars, sedans, compact cars, and cars with white-walled tires, you are likely to be confused, even if you somehow manage to get them all into the categories.

A good example of this is the occasional argument that the United States Supreme Court, in its decisions in recent years, has been "favoring communism." The category of communism-favoring decisions might be a significant one, but when the attackers break it down into its subclasses, they turn out to consist of decisions limiting certain police practices, decisions prohibiting a state from requiring a prayer of school children, decisions enlarging the First Amendment freedoms of speech, decisions in which a Communist or Communist sympathizer was involved, even though the basic question was a government employee's right to a hearing if he is fired—and other miscellaneous cases. As long as no attention is paid to the merits of the cases or the constitutional issues, they may look all of a piece, but it would take a considerable amount of analysis to discover how many bases of division are involved in this ranking.

A classification that violates the rule about a single basis of division is said to commit the **fallacy of cross-ranking.**

A classification groups certain things together and separates other things. A *significant* classification puts together things that really do belong together. Even though a classification may be entirely arbitrary—dividing at each rank on any basis that suggests itself—it will still be correct if it avoids the fallacy of cross-ranking. But one way of classifying a collection of things will be better than another for certain purposes: the distinctions that interest a theologian may not interest a social worker. Whatever your purpose in classifying may be, however, you want your categories to be *significant.* A significant classification is one whose ranks include some fundamental distinctions—and if it is an orderly one, the most fundamental distinctions will be those on the highest ranks.

The notion of fundamentalness cannot be made very precise without a good deal of discussion, but for our purpose it will be enough to show in a rough way what it involves. Some distinctions, we say, cut deeper than others—that is, the basis of division is a characteristic on which a number of other characteristics depend, so that when we have made the division on that basis, we find that the things in those categories have other noteworthy characteristics in common. Biological classifications bring this out clearly. It would be very superficial to begin classifying fish, for example, by distinguishing between those with pink patches and those without pink patches: we would not expect the pink-patched ones to share many other particular characteristics. But if we begin with certain basic physiological and anatomical differences, we find that other things depend on these—a certain kind of heart or gill or whatever determines other features of the organism. When a new kind of deep-sea creature, the pogonophore, turned up some years ago—a sort of very slender worm up to two feet long, with no digestive or excretory system and no means of breathing, but with a tiny brain—zoologists were baffled as to how to classify it. Their problem was not to find a larger class under which to subsume it (the description of the creature just given provides several such classes), but rather to know how to fit it into the fundamental categories already in existence, namely, the phyla into which all living things are basically divided. Finally they gave it a new phylum of its own.

A classification is not a generalization, as we have seen, but the significance of a classification depends on what generalizations are known to be true. That is why, as our knowledge of any group of things increases, we revise our classifications; for we learn that certain characteristics are more fundamental than others. The more true generalizations we have about all or most *X*, the more fundamental that category becomes. Not long ago a magazine suggested that present day Americans could be classified as highbrow, middlebrow, and lowbrow. How significant would such a classification be? It depends on what can be predicted from it. These categories were actually defined in terms of people's preferences as economic consumers: their taste in salads, television programs, sports, cars, spouses, beverages, and so on. If firm correlations can be found among these things, so that, for example, a fondness for tossed salads generally goes with having a Van Gogh reproduction in one's living room and preferring basketball to baseball, then the classification might turn out to be fairly significant. But it would probably not be as significant as more basic sociological classifications, in terms of economic status or type of employment.

Classification arises from comparison, that is, noting the similarities and differences of things. But there is another form of comparison that is also very important in our thinking. Consider the following passage:

> Let me explain to you the socialistic, or New Deal, theory of grading papers, which is like the income taxes, corporate profits taxes, anti-poverty programs, redevelopment giveaways, and so on, that are so

> much a part of our economy. When one of my bright or harder-working pupils makes a grade of 95 on a test, I take away 20 points and give them to a student who has made only 55 points. This creates a "common ownership" of grade points, from which each pupil draws the 70 to 80 points he needs for survival. Thus each contributes according to his ability and—since both receive a passing mark—each receives according to his need.

This speaker is drawing an **analogy** between certain economic procedures and certain (imaginary) grading procedures. Let us see what are the essential features of an analogy.

First, of course, an analogy is a comparison: we say that two things have certain characteristics in common. But we do not generally call a similarity an analogy unless it is somewhat complex. Two white things are similar, but not analogous. But if two things have several characteristics in common, and especially if these characteristics are systematically related to each other, then there is a structural similarity between the two things. A map has an analogy to the territory it maps, because the order of points on the map corresponds to the order of cities in the territory. Certain passages of music have an analogy to certain psychological processes, feelings and emotions, because the path the music follows (as it speeds and slows, intensifies and relaxes, gets loud and soft) matches in some degree those psychological processes. Finally, we do not usually speak of even a complex similarity as an analogy unless the two things we are comparing belong to basically different categories of things. Two Wyoming road maps are extremely similar, but they are not analogous; two eggs may be indistinguishable, but they are not analogues of each other. The map and its territory, however, are very different kinds of things; the former lacks certain essential characteristics of the latter. So their likeness, striking as it is, reaches across a deep contrast in kind. The auditory process of music and psychological processes in the mind would not belong together in an ordinary classification; to discover so close a similarity *despite* so great a disparity is to discover something unexpected and impressive.

I propose to define an analogy, then, as a complex set of similarities between two things of basically different kinds. I confess at once that the line between analogies and ordinary similarities cannot be made sharp by this definition, but that cannot be helped.

To recognize an analogy, or to draw one, may be extremely helpful to our thinking. Certainly the one just drawn puts the graduated income tax in an interesting light—or perhaps darkness. An analogy can help us understand complicated things in terms of simpler ones—as when a lecturer fashions pretty colored balls into a model of the structure of the DNA molecule, or explains the operation of the municipal government in terms of the internal-combustion engine. Even to say that radio waves "bounce off" the Van Allen magnetic belt or that the local antipoverty program will generate a "self-winding machinery of progress" is to speak somewhat analogically, to give a partial analogy, though these are strictly metaphors (metaphor will come in for consideration later, in Chapter 5). An analogy can also be very fruitful in suggesting new hypotheses to test out. When we are stuck on a problem and don't know where to turn next, the sudden perception of an analogy with even a fairly remote phenomenon may give us some ideas to try. This is the classic case of Kukulé's dream of the serpent with its tail in its mouth that suggested a possible structure of the benzene molecule —though of course he didn't believe that he *knew* the structure just because of his dream; he went to his laboratory for the final test. In our own day, the concept of the brain as a kind of computer, receiving its "inputs" and processing them into "outputs" has suggested a number of fruitful theories about the nature of thinking, about memory, about what causes dreams, and so on.

Analogies help clarify thinking—if not pushed too far—and they help inspire fresh and creative thinking. The logical problem arises, however, when they are put to another use, namely as the basis of an argument. Suppose the speaker already quoted went on in some such fashion as this:

> From what I have said you can draw your own conclusion. Just as the socialistic grading system would sooner or later destroy initiative, by encouraging all the pupils to give up working and let others earn their grades, so inevitably the taxation process must destroy economic creativity and lower the total productiveness on which we all depend. Moreover, after the grades had begun to go down, the teacher would have to resort to totalitarian methods—severe punishments and long hours of study—to get the grades up again. By the same token, the taxation system will produce a government which, in order to insure survival for all, will substitute forced labor, compulsory service, and prison camps, for the free market.

Here the speaker is not merely stating his analogy between taxation and "socialistic grading," but is drawing from that analogy a conclusion about one of the two things under comparison. This is an **argument from analogy.**

The pattern of this inference can be abstractly represented in this way:

X has characteristics *a, b, c, . . .*
Y has characteristics *a, b, c, . . .*
X also has the further characteristic *q*.

Y has the characteristic *q*.

In the example at hand, *X* is some particular classroom case of "socialistic grading," and *Y* is the United States government's internal revenue activities. The characteristics *a, b, c,* and so forth, are the allegedly common properties (sharing the income, whether grades or money). The characteristic *q* can be either one (or both) of the predicted outcomes: that the income will decline and/or that force will be exerted to bring it up. The inference is that because this would happen in one case, it will (probably) happen in the other. The argument is complete and self-contained, in that it does not fall back on any other information about the two cases involved. The underlying logical principle is that the more characteristics (*any* characteristics) two things from different categories have in common, the more probable it is that any further characteristic found in one is also present in the other.

Since this is a familiar form of argument, and quite obviously an inductive one, you may well question why I said earlier that there are only two kinds of inductive argument: generalization arguments and hypothesis arguments. For the conclusion in this case is not a generalization, nor is it an explanation of anything, so that the argument doesn't fall into either of the two categories of induction.

There is, it must be admitted, some difference of opinion about this matter among logicians, and there is no excuse, therefore, for being dogmatic. But the account to be given here seems to me to be the soundest, as far as it goes (and it would have to be refined in a fuller treatment). The argument from analogy is a distinct kind of argument, in its pure and strict form. But it is not an acceptable form of argument. However plausible it seems at first, it does not really succeed by itself in giving any probability to the conclusion, and is therefore no rival to the two sound forms of induction.

This can be seen at once, I think, if we put in arbitrary characteristics for the letters. Let *X* be brown, round, hard, cool, and small; let *Y* be brown, round, hard, cool. If this is all we know about them, do we have the slightest reason to believe that *Y* is also small? Add all the common characteristics you wish, and still there is no strength to the argument. Now, sooner or later, you *will* hit on a characteristic that does make a sudden difference. Suppose you add the characteristic *being a seed.* As soon as you know that *this* is what *Y* is, you can say, Yes, indeed, then it almost certainly is small. Why, then, do some characteristics add probability to the conclusion, while others (like brownness) do not? Why are there *telling* characteristics? Obviously because we already know a generalization connecting the telling ones with the inferred one: "Most seeds are small." But if we are allowed to assume this, we can make a new argument, instead of the original one:

Most seeds are small.
Y is a seed.

Y is more likely than not to be small.

In this streamlined version, not much is left of our original argument. The conclusion follows, to be sure—indeed, too well. For this is not an inductive, but a deductive argument. It consists in the application of a known generalization to a new instance—a common form of reasoning, but very different from the argument from analogy. In this argument the analogy no longer matters; all the other common characteristics (such as brownness and roundness) become irrelevant.

It may not be obvious, by the way, that this argument actually *is* deductive, for it is different from any deductive arguments we have considered, and it may easily be confused with a similar argument that is inductive. Consider:

Most seeds are small.
Y is a seed.
- - - - - - - - - - - - - - - - - -
Y is small.

This is not a *valid* deductive argument, of course; yet it lends the conclusion some degree of probability, so it can be called inductive. If, however, we put that probability into the conclusion, as with the argument just before this one, then the conclusion merely states in terms of probability what the premises give in terms of frequency. This is easily seen in cases where the inference is quantitative:

90 per cent of all seeds are small.
Y is a seed.

The chances are 9 in 10 that *Y* is small.

This is, of course, deductive—and valid.

The mere multiplication of common characteristics gives no basis for an inductive inference, then, as the argument from analogy claims. But, though it is always fallacious, we can never dismiss an argument from analogy out of hand. For the germs of another and better argument, as we have seen, may be lurking behind it. No matter how the ingenious comparisons between the "socialistic grading system" and the internal revenue operations are worked out—and a clever orator can work wonders with such comparisons—nothing will be proved about the evils of the national economy. But as the analogy brings out various features of the national economy, some of them may turn out to be in fact telling—if we happen to know the relevant generalizations. Suppose it is true that in an examination system, if we took away points from the best papers we would defeat the whole purpose of the examination and discourage people from trying very hard. (I'm not convinced that this is always true, but let it stand.) It doesn't follow at all that taxing the wealthy discourages people from bothering to make money; in fact, as taxes have increased in recent decades, so has the size of big corporations and so has the number of millionaires. Maybe taxation works in this situation like a challenge, a stimulating handicap. However the analogy does raise an interesting question about the motivation of people in reward situations of certain sorts—and if we are reasonable, we may turn to the social psychologist to see if he has any general laws about motivation that will enable us to carry out the required reasoning:

In such-and-such situations, motivation is decreased.
The tax system is such-and-such a situation.
____
The motivation to make profits will decrease.

If we do come up with this argument (by finding the right premise) then the argument from analogy will turn out to be of some use after all—not as an argument, but as a hint in the direction of one. But the argument would not be a very ambitious one; the real inductive work, so to speak, would already have been done when the generalization was being established in the first place. That took a certain amount of investigation. The argument from analogy is a short-cut method of getting the same results as generalization without going through the work—and it is no substitute for the real thing.

In meeting an argument from analogy, then, the first thing to point out is that it is no proof. The second thing is to see whether the conclusion can be supported with the help of relevant generalizations that are already available. If not, then the third thing is to find a way of showing the arguer why his argument won't work. This is not strictly a logical matter, but sometimes it is needed to shake him loose from the spell his analogy casts upon him. One way to do this is to caricature his analogy by extending it to the breaking point. Here is an interesting argument:

> Mrs. Cleo Maletis, Mrs. America of 1956, today demanded legislation to force every prospective bride to pass cooking tests before receiving a marriage license. . . . "If a state can require a blood test before marriage, it can certainly pass a law for compulsory cooking tests," she said.

What are the differences between the two kinds of thing compared? Well, for one thing, the blood test protects the general public, as well as the spouse; the cooking test, one might say, protects only the husband. If Mrs. Maletis' argument is legitimate, we can just as easily extend it to every respect in which a husband might conceivably want to be assured by law that his wife is all that he believes her to be. Shouldn't there be a law to insure that she has no unadmitted artificial parts? That her complete medical history is read out as part of the wedding service? That she pass sewing tests, ironing tests, secretarial tests, driving tests, and so forth, before a marriage license is issued? And what about the husband? Should not *his* medical and financial and moral history be made a matter of record, and his skills in carpentry, plumbing, gardening, and so forth, be proved? Of course none of these follows from the acceptance of a Wasserman test, any more than Mrs. Maletis' conclusion does—but by drawing enough of them, if they really follow no less than hers, we may be able to show that the whole argument is wrong. This method of extending the analogy is a reduction to absurdity—showing that in the end it leads to silliness.

A Check-up Quiz Which of the following are arguments from analogy? State the assumed common characteristics, and the conclusion, in each argument.

1. Reason uses the senses for help as the blind man uses his cane [Leibniz, in a letter to Queen Charlotte of Prussia, 1702].
2. To THE EDITOR: Every living fetus is truly a human person just as you and I. To treat a fetus in the manner suggested by your editorial is to make a human person into a thing. Consequently

every direct abortion, no matter what may be the motive, is just as much a crime as the assassination of President Kennedy or Hitler's condemning rabbis to the gas chamber.

3. When someone asked Bertold Brecht, toward the end of his life, why he had elected to stay in East Germany, though he could have gone to the West, he likened himself to a doctor with a limited supply of drugs who is forced to choose between two patients—a syphilitic old roué and a diseased prostitute who is, however, pregnant.
4. Medical experts testifying on proposals to require labeling of cigarettes as injurious to health refused to flip tops over the suspected link between cigarette smoking and lung cancer. Dr. William B. Ober, of Knickerbocker Hospital, described the "Puritan school" of cancer theorists as believing "that smoking causes lung cancer, sexual intercourse causes cancer of the cervix, and drinking causes cancer of the throat. Lord help us all!"
5. "Once upon a time," says John Keats in his new book, "the American met the Automobile and fell in love. Unfortunately, this led him into matrimony, and so he did not live happily ever after." This analogy merits extrapolation. The American automobile, according to Keats, has grown fat and insolent, demanding and expensive. Entrenched and no longer young, this mechanical bride has bedecked herself with chrome and falsies. . . . The sweetheart turned wife has grown vulgar and ostentatious.

   Pursuing the thought further, we can liken the European car to the Other Woman, a svelte and sophisticated siren, potent and petite, gay and inexpensive, with the appeal of the exotic and the promise that her lover will be accorded jealous admiration from others who are still in bondage to their bulging brides. Meanwhile, back home in Detroit, the bride's enraged parents . . . but why go on? [A. C. Spectorsky in *The New York Times Book Review*].

For Further Study L. S. Stebbing, *Thinking to Some Purpose,* Ch. 9. Baltimore, Md.: Pelican Books, 1939. Irving M. Copi, *Introduction to Logic,* 2nd ed., Ch. 11. New York: The Macmillan Company, 1961. James D. Carney and Richard K. Scheer, *Fundamentals of Logic,* Ch. 5. New York: The Macmillan Company, 1964.

OUTLINE-SUMMARY: chapter three

There are two forms of inductive argument:

In a *generalization argument,* the conclusion is a general statement, describing the distribution of some characteristic among the members of a class; and the evidence supports the conclusion by reporting instances of it. (Each red barn is an instance of the generalization "All barns are red.") The class referred to in the generalization is the population under investigation; the subclass which has been examined as a basis of the generalization is a sample of that population. The more assurance we have that the sample is representative of the whole population, the more probable the conclusion is; and this assurance is increased by the *size* of the sample, relative to the whole, and by the *randomness* of the sample. To generalize from too small or biased a sample is to commit the fallacy of *hasty generalization.* A special case of this fallacy, in dealing with causal generalizations, is the inference that because one event follows another it must be an effect of it (*post hoc, ergo propter hoc*).

In a *hypothesis argument,* the conclusion is a singular statement, describing an event or state of affairs; and the evidence supports the conclusion by reporting other observed events or states of affairs that can be explained by the hypothesis. (The hypothesis, or explaining statement, "Someone left the freezer door open" explains the condition reported in the statement to be explained, "The freezer is heavily frosted.") The more superior a hypothesis is to alternative explanations of the same available facts, the more acceptable, or probable, it is; and the criteria of superiority are *frequency* (the statistical frequency of events of that sort) and *simplicity* (the fewness of the events and objects involved in the hypothesis). To accept a hypothesis when a more frequent and/or simpler one can readily be found is to commit the fallacy of *far-fetched hypothesis.*

To make a *classification* is to set forth the relationships among various classes, showing which are parts of, or subordinate to, others (as green men form a subclass of Martians), and which are coordinate with others (as green men and Caucasians are both races of men). The principle of good classification is to insure that at every rank there is one and only one *basis of division* (that is, a single characteristic, such as race, color, or creed, in terms of which the division is made). A classification that violates this rule commits the fallacy of *cross-ranking.*

An *analogy* is a complex similarity between two things that belong to basically different categories (as between organized crime and an octopus). The *argument from analogy* reasons that because two things have a number of common characteristics, it is probable that a further characteristic found in one is also present in the other (because organized crime is like an octopus, and because an octopus is to be dealt with in certain ways, then organized crime is to be dealt with in the same way). This argument is always fallacious as it stands, but it may suggest a valid deductive argument, if we already know a generalization that connects one of the common characteristics with the inferred one.

Exercise 11

Discuss the dependability of the following generalizations. What weaknesses, if any, can you find in the argument? What further information would you wish to have before accepting the conclusion?

1. QUESTION: Dear Dr. Molner: My daughter, a freshman in high school, has to ride on the bus a full hour to get to school. Because she gets sick on the bus, she can't eat any breakfast. This morning she had only two salty crackers and a glass of milk. Can you possibly suggest something substantial she could eat so early in the morning—6:30 A.M.? The bus ride home doesn't bother her.

ANSWER: Since the bus ride bothers her in the morning but not in the afternoon, I suspect that her troubles—both the car sickness and the inability to eat—are psychological rather than physical. Keep in mind the fact that she is a freshman.

2. DEAR ABBY: In regard to the husband who wrote you recently that his wife "sweet-talks" all her plants and flowers, and this makes them grow well. I have tested out this theory by sitting in my front yard and cussing the weeds and crabgrass; but it doesn't seem to discourage them at all. It seems to me that the theory must be wrong.

3. A team of researchers from the University of Colorado has found that religious people who are drawn to the mystical qualities of life make the safest drivers. According to their report to the American Psychiatric Association meeting, the subjects of the study were 264 airmen at the Lowry Air Force Base in Denver, whose accident records were known. According to the Vernon-Allport definition, the religious man is one who is "concerned with the supernatural meaning of all existence and particularly his place in it." Subjects who belonged to this type, according to the test, had collisionless records in 73 per cent of the cases. The scientists said that the higher accident scores of the nonreligious types (the aesthetic and theoretic types) was due to "a general tendency to be less conventional, psychologically

more complex and conflicted, more in disharmony with their everyday environment, and more ready to resort to complex defensive operations as a protection against anxiety."

4. Anyone who keeps up on the Internal Revenue Service's attempts to get people to pay their income tax, as reported in the newspapers, can see that the rich are far more given to thumbing their noses at the income tax law than the poor. Every week or so we read of people from whom the government has collected back taxes, either through court action or by the threat of it, and the sums are always substantial amounts.

5. The Illinois state highway department has reported that small cars are neither more nor less hazardous to drive than larger ones, though they have worse records in several categories of accident. Small cars, both domestic and foreign (defined as one weighing less than 2,800 pounds), were involved in 85, or 5.7 per cent, of the 1,473 fatal accidents in Illinois last year; and they make up 5.8 per cent of the cars registered in the state. In the category of deaths caused by driving to the left of the center line, the small cars had a bad record, for 20.8 per cent of their fatal accidents occurred on the left side, as against the bigger cars' score of 14.9 per cent. It was also noted that the proportion of accidents in which the driver had disregarded traffic signals was greater among small cars than big cars. The age group with the worst record was from 20 to 24 years and this applied to both types of car.

6. After a lot of parents complained because their children were getting failing marks, Principal Edwin Anderson of the Prosser, Washington, high school made a survey, ventured an answer: an educational mixture too rich in gasoline. His figures: of seniors with A or B grades, only 11 per cent own cars or have the use of them regularly. Among C grade seniors, 33 per cent have cars, and 62 per cent of the C-minus-to-failing seniors are motorized. Cars owned by juniors with A or B grades, none; with C grades, 31 per cent; and with C-minus-to-failing marks, 39 per cent.

The tabulations, Anderson added, did not include youths who had quit school to buy gas, parts, and polish for their jalopies.

7. A psychologist studied the affective qualities of music. Parts of three movements (finales of Beethoven's *A Major Symphony* and *E-flat Major Piano Concerto* and the first movement of Mendelssohn's *Symphony in A Major*) were described as "joyful" by all subjects; they contain several rising thirds. Parts of ten arias from Bach's *St.*

Matthew Passion were described as "sad"; they contain several falling major and minor seconds. He concluded that pieces with rising thirds sound joyful and pieces with falling seconds sound sad. This conclusion was further substantiated by a study of two larger groups of compositions. In one group, every piece was described as "sad," "gloomy," and so forth, and in the other every piece was described as "gay," "happy," "joyful," and so forth. The first group averaged 45 per cent more falling seconds per 100 measures than the second group; the second group averaged 32 per cent more rising thirds per 100 measures. This shows that falling seconds tend to make a piece sad; rising thirds tend to make it joyful.

8. The high degree of intellectualization of the modern American college campus is shown by our study of general conditions. According to the National Education Association, the national median salary for full professors is $10,327, whereas that for head football coaches is only $8,554. In most colleges the contents of the library cost more than the athletic equipment. Attendance at class and adequate performance on examinations is still considered indispensable to remaining in college, and fraternities are not generally allowed to practice the kind of disruptive hazing that used to be widespread. The number of goldfish swallowed and of panties raided has declined, and the number of paperbound books purchased in college bookstores has increased.

9. On second thought, the inaccuracies in Gilbert Highet's book, *The Powers of Poetry,* are more likely the result of an imprecision of thought and crudeness of attitude which are abundantly present in Professor Highet's observations on matters nonpoetic. We are reminded, for example, of "some aspects of the Italian character—in particular, the treacherous cunning which we know from the Mafia." So much for the Italians. A little later on, a reference to "the intellectual with his nagging sense of inadequacy and frustration" fixes another set of wagons. But my favorite example of the generalization unleashed comes in the chapter on the Japanese haiku: "Yet the oddest thing about these exquisite poems . . . is that they should have been produced by a nation which is also capable of beastly treachery, violence, and cruelty." Come to think of it, there's something odd about Inquisition Spain producing the universal wisdom of Cervantes and the spiritual insight of Calderon, or Germany producing a Hitler and a Rilke at nearly the same time—or, for that matter, a nation in which lynching and mob violence are not unknown producing the delicate art of Emily Dickinson and Wallace Stevens.

Professor Highet's generalizations may be at times, a little annoying, but his chapters on poetic technique are a sheer delight. He's especially interested in alliteration: "*s* shows hatred, *t* disgust, *l* and *v* soft affection, and so forth." As we continue, we discover that *s* has become "the letter of disgust and sinister cunning," and a page later, simply a "soft" sound [from *The New Republic*].

10. In a scientific symposium at the 150th anniversary convocation of the Massachusetts General Hospital, Dr. Henry K. Beecher reported that the well-known placebo effect of the sugar pill can be extended to surgery as well. According to Dr. Beecher, the average placebo effect of pills (that is, pills with no pharmaco-dynamic or specific chemical properties) can rise as high as 25 per cent. The operation he spoke of consists in internal mammary artery ligation for treatment of angina pectoris. The mammary arteries are tied off to increase the flow of blood to the heart by diverting some blood flow from the chest. In a series of surgical tests the patients were placed on the operating table; their mammary arteries were exposed and a piece of surgical suture material was placed around the artery. But the knot was not tied, and the arteries remained untouched. These patients were then compared with patients who had had the actual operation. The improvement in both groups was about the same: patients reported feeling better and they were able to take more exercise without ill effects.

Exercise 12

Examine the following pieces of reasoning. Discuss the frequency and simplicity of the hypothesis in comparison with an available alternative, and give examples of evidence that would, if obtained, decide between the two hypotheses.

1. A German missionary has just brought back from thirteen years in Tibet a photograph of the "abominable snowman" of the Himalayas, the mysterious creature of the snowy slopes who has been credited with leaving enormous footprints and has been fleetingly glimpsed from time to time by terrified travelers. The Reverend Franz Eichinger says that the "abominable snowmen" are native priests living nude (except when meeting strangers) in the subzero temperatures of the icy wilderness of the inaccessible mountain ranges. "In a way which we cannot understand, they are immune from the influence of nature and the needs of human life," he said. The picture showed the snowman in a loincloth with wild hair and eyes closed. "To be the first Euro-

pean to meet one of these people is the most unforgettable experience of my thirteen years in China," wrote Reverend Eichinger.

2. After making a thorough study of the "abominable snowman," The Reverend Swami Pranavananda has concluded that what travelers have seen is a large bear walking on his hind legs, and standing seven feet tall. He pointed out that the footprints of bears are frequently mistaken for those of men, that bears stand and walk erect occasionally, and that the Himalayan red bear is found at altitudes from 10,000 to 21,000 feet. He suggested that the superstitious shepherds would naturally think that the bear's footprints, especially when enlarged by partial melting under the summer sun, were those of a gigantic 1,000-year-old Yogi or other legendary character. The term "abominable snowman" is a bad translation of the local Tibetan phrase, "man-bear." Reverend Pranavananda rejected the view proposed by some anthropologists that the footprints are those of *Gigantopithecus blacki,* an extinct giant ape that may have survived in the Himalayas, if it ever existed—the only evidence for its existence being three teeth that turned up in a Chinese drugstore.

3. Landstuhl, Germany, January 27, ———. When United States Army private A—— B——, stationed at Amsbach, Germany, broke out in a rash recently, his twin brother, miles away in Berlin, broke out in an identical rash at the same time. The 22-year-old Pittsburgh twins were transferred to the Second General Hospital here. It turned out to be an old story with them; on several previous occasions, when something happened to one, it also happened to the other. Doctors said they had never seen such conclusive proof of that mysterious psychic relationship between twins, by which unconsciously and unwittingly one can cause sympathetic effects in the other.

4. Gerald Hawkins studied the layout of the great trilithons (three-stone archways) at Stonehenge, on Salisbury Plain, built between 2000 and 1500 B.C.—the uprights weighing 50 tons, the crosspieces 6 tons. He asked: Why was Stonehenge built? It had already been noted that if you stand in the center on a clear midsummer morning (around the summer solstice, June 22) and look down the "avenue," you see the sun rise almost exactly over the distant "heelstone." With the help of astronomical data and a computer, he proved that back before 1500 B.C. there were 24 significant positions of the sun and moon that could be sighted at different times of the year through Stonehenge in various directions. He concluded that Stonehenge was built as an astronomical observatory: a calendar to predict changes of season, perhaps also eclipses.

5. To the Editor: I'm sorry, but in a paper as fine and honest in its reporting as *The Evening Bulletin,* it makes me mad to see a writer —whoever wrote "Mystery in the Sky"—apparently knuckling under to Pentagon pressure.

Everyone who knows anything about the subject knows how the Air Force is suppressing for all it is worth anything and everything connected with U.F.O.'s (Unidentified Flying Objects) such as the color movie taken at 11:10 a.m., MST, on July 2, 1952, by W. C. Newhouse seven miles north of Tremonton, Utah, on U.S. 30, of 12 to 14 U.F.O.'s; the CAB report of the near collision of United Airlines Flight No. 193 on April 14, 1954, with a U.F.O.; the report of Captain Adriance, of Pan American Airlines, about the incredible speed with which a U.F.O. passed him and caught up with the plane ahead on April 23, 1954; and literally thousands of more sightings, not by men in the street but by airline pilots, Air Force detachments, and innumerable well-qualified people, including astronomers.

Doesn't your editor know about the Air Force's ruling—passed when it got panicky—which not only directs all personnel reporting unidentified flying objects to do so immediately to the Secretary of Defense in Washington, who will transmit copies to the CIA, and so forth—but which directs that *only reports of objects that are identified as natural* can be released to the press. . . .

In a fright over the latest rash of sightings, they got Professor Menzel, at Harvard, to say again that all these reports were just mirages, hot air bubbles in the atmosphere. Oh, sure, that was what the C. G. Cutter *Sebago* tracked on its radar at 1,000 mph; mirages that turned off car lights and radios and left batteries steaming on November 3; a mirage that got James Stokes, electronic engineer, out of his car at Alamagordo and gave him a severe sunburn last week.

I bet the Air Force considers it a doggone shame that the ice that has fallen in Kensington and elsewhere around here can be put in freezers and tested in labs, or they could claim it was a mirage, too!

6. Still unsolved is the famous mystery of the disappearance of Judge Crater. Acting on a tip from a butcher, *Life* magazine dug up a Yonkers backyard in 1960, looking for his body but not finding it. Joseph Force Crater, 41-year-old justice of the New York State Supreme Court, had a Columbia University law degree; he had worked hard at law and politics and headed a Tammany club; he had been a secretary to Senator Wagner. In 1916 he married a woman seven days after he got her a divorce. Before his disappearance he was

maintaining an attractive divorcée in a midtown apartment, was often seen escorting Ziegfeld Follies girls to nightclubs, and was known as "Goodtime Joe" in the Broadway area. On the morning of Sunday, August 3, 1930, when he was at Belgrade Lakes, Maine, he received a call from New York City, and told his wife, "I've got to straighten those fellows out." On Monday he was seen entering his apartment in New York City. On Wednesday he had his assistant cash two checks totalling $5,150, and he took two locked briefcases to his apartment (these disappeared with him). He tried to buy a ticket to a play that evening and ate at a restaurant with some theatrical friends. At 9:15 he waved good-bye, and has not returned since. A long investigation, following up hundreds of false claims to have seen him, led nowhere. In 1937 Mrs. Crater sued three insurance companies for double indemnity—$50,000—claiming that her husband had been blackmailed by a woman and murdered by her gangster friends because he couldn't produce enough money to satisfy them. Double indemnity was not awarded (Mrs. Crater was paid $20,561), but the judge was declared legally dead in 1939.

7. A fortnight ago, three archaeologists of excellent reputation announced the discovery of drawings on the wall of a cave near Perigueux, in southwestern France. They said that the paintings—which depict mammoths and other prehistoric animals, including big two-horned rhinoceroses—were made 20,000 years ago by cavemen. "A great discovery," the Poitiers Conference of Archaeologists was told. But William Martin, a speleologist and former president of the Perigueux Speleo Club, said that he spent three years exploring that cave eight to ten years earlier, and that there were no paintings on the walls then. He said the paintings are "phonies, put in by people since. Believe me, none of these paintings dates back more than eight or ten years." Newspapers pointed out that some years ago scientists discovered a cave in North Africa decorated with highly realistic drawings of animals; there was great excitement in archaeological circles until an expert discovered a previously overlooked drawing, in the same style and technique, of a twentieth-century locomotive. As for the Perigueux drawings, Abbé Henri Brouil, a specialist on prehistoric art, told newspapers: "I declare the figures perfectly authentic."

8. Tektites are bits of semitransparent glassy stuff, mostly black or dark green, found in many parts of the world. They have not been explained as earthly minerals, so many scientists believe they come,

like meteorites, from outer space. In a recent issue of *The Scientific Monthly*, physicist Ralph Stair of the National Bureau of Standards tells how he thinks they were formed and scattered. According to his theory, tektites come from a "lost planet" that once revolved in an orbit between Mars and Jupiter, which broke up and filled the solar system with debris. On the surface of this planet, Stair thinks, was light, glassy material that had separated like cream as the heavier rock sank toward the center of the planet. When the planet broke up, chunks of the surface glass flew around the solar system, and when they hit the earth's atmosphere broke up into small fragments from the heat.

9. The latest Communist-inspired conspiracy against the American people is the bill before Congress which proposes a grant to Alaska to build up its mental-health facilities. Thank God Alaska has so far kept its fine insanity laws, which provide that a person can be declared insane only by a jury of his peers, and if he is insane he is put in jail until he can be taken by the United States Marshal to Oregon. This new bill, by introducing a lot of mental care, psychiatry, and confused coddling, will transform Alaska into Siberia, U.S.A. Why? The bill allows the governor of Alaska to arrange with governors of other states for transfer of mental patients to other states. This is nothing short of a banishment bill—its underlying purpose is obviously to let the governor dispatch anyone who has been active against New Dealers and their one-world schemes of slavery. This is part and parcel of the whole phony mental-health crusade, which we have been fighting for years along with the American Public Relations Forum, Inc., of Burbank, California, and that great patriot, John Kasper, of Merchantville, New Jersey, and the Association of American Physicians and Surgeons, which has been waging its battle against socialized medicine. Every enlargement of mental-care facilities, hospitals, and clinics is a transparent attempt to prepare the way for locking up anti-Communists as mental cases. Already the pseudopsychology people are saying that anti-Semitism is neurotic, and that objections to race-mixing and other things proceed from an unbalanced mind, and that General Walker, in leading the defense of the University of Mississippi, was mentally ill. Their plan is to send all true anti-Communists to insane asylums, so there will be no one to protect the country from going Red.

10. The so-called *déjà-vu* ("already seen") phenomenon has happened to many people: you find yourself in a new place, and suddenly

you have the powerful feeling that you have already seen it, that you know every bit of it, though you are sure you have never been there before. There are different explanations of this phenomenon. One theory (put forth by A. L. Wigan in the nineteenth century) is that the two hemispheres of the cerebrum are capable of independent action; when the mind is exhausted or for some other reason not very attentive, one part of the brain registers the scene without our becoming fully conscious of it, and when the other part is aroused to full attention, there is the vague sense that these images have passed through the mind before. They have indeed passed through the mind before, but not in some earlier incarnation (as some believe), but only a split second earlier. Another version of Wigan's theory is that the *déjà-vu* phenomenon is a product of mental fatigue, in which the mind is too slack to distinguish between the new and the old, the present and the past. This was proposed by Michel Leon-Kindberg and Havelock Ellis, who said the illusion occurs not in perception, but in "apperception," the conscious registering of what is seen. What is really a new perception flows so rapidly through the mind, in its relaxed state, and is so effortlessly grasped, that it feels like a memory.

Exercise 13

Improve upon the following classifications; revise them so that they do not involve cross-ranking; put the more significant categories in the higher ranks; fill out the scheme where there are apparent gaps. It may be helpful, in doing this exercise, to choose a point of view for each of the examples—that is, a set of intellectual or practical interests in terms of which certain categories will become more significant than others.

1.

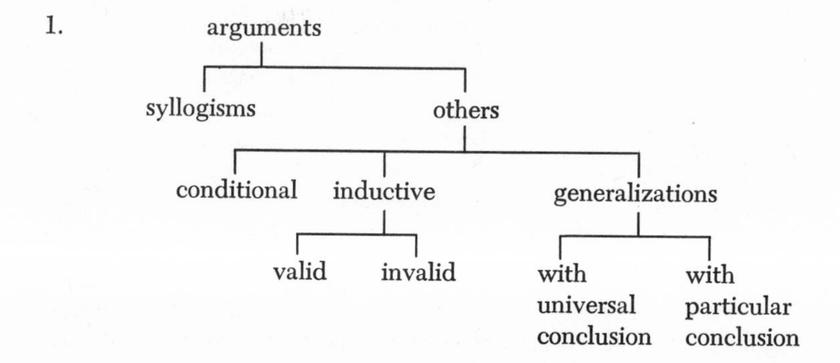

2.

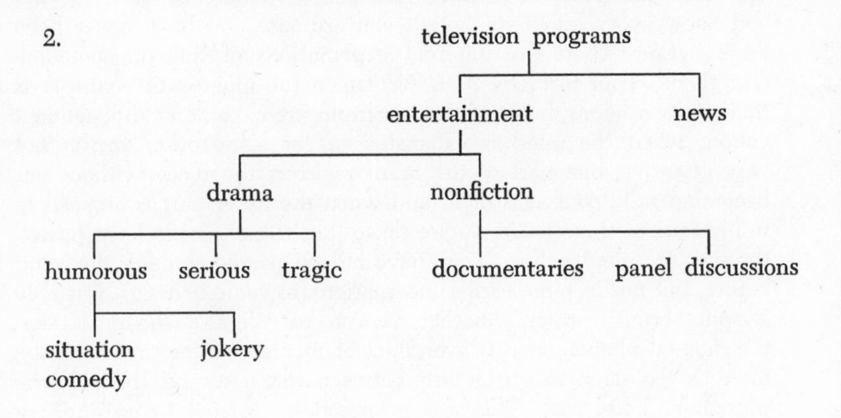

3.

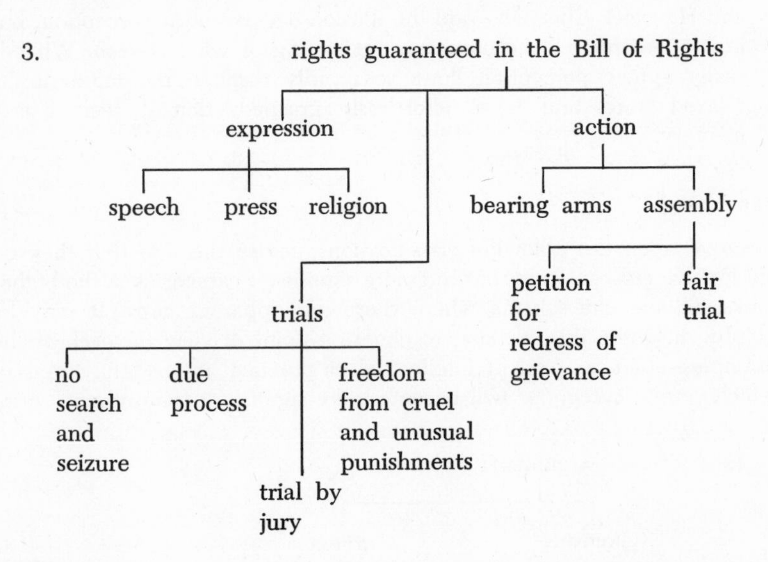

Exercise 14

Examine carefully the following arguments from analogy. Exactly what does each assume, and what does it try to prove? How would you reply to each of them?

1. To the Editor: In view of your article in Sunday's *Times*, you seemingly encourage the hiring of people with left-wing associations in radio, television, and the theatre. You say "it is only right that the

independent producers of motion pictures should be free to choose those whom they wish to employ as actors and writers." But by the same token, shall we let the producers of dairy products be free to employ people with communicable diseases to handle the food products? Ridiculous, outlandish comparison, you say? Food producers have a public trust; they are regulated by agencies which see to it that the physical health of the population is safeguarded. Is the mental and moral health of the public of any lesser importance?

2. COLLINGWOOD: How are we going to stop the spread of infection from Castro's Cuba to the rest of Latin America?

LIPPMANN: You throw off infection by being healthy, and South America is not healthy. Again and again, in most countries, you have a problem of poverty and riches, of backwardness, of illiteracy, not in all of them, which has to be cured. . . . That's what the Alliance for Progress is.

3. Suppose *The New York Times* suddenly adopted a new policy, according to which every advertiser would have to supply ten adjacent columns of news and views for every column of advertising he buys. Would Macy's and Gimbel's be willing to sponsor an analysis of the Communist Party Congress in Moscow, or bad news about military reverses in Southeast Asia? Or would it be more likely to sponsor some sordid story about a Hollywood star's love life, to attract more attention to its ad? Sounds absurd, but this is exactly the system that is used on radio and television, and the advertising agency executives who testified before the FCC last month said that it couldn't be changed—that there is no other practical method of making up programs.

4. If we say that the aim of any activity is merely our pleasure and define it solely by that pleasure, our definition will evidently be a false one. But this is precisely what has occurred in the efforts to define art. Now if we consider the food question it will not occur to any one to affirm that the importance of food consists in the pleasure we receive when eating it. Everybody understands that the satisfaction of our taste cannot serve as a basis for our definition of the merits of food, and that we have therefore no right to presuppose that dinners with cayenne pepper, Limburg cheese, alcohol, and so on, to which we are accustomed, and which please us, form the very best human food.

In the same way beauty, or that which pleases us, can in no sense serve as a basis for the definition of art; nor can a series of objects which afford us pleasure serve as the model of what art should be [from Leo Tolstoy, *What is Art?*].

5. From before the Revolution until after the Civil War fire fighting was done by volunteer fire brigades, with haphazard, often inadequate, equipment. These were organizations in which the colorful uniform and the social functions were as much a part of their activity as was the fire fighting they were called upon to do.

The services of these fire brigades were not available to all who needed them, but only to the property owner who was insured and indicated his insurance by an ornate plaque attached prominently to the front of his building. These plaques were known as "fire marks" and have become collectors' items. Some of the insurance companies in the large cities formed their own brigades in an effort to bring some reliability to fire fighting. However, most of the brigades worked freelance and responded to as many fires as they could; they were assured of payment for their work by the insurance company indicated by the fire mark. Sometimes they were met at the fire by a rival brigade, and before either could get down to the business of extinguishing the fire a fight ensued to eliminate one of the brigades. The rivalry between brigades also included hiding the source of the water supply, or damaging the other brigade's equipment. A homeowner whose fire mark indicated an insurance company which drove a hard bargain in the payment following a fire sometimes found it necessary to fight a fire himself. Probably the worst defect of this free enterprise system was that some of the brigades were too enterprising. Incendiarism by the very brigades who later were to collect from the insurance company became a tremendous burden to the underwriters.

The first efforts of the insurance companies to offset losses from ineffective fire control and incendiarism came in 1866 when 75 companies convened and organized the National Board of Fire Underwriters. On October 8, 1871, the great Chicago fire brought bankruptcy to more than 100 fire insurance companies. It was then that the 5-year-old National Board realized that the insurance companies could no longer remain solvent when dependent upon amateur, dishonest, unreliable fire-fighting organizations. Professionally trained and properly equipped fire departments were necessary. By 1876, 275 cities, towns, and villages had paid, full-time fire departments with an adequate standard of equipment.

All this came not at the insistence of politicians or the government, but as the result of pressure from the insurance companies through the National Board of Fire Underwriters. Through the years this pressure set the standards of fire-fighting facilities until the underwriting of fire insurance became a profitable enterprise.

Is there any indication that sickness fighters may feel the same kind of pressure from a relative source, the health insurance industry? Now that the medical profession's insurance, Blue Shield, has proven to commercial companies that health insurance is sound, and competition for this business becomes intense, is the practitioner going to be affected? Will the insurance industry find that indemnities following the services of a well-trained surgeon are less than the payments made after the use of a poorly trained surgeon? Will they find that severe illnesses cared for by the well-trained internist are less expensive to them than those cared for by the general practitioner? Will their surveys show that treatment by physicians attached to certain types of hospitals is more desirable from a profit viewpoint than by those attached to less adequate hospitals? Is there a possibility that the larger companies in the big cities will organize their own "brigades"? Will they hold the threat of underwriting boycott until standards are met? Above all, is there any evidence that the insurance forces will go so far as to insist that the medical profession become governmentalized to bring about actuarial soundness? [Dr. V. R. DeYoung, Jr., in *The Progressive,* December 1958; quoted by permission].

chapter four | SOME PITFALLS OF LANGUAGE

When we study the principles of deductive and inductive logic, as we have been doing in the past two chapters, we are concerned with what might be called the *strategy* of argument: the management of over-all structure, control over the main lines of force that hold the argument together. When we turn to the language in which the argument is formulated, and the ways in which that language can help or hinder the course of the argument, we are concerned with *tactics*. This is no less important than strategy, if the argument is to succeed.

For the problem we face in constructing an argument is not only to build with an eye to the logical coherence of the whole, but also to make sure that the full subtlety and force of the argument comes through to our audience. It must not be fallacious; it must not even *appear* fallacious because of careless choice of words or fumbling syntax. And in trying to grasp an argument and find out what it has to offer from a logical point of view, our problem is not only to get a broad impression of how the argument is proceeding, but to make sure that some serious flaw has not crept in through a far from obvious play on words or through the confusion of one concept with another.

Language is such a complex thing that a study of its phenomena can be almost endlessly interesting. For practical logical purposes, however, we can limit our study to certain aspects of language. And the first thing to do is examine with some care certain very fundamental and pervasive features of language that are the sources of the main troubles we have in managing it. As with many things in this book, these troublesome characteristics of language will not by any means be strange to you. But you have probably not examined them as closely or systematically as we shall do here. By distinguishing them carefully, and giving them different names, we come to notice them readily—as a critical reader must—when we run across them. Then it is much less easy for them to impose upon us.

§12. ambiguity

Almost all the words in our language—except for technical terms that have been too recently coined to collect them—have a number of meanings, or senses. This is a fundamental feature of our language. And it is certainly an advantage, for once we learn a new word, the more work we can make it do for us, the more valuable it is. Without much trouble, we can easily think of a variety of senses for most of our simple and common words: consider, for example, what the noun "bolt" means when we speak of (1) a bolt of cloth, (2) a bolt of lightning, (3) a bolt that fastens pieces of wood or metal, (4) a bolt of delegates from a political party convention. There is very little that these meanings have in common; (1) and (3) are objects, whereas (2) and (4) are events; (1) doesn't look any more like (2) than (3) looks like (4). There is no danger of confusing these senses, because in each example the *context* makes it quite clear which sense the word has. Whether "lox" means smoked salmon or liquid oxygen propellant is pretty well indicated by the subject of conversation: food or rocketry.

This is a second fundamental feature of our language: that the senses of a word are subject to control by context. If someone merely referred to a "bolt," we would be at a loss as to how to interpret the reference. If he said that the bolt was picked up, we could rule out lightning and party bolts. If he said "bolt of cloth," we would be able to single out the required sense right away: *a compact roll, containing probably about forty yards*. That is the only one of the four senses that makes sense with "cloth." For if we tried to read "bolt of cloth" as "a threaded pin with head and nut, made of cloth," we would encounter something of an impossibility. If all the senses but one involve impossibility, that remaining sense is the one the context requires.

It is congruence with context, then, that usually indicates the relevant sense of a word (or phrase). The **context** (in *this* context) includes at least the words immediately before and after. A word may shift its sense very rapidly. When the fatalist says "What will be, will be," the second "will be" has a slightly different context from the first—enough to give it a very different sense. When Coolidge said, "The business of America is business," he was certainly not saying something trivial, or even true. There are clearly two senses of "business": (1) *main or most important occupation,* and (2) *commercial and/or industrial activity.* The larger context may be the whole discourse, or even the whole group of discourses in which the word appears—the books of the New Testament, the complete works of a novelist, or the file of a newspaper.

A word that has different senses in different contexts will be said to have **variable meaning.** The dictionary records a variety of senses, and perhaps gives some indication of the kinds of contexts in which these senses are operative—as law, medicine, heraldry, carpentry. And the dictionary distinguishes these different senses by giving different *synonyms* of the word. Take "noisome," for example —a word often misused. It has two distinct senses. One is the same as that of "harmful"; the other is the same as that of "smelly." In certain contexts, "noisome" and "harmful" could be substituted for each other, without materially affecting the meaning: "The place was filled with sweet-smelling but noisome (harmful) plants." In certain other contexts, "noisome" and "smelly" could be substituted for each other: "They could hardly breathe; the air was hot and noisome (smelly)." I do not want to say that these pairs of words have exactly the same meaning in any context. But they may have approximately the same meaning. When two words have a very similar meaning throughout some range of contexts, I shall say they have the same *sense* and are **synonymous** in those contexts.

How do we know when a word has the same sense in two contexts, or a different sense? This question cannot be fully answered without a study of several problems about meaning. But practical advice can be given, and it will often be found helpful. Suppose the same word occurs in two different statements; for example:

(1) The experimenter's *induction* from the evidence was sound.

(2) It was the day of his *induction* into the Army.

These are apparently different senses; the problem is to *show* that they are different. The method is to look for another word or phrase that can be substituted for "induction" in one of these contexts, but cannot sensibly be substituted for "induction" in the other context. And this is fairly easy. We can rewrite (1) as

(1′) The experimenter's *process of drawing a probable conclusion* from the evidence was sound.

This is not ideal syntax, but it is intelligible, and with a little re-arrangement it could be made all right. But we cannot write:

(2′) It was the day of his *process of drawing a probable conclusion* into the Army.

The first sense of "induction" is ruled out for the second sentence. On the other hand, if we found a synonym to mark the second sense of "induction," it would not have worked in the first statement.

(2″) It was the day of his *formal admission* into the Army.

But not:

(1″) The experimenter's *formal admission* from the evidence was sound.

If you can find a satisfactory substitute that will work in one context but not in the other, you can demonstrate that the word does not have exactly the same sense in both contexts. This is not an absolutely conclusive proof, because it is conceivable that even if the word has the same sense in both contexts, you might hit on a synonym that is more affected by being transferred from one context to the other. But the method gives a result that deserves acceptance in most cases—especially if it is used in both directions.

Suppose, on the other hand, that the problem is to show that a word has the *same* sense in two contexts. Then you look for a synonym that can be substituted in both contexts without doing violence to the meaning. Compare (2) with

(3) After her *induction* into Phi Beta Kappa, she graduated with honors.

The same phrase, "formal admission," can be substituted for "induction" in both (2) and (3). And this is evidence that "induction" has the same sense in both. Again, it is not conclusive; for it might happen that the substitute phrase had a similar pattern of variability, so that the change of context shifted its sense in a way parallel to the shift of "induction." But to find a phrase that is synonymous in both contexts—and especially to find a second phrase (say, "official entrance") that is synonymous in both contexts—is a good indication that the original word has a constant sense through this change of context.

In the examples we have examined so far, the contextual control is firm enough to single out one sense from all the possibilities. But it also commonly happens that the control is not complete, and more than one choice is left open. When a word can have either (but not both) of two (or more) distinct meanings in a certain context, we shall say that the word is **ambiguous** *in that context.*

The ambiguity of a word is always relative to a context; no word is ambiguous in itself. Thus ambiguity is not at all the same thing as variability of meaning. It is true that some words with variable meaning are ambiguous in a great many contexts—they are complicated, tricky, or slippery, and hard to keep under contextual control. It is hardly ever safe to assume that their sense will take care of itself; some thought has to be given to preparing the context. For example: "liberty," "love," "faith," "equality"—very important words, all of them, and worth the effort they require. But there are many other words whose senses vary enormously from context to context but which are hardly ever ambiguous, since it doesn't take much of a context to select a single sense. "Bolt" is one of them; "point," "bond," "bill," "run" are others. With some ingenuity, you can construct short sentences in which these are ambiguous, but in any very long sentence, the ambiguity is almost certain to be lost.

There is another important mode of meaning that must be kept clearly distinct from ambiguity. When we have ambiguity, we have at least two senses in mind, but we are left in doubt; we cannot choose. When we have **multiple meaning,** we have at least two senses in mind, but we do not have to choose; indeed, we are invited to take in both at once. Puns exploit this possibility. When, for example, a book review says that a certain novel should not have a jacket but a negligee, the point of the pun (if I may perform the painful operation of analyzing it) depends on thinking of *both* senses of "jacket"—an article of clothing and a paper cover around a book. This is not a case of doubtful meaning, but of double meaning. The most moving examples of multiple meaning are, of course, in poems. When the speaker in Keats' "Ode to a Nightingale" says:

> Thou wast not born for death, immortal Bird!

he is saying (1) that the bird is not destined to be killed (since it is not particularly edible, and so is spared being hunted); (2) that the bird ought to live forever; and (3) that the bird's song places it among the artists who overcome death as their creations live on. These senses are in there together, all at once; and they are part of what makes the poem rich and beautiful.

Unfortunately, what I am calling "multiple meaning" is often called "ambiguity," but it would be valuable to preserve two distinct terms for these very different phenomena—one of which is such an infirmity in any discourse, the other such an asset to some kinds of discourse.

There are a number of ways in which a context can fall short of fixing meaning decisively. They can be classified under two general and convenient headings to give us two types of ambiguity, which arise from the two fundamental aspects of a word. We can speak of a word's relationships to the things in the world, or to things that might be in the world; or we can speak of its relationships to other words. When we say that a word *means* something, or (as we have been doing) that it has various senses, we are talking about the **semantical** aspect of the word; and more will be said about this in the remainder of this book. When, on the other hand, we say that a word is a noun or adjective, that it is a transitive or intransitive verb, that it occurs as direct or indirect object of the verb in a certain sentence, then we are talking about the **syntactical** aspect of the word—its grammatical properties and functions. All words in our language have both aspects. And when we are confronted by an ambiguity, we may be in doubt about either of these aspects of words—about their sense or about their syntax.

A word (or, indeed, any piece of language) is **syntactically ambiguous** in a certain context if there is more than one way, consistent with the context, of construing its grammatical relationships. There are a number of ways in which this can happen. There are common elliptical expressions, like "Chinese historian," which can mean either a historian who is Chinese or one who studies Chinese history. (On the other hand, the hyphen shows that a head-hunter is one who hunts heads, not one who heads hunts.) There are uncertainties about what modifies what: "Rehearsing with a male trainer, she entered a cage holding four lions. Two immediately attacked and knocked her down." (Evidently they didn't care to be held by her.) There are loose connections of pronouns with their antecedents: "The Air Force admitted today that it had issued an 'on-the-job-training' manual instructing G.I.'s how to wash an officer's dog, make his bed, and mix his drinks." There are constructions that give an odd emphasis and create an unexpected comparison or contrast: "A major New York agency needs TV writer-director combinations. If you can write TV you don't have to sit around and wring your hands while someone else botches your work. Here you direct it *yourself*."

Syntactical ambiguity is cleared up when the grammatical relationships are made determinate—and of course to expose the ambiguity, you have to resolve it both ways. This may involve changing the order of words, changing the voice of a verb, filling out an ellipsis—that is, supplying what is taken for granted. For example, the headline

> FERTILIZERS HAVE
> NO EFFECT UPON
> CANNED TOMATOES

obviously has a sensible and a silly interpretation. The ambiguity concerns the relationship between the time of applying the fertilizers and the time of canning the tomatoes. Thus we can write: "Canned tomatoes are not affected by fertilizer used in growing them," or "Tomatoes in cans are not affected by the application of fertilizer." In these statements the syntactical ambiguity has been resolved—though in different directions. Take one of the famous questions used not long ago in voter registration tests in the state of Alabama to confuse the poor registrant.

> Question 18: Will you give aid and comfort to the enemies of the United States government or the government of the State of Alabama?

It is not surprising that some people taking the test answered "Alabama." They figured that if they *had* to make a choice they would rather help Alabama than hurt the federal government. To eliminate the syntactical ambiguity here, we have to write something like:

(1) Will you give aid and comfort to the enemies of the United States government or will you give it, instead, to the government of the State of Alabama?

(2) Will you give aid and comfort to those who are either enemies of the United States government or enemies of the State of Alabama?

This example, by the way, illustrates a common type of syntactical ambiguity that is due to inadequate indication of the scope of a word—what is covered by a preposition, a connective, a verb, or a modifier.

A word is **semantically ambiguous** in a certain context if there is more than one sense that it can have in that context. The newspaper reports that "The Spokane Press Club's exhibition of the paintings of Leonard Lopp, scheduled for June 4 to 16, may have several pieces of Lopp's wife, Margaret, as an added attraction." If you want to be very exact, you can argue that this sentence is not ambiguous, but simply states unambiguously something that is obviously untrue. For what it ought to say is (1) that the exhibition may include several *paintings by* Lopp's wife; and what it does say is (2) that the exhibition may include several *portions of* Lopp's wife. But if there is ambiguity, it is semantical ambiguity, because it depends on two very different senses of "pieces." One way of removing the ambiguity is to substitute two synonyms, as I have done. The other is to build up the context so there can no longer be any question: (1) "may include several pieces painted by Lopp's wife," (2) "may include several pieces of Mrs. Lopp's anatomy."

For a serious example, we can go to the provision in the United States Constitution that "No person except a natural born Citizen . . . shall be eligible to the office of the President." Does "natural born" mean (1) born a citizen (as, for example, being born to parents who are citizens), or (2) native born (born in this country)? The correct sense has never been ruled on by the courts, and no doubt the issue will not arise until we have a presidential candidate who is natural born in the first sense but not in the second.

Most of the usual cases of ambiguity can be classified as belonging to one and only one of the two types; but some cases can be said to be mixed. Syntactical ambiguity often carries along with it some difference in sense:

BEAT POLICE TESTING
TINY 2-WAY RADIO

The sense of "beat" depends on whether it is taken as an adjective or as a transitive verb. In analyzing ambiguity, it is a good idea to follow a certain order. First, consider whether there is any doubt about syntax—for example, whether "beat" is an adjective or a verb. If not, take up the question of semantical ambiguity. If there is syntactical ambiguity, then resolve it in the two (or more) possible ways: (1) Some beat policemen are testing a tiny two-way radio. (2) Someone has beaten policemen testing a tiny two-way radio. (3) (You should) beat any policemen who test a tiny two-way radio. Once the syntactical ambiguity is removed, the doubt about the sense may also be removed: in (3), "beat" has to mean "hit"; but in (1), "beat" policemen may be either those assigned to a beat or those who have taken up bohemian (that is, off-beat) ways. When all traces of doubt about the sense disappear along with the syntactical ambiguity, then we shall say that it is a case of syntactical ambiguity, pure and simple. If we find that elimination of the syntactical ambiguity still leaves us with a residue of semantical ambiguity, then the case is mixed. For example, our translation (2) is syntactically unambiguous, and yet a question remains as to the sense of "beat," which in this context can still mean (a) hit, or (b) win over, as in a race.

This example raises another question, however, which perhaps should be considered briefly. It may seem that to interpret "beat" as "beatnik" in this example—or to interpret "beat" as "win over" in translation (2b) above—is rather far-fetched. If we put our mind to it, we can no doubt turn up all sorts of possible ambiguities that would ordinarily escape our notice, and are quite unlikely to mislead anyone. A few years ago a computer at Harvard was given the rules of English syntax and a method of distinguishing senses, and set to work analyzing English sentences. It found, for example, that the innocent sentence, "Time flies like an arrow," could conceivably mean "Determine the speed of flies as quickly as you can," and "A species of fly, called *time flies,* enjoy an arrow." The original sentence is very short, so there is not much of a context; therefore it is not surprising that these ambiguities should occur, even though they are not troublesome and for most practical purposes could be ignored.

When a word is ambiguous, the possible interpretations may be more or less apparent, and more or less likely to be relevant to some plausible context. It is hard to think of any reason why anyone would want to talk about time flies, since there are no such things, and on any occasion where orders would be given to measure the velocity of flies, the order would probably not be given metaphorically. So let us speak (roughly) of *degrees of prominence* among the possible meanings; and add that ambiguity is likely to cause trouble only when the meanings are fairly prominent.

The troubles caused by ambiguity are principally two. First, when a word is ambiguous, the reader may be baffled, since he does not know how to take it; indeed, there is nothing to take, for the writer has not succeeded in saying either of the two things until he has succeeded in *not* saying the other. Second, and more seriously, the writer may fail to recognize the ambiguity, and think he has said one thing; and the reader may also fail to recognize the ambiguity, and think that the other thing has been said. Then there is a real breakdown in communication. An example of this has been described by Thomas Merton, writing in the *Sewanee Review:*

> Governor Chandler of Kentucky, "Happy" Chandler: he came to the monastery with a party of friends and stood in the bright sun on the steps of the old guest house. . . . "You monks," he said, "know you cannot be happy because you have material possessions." I spoke of this later to the novices, pointing out the exact meaning of these words —that we were in despair because of our great possessions. One novice protested at once: "that was not what he *meant.*" Naturally. What he meant was that we monks knew that poverty and not possessions would make men happy. How true it is that everyone instinctively pays attention not to what a politician actually says, but to what he seems to want to say.

Thomas Merton may be right in saying that there is only one way the remark can reasonably be understood—but it seems to me that the remark really was ambiguous. And if the occasion had been more important—say, if the governor had been looking for votes— the misundersanding could have been serious.

Ambiguity is most deceptive when one of the meanings is much more obvious than the other. No doubt many purchasers of a recent record album entitled "Best of the Beatles" were somewhat annoyed to find that it featured Peter Best, who was with the Beatles for a time in 1961.

We are now in a position to give a more exact meaning to a logical term that was used in Chapter 2, in our discussion of syllogisms. A **term,** in this technical sense, is a word or phrase *taken in a certain sense.* "Bolt" is the same *word,* if you will, in "bolt of cloth" and "bolt of lightning"; but since it has two senses, we shall say that it is two different *terms.* It is convenient, for logical purposes, to define absence of ambiguity into the meaning of "term" just as, in speaking of statements, it will be convenient to say that if the same sentence (because it contains an ambiguity) can be taken in two different ways, then there are two different statements that it can be.

A Check-up Quiz Which of the following headlines are syntactically ambiguous? Which are semantically ambiguous?

1. BLENKINSOP SWORN IN AS PRESIDENTIAL AIDE
2. REDS THREATEN TO TRY YANKS AS SPIES

3. EDEN GRIM ON SUEZ ISSUE; BARS PEACE AT ANY PRICE
4. COLOR TV DATA GIVEN FCC TO END FEUDING
5. NANNIE DOSS GETS LIFE TERM FOR POISONING FIFTH HUSBAND
6. WARNS AGAINST ABUSE OF FIFTH AMENDMENT
7. DAVIS CUP MATCH WON BY AUSTRALIAN
8. YOUNG DEMOCRATS ELECT BONE HEAD
9. FATHER OF 11 FINED $200 FOR FAILING TO STOP
10. DOCTOR COMPILES LIST OF POISONS CHILDREN MAY DRINK AT HOME
11. BOY CRITICAL AFTER BEING HIT BY TRUCK
12. ARMY DROPS PLANS TO ROTATE TROOPS WITHOUT FAMILIES
13. PARENTS SATISFIED TO HAVE GIRL OR BOY BABIES
14. HEARING SCHEDULED BY HUMAN RELATIONS COMMISSION
15. NEW ZEALAND TAXES SLOW BEER DRINKER

For Further Study Simeon Potter, *Our Language,* Chs. 7, 9. Baltimore, Md.: Penguin Books, Inc., 1950. Hugh R. Walpole, *Semantics,* Chs. 1, 5. New York: W. W. Norton & Company, Inc., 1941. L. M. Myers, *American English,* Chs. 15, 16, 19. Englewood Cliffs, N.J.: Prentice-Hall, Inc., 1952.

§13. equivocation

We have seen that words can be quite stable in their meanings, or quite volatile: a word may preserve a single definite sense intact through great changes in its context; it may take on one clear sense in one context and another in another; it may hover between two meanings without alighting on either; or it may shift rapidly from one sense to another in the same discourse, even in the same sentence. It is this last ability that gives rise to one of the most important fallacies, when the shift takes place in such a way that it can be overlooked by the writer (or speaker) or by the reader (or listener).

Suppose someone argued this way:

All pickpockets are men.
Therefore, all red-headed pickpockets are red-headed men.

This is evidently a sound deductive argument, so far as it goes. But suppose someone else, reasoning along analogous lines, were to argue:

All pickpockets are men.
He is a good pickpocket.
Therefore, he is a good man.

This is something else again. Even if the premise is true, the conclusion doesn't follow. Yet if the first one is validated by some rule of deductive inference, it seems that the second must also be. What is the difference?

By examining the argument carefully, we can track down the source of its trouble. When we say that someone is a good pickpocket we mean that he is good *as* a pickpocket; and this implies certain criteria of excellence in pocket-picking: manual dexterity, experience in judging fruitful quarries, skill in "scruffing," "moll buzzing," "lush working," and so forth. When we say that he is a good man, we imply quite different criteria of excellence: the possession of certain moral and intellectual virtues, shall we say. The word "good" is a complicated one, for all its apparent plainness, and it is oversimplifying things a bit to say that the word has a different *meaning* as applied to "pickpocket" from what it has when applied to "man." But in the broad sense in which we are using the term "meaning," we can say so. "Good" has changed from one sense to another in the course of the argument. And since the validity of a deductive argument requires that the same *terms* be used throughout (that is, words in the same senses), the argument is fallacious. It commits the fallacy of **equivocation.**

This fallacy does not depend on whether or not the change of sense is deliberate, or on whether or not it succeeds in fooling anyone. Even if it is quite transparent, we can still say that to use the same word throughout an argument is implicitly to claim that the same meaning is attached; therefore, any change in meaning is at least to some extent disguised by the identity of word—and it may be so well disguised that only very careful reading can expose it.

Equivocation is, in a way, the inverse of *elegant variation,* where a writer uses different words with the same meaning in the course of an argument—this does not necessarily make the argument invalid, but it is confusing, for the change of word strongly suggests a change in meaning.

The most misleading equivocations are those that are carried out in longer passages. The longer the argument, the better the opportunity to slide from sense to sense by gradual stages, so that the transition is well concealed. The most instructive examples are books and substantial articles in which the writer plays with various senses of a word and builds up an apparently compelling argument on a series of equivocations. Thus suppose someone is arguing against a proposed bill before Congress which would impose certain restrictions on the packaging and labeling of groceries. Such a so-called "truth-in-packaging" bill might, for example, require that the "Giant Economy Size" be priced so that the contents are cheaper per ounce than the "Economy Size" (which they sometimes aren't)—or that the size of a box have some proportion to the quantity of its contents. Suppose a critic of this bill wants to show that it is an unwarranted interference with freedom of competition in the packaged-goods industry. This claim may not be very plausible if baldly stated, but it can be made to appear plausible by equivocation. The critic starts out, perhaps, by arguing for freedom of competition in a fairly narrow sense of the term—the industry's freedom to sell its goods at competitive prices, to choose the quantities offered for sale, and to put the goods in attractive packages. But as the argument moves along, "freedom of competition" may gradually be given a broader sense, so that it comes to mean lack of any restriction on packaging and labeling. If the equivocation is carried through smoothly, so that the reader does not notice what is happening, he will find himself agreeing that there should be freedom of competition in the broad sense because he has agreed that there should be freedom of competition in the narrow sense.

In shorter passages, equivocation is a good deal harder to cover up. Yet even when you see that something odd is going on, you may not find it easy to explain exactly what is wrong.

> Now, I am no lawyer, but I know that the Fifth Amendment says: "No person shall be compelled to testify against himself." In plain words, you can plead the Fifth only when you're guilty; ergo, if you take it, you're guilty.

To track down the equivocation here, it is best to set the argument out in a fairly formal way:

Anyone who testifies against himself is providing the proof of his guilt.

Therefore, anyone who testifies against himself is admitting his guilt.

Therefore, anyone who refuses to testify against himself is refusing to admit his guilt.

Therefore, anyone who refuses to testify against himself is guilty.

But anyone who pleads the Fifth Amendment is one who refuses to testify against himself.

Therefore, anyone who pleads the Fifth Amendment is guilty.

The last three statements make a syllogism; the others are background. And the equivocation emerges pretty clearly: the phrase "to testify against himself" has shifted its meaning from one premise of the syllogism to the next. In the first premise it means something like *to present proof of his own guilt;* and in the second premise it means *to present evidence pointing toward his own guilt.* Of course, even if a man is completely innocent, there may be evidence pointing toward his guilt; even if he has a perfect alibi, someone may claim to have seen him on the scene, and that testimony points toward his guilt, though it doesn't establish his guilt.

This fallacious argument, then, takes the Fifth Amendment plea to indicate that a person has *knowledge* of his own guilt, which he is concealing—and implies that unless a person knows he is guilty, he has no right to plead the Fifth Amendment. This is absurd, of course, for no one has ever understood the Fifth Amendment to be a protection only for the guilty, but rather a protection for those who may unknowingly or unwittingly incriminate themselves by providing facts that can be used unfairly by an overzealous prosecutor to build up a false case against them. The argument would have no plausibility without the equivocation, for it would look as fallacious as it is. We can show this by substituting synonyms for the two senses involved.

Anyone who refuses to present *evidence proving* his own guilt is guilty.

Anyone who pleads the Fifth Amendment is one who refuses to present *evidence pointing toward* his own guilt.

Therefore, anyone who pleads the Fifth Amendment is guilty.

This is not even a syllogism, since it has not three, but four, different terms.

A special case of equivocation is that involving two people, one of whom makes a statement using a word in one sense, and the other of whom, in his reply, gives the word a different sense. This may be harmless conversation:

> INTERVIEWER: "Speaking of your wife, I understand you have a large family."
>
> MAX SHULMAN: "No! It's small, but there are a lot of them, one small wife, three small sons and one small daughter."

The point of the joke might be to suggest that the interviewer's remark was ambiguous, but strictly speaking it was not. The interviewee has to go quite far out of his way to make the second meaning of "large family" stick: *family of large people*, rather than *family of several people*. (In this example, of course, there is the added complication that in replying, Mr. Shulman doesn't use the original term, but its negative.)

This trivial example is not really an equivocation, because no argument is involved. But now suppose we have an argument involving two people, of whom one is defending an assertion and the other trying to disprove it. That is a *dispute*. There will be an equivocation if, in arguing against *A*'s assertion, *B* picks up a word from *A*'s argument and gives it a new meaning.

> *A says:* "I have tried to listen to the compositions of Boulez, Stockhausen, and the other far-out composers, but with no success. There is no order there, only disconnected cacophony—as far as my hearing goes, anyway. I can no longer force myself even to listen."
>
> *B replies:* "You can hardly call these sounds 'disconnected cacophony.' This music is as carefully ordered as Bach's *Art of Fugue*. Once you are told the mathematical formulas used in working out the details of pitch, note length, dynamics, and so forth, according to a preset scheme, and study the score, you realize that there is indeed order here."

This is a dispute all right, since *B* denies the statement that *A* affirms: "This music does not have order." The question is: has *B* really answered *A*'s argument?

When we examine the two contexts of the key word, "order," a significant difference appears. *A* is clearly thinking of musical order as something that you can hear in it—what he misses are those audible interconnections and interrelationships of musical parts that he is used to in pre-World-War-II music. "Order" for him means *auditory relationships*. *B*, on the other hand, proves that there is "order" by referring, not to the music itself, but to the mathematical formulas used in composing it and revealed in the written score. "Order" for him means *mathematical relationships*. There is clearly a big difference between these two senses, since you can't hear mathematical relationships. To bring out that *B* is equivocating, and that his reply simply misses the mark, and has no force against *A*'s assertion, we can substitute the (rough) synonyms, and abbreviate:

A: "This music lacks auditory relationships."

B: "On the contrary, it possesses mathematical relationships."

These two statements are at cross-purposes.

B could argue, of course, that any music that has mathematical relationships will also have auditory relationships. And if he could prove this generalization, he would make a strong connection between the two things. But by slipping from one sense to another, he tries to get around the necessity of supporting the generalization—which he may not be able to support. Nor can he take it for granted; that would be begging the question at issue, since it is just what *A* would undoubtedly deny. *A* would certainly want to say that no matter what complicated mathematical formulas you use in composing music, the music may still *sound* like auditory hash. The only way to refute *A*'s position is to show him that there are audible connections between parts of the music (thematic or rhythmic or harmonic echoes, for example) that he has missed, and to get him to hear them.

In this little dispute, then, *B*'s reply can be dismissed as soon as the equivocation is exposed. And when a dispute evaporates in this fashion, we know that it was a *verbal dispute*—that is, a dispute that only seemed genuine because of equivocation. It is a satisfaction to be able to do away with futile disputes in this fashion, by showing that they are based on misuse of words; and sometimes it may be encouraging to do so, because we find out perhaps that we were not so far apart after all, and didn't really disagree as much as we thought we did. Now that *A* and *B*, in the dispute above, have cleared up their confusion, they may be on the road to a meeting of minds on the subject of contemporary music. Or at least, if they continue to disagree about other things, their disagreement will be real.

But we must not let our exhilaration beguile us into dismissing disputes too fast, just because there are verbal confusions in them. A verbal dispute may have substance to it that remains even after we have cleared away the confusions. Indeed, the main value of eliminating verbal confusions is not to cut down on the number of disputes—for it is through serious and well-conducted disputes that we often learn from each other and come closer to the truth—but to turn fruitless ones into fruitful ones that have some chance of success.

A Check-up Quiz Which of the following arguments involve equivocation? Point out the terms that shift their meaning.

1. Peanuts must be a basic necessity in our diet, and we should be sure to eat them regularly, for they are listed by the Department of Agriculture, along with rice, corn, cotton, wheat, and tobacco as "basic crops."
2. The unintelligibility of modern poetry needs no proof. Much of it can obviously not be understood clearly by the ordinary reader. But what is unintelligible is nonsense, and what is nonsense is not worth writing.
3. It is useless to try to found a just social order on war and revolution, which can never establish one. For you cannot have justice without peace, and a peaceful society obviously cannot be founded on a basis of violence and disorder.
4. Industrial wastes and raw sewage are more and more polluting our streams and lakes. If we are going to preserve them for recreation and as sources of drinking water, we will have to pass severe laws to prevent further pollution.
5. The company admitted that it had no good reason for changing the shift periods; in other words, its action was arbitrary. And that is why the union is strongly opposing the change, for how can we bow to arbitrary and capricious company decisions, when an arbitrary decision is one taken despite good reasons to the contrary?

For Further Study Robert H. Thouless, *Straight and Crooked Thinking,* Chs. 9, 10. New York: Simon and Schuster, Inc., 1932.

§14. vagueness

The main—though not the sole—purpose of an assertive discourse is, of course, to effect a *communication* between a sender and a receiver. This is just as true when the sender wishes to deceive or misinform the receiver as when he is concerned to share his knowledge. Much of the thinking required of us as members of society is group thinking—thinking in which a number of people cooperate —and successful communication is indispensable to it. There are four significant features of a discourse that can frustrate or prevent communication.

The first of these we have already discussed: it is ambiguity. When a discourse is ambiguous in a material and important respect, it leaves the receiver unable to choose between the alternative possibilities. He can only wait for—or request—a further message that will provide a large enough context to remove the ambiguity.

The second source of trouble is **obscurity.** Obscurity is difficulty of comprehension, in so far as that difficulty is due to the misleadingness of the syntax and to clashes between implicit meanings of the words. The notions of "misleadingness" and of "clashes of meaning" will become clearer in the following chapter, but a few examples may be sufficient for the present. "He wasn't the only one who didn't refuse to remain uncommitted" is more obscure than "Others besides him agreed to remain uncommitted." These two statements may not have exactly the same meaning; the negations in the first one add something. But what they add interferes with the main part of the message, which the second statement presents without unnecessary grammatical complications. Again, "He spontaneously relegated his employment opportunity to an alternative applicant" is more obscure than "He spontaneously offered his chance for a job to someone else." Again, these statements do not have the same meaning. But what the second one means is included in what the first one means; and to extract that meaning from the first one is more of an effort than to extract it from the second one.

A discourse on a specialized subject may be difficult to follow if you are unused to that style of thinking or do not know the definitions of technical terms. Here is Bertrand Russell explaining a point of mathematical philosophy:

> The multiplicative axiom has been shown by Zermelo, in the abovementioned proof, to be equivalent to the proposition that every class can be well ordered, i.e., can be arranged in a series in which every subclass has a first term (except, of course, the null-class). . . .

This cannot be understood without close attention, but it is not in the least obscure; every word is carefully defined, the combinations of words are perfectly intelligible, and the syntax is completely clear. Compare this passage from a periodical devoted to avant garde music:

> Differentiation of the intended permutation of timbres is obtained from the complexity resulting from the simultaneous combination of the six formant regions within one sound process, from the varying of the elements or groups of elements, in all their components, according to the series and of coordinating a special intervallic scale of partials or of medium frequency width ratios in each formant octave.

These technical terms have well-defined scientific senses, but they are combined in ways that apparently don't make sense. The whole passage is almost unreadable. Of course, it *may* be saying something important, something we would like to know. But it is hard to tell ahead of time whether its message will be worth the effort of decoding it.

Of course, if a passage is nonsense—if it has no meaning as a whole—then it is not obscure. We call a passage obscure if it *has* a meaning which the style makes troublesome to discern. An obscure passage may or may not be ambiguous—we can't tell whether it has two possible meanings until we have succeeded in finding at least one.

The third potentially troublesome feature of discourse may be called **indefiniteness.** And this, too, is relative to what is expected or required. If *A* says to *B*, "Someone called me on the phone yesterday," he is giving certain information, but, of course, withholding a great deal as well. Who called? When? Why? Perhaps, knowing *B* as he does, *A* realizes that the statement is not *too* uninformative, since *B* will probably not care to know any more than this—if indeed he even cares to know this much. On the other hand, if *A* says to *B*, "Someone called *you* on the phone yesterday," *B* will probably prick up his ears. "Who was it? What did she say?" From *B*'s point of view, this statement is probably too indefinite. Given two statements, *P* and *Q*, *P* is more definite than *Q* when *P* gives all the information that *Q* does, and also adds further information. "Joe Jones called me" is more definite than "Someone called me." "Joe Jones called me" is more definite than "Joe Jones got in touch with me."

Indefiniteness is not in itself a fault, of course. The question is whether a statement is less definite than it ought to be, and that depends on what is at stake in the discourse. When we know what conclusion is to be proved, or what practical goal is to be attained, we may be able to say that not enough information has been given. The statement may be too *general,* for example. To say that something is an animal is to talk in very general terms; to call it a fish or a trout is to be more *specific,* and thus to convey more information.

A few years ago, Senator Barry Goldwater recommended that the Republican party adopt no platform—since platforms promise specific legislation that, as often as not, never gets passed—but substitute a "declaration of principles." "Say we included a simple statement like 'We believe in the freedom of the individual.' All right, Senator Javits can take that in New York and apply it to civil rights. . . . I can take it and apply it to 'right to work.' I can apply it to states' rights." It may be stretching things a bit to say that "the freedom of the individual" includes *states'* rights, but in any case it certainly does include (or may be made to include) a great many things: it has a very high degree of generality. Whether it is more general than is desirable for one political purpose or another is not for this book to decide: the only advice that can be given (and it is very general advice, to be sure) is that we must always be prepared to notice *how* definite or indefinite a statement is, so that we do not expect too much of it or think it says more than it really does.

The fourth feature that can cause a breakdown in communication is **vagueness.** This merits somewhat more extensive discussion.

As we saw earlier when we were discussing classification, words mark distinctions, and enable us to divide our world so that we can grasp and order its varied contents. There are two basically different ways in which this is done: there are distinctions of *kind* and distinctions of *degree.* The words that mark the kinds, or classes, of things in the world, are (at least on their face) *either/or* words: something is either a tree or it is not; it is either a dachshund or it is not. And a statement is either true or false, or it is not—when we speak of a "half-truth" we mean a statement that is false but would become true if it were qualified in some way. The words that mark the degrees of things, that is, compare them with respect to the extent to which they possess some characteristic, are *more-or-less* words. A tree is more or less tall, a dachshund more or less lively. It makes sense to ask "*How* tall is the tree? *How* lively is the dachshund?"

For many purposes it is convenient to turn distinctions of degree into distinctions of kind. Given that trees vary in tallness, over a wide range, we can select some part of this range and make that a category: thus besides talking about trees as more or less tall—as taller or shorter than others—we may decide to divide them into two complementary subclasses, tall ones and nontall ones. A great many of the groupings that play a role in our thinking about practical affairs are made in this way: educated persons, stable governments, unskilled labor, good schools, safe highways. When we are wondering whether to put something into such a category, we do not ask whether or not it has some characteristic, but to what *degree* it has some characteristic. *How* hard must wood be to be called "hard wood"? *How* stable must a government be to be called "stable"? *How* safe must a highway be to be called "safe"?

These are very natural questions, but they do not always have exact answers. How much does a person have to eat in order to be a hearty eater? How many times does he have to forget something in order to be absent-minded? How well does he have to swim to be a good swimmer? We have never come to an agreement, tacit or explicit, about these words, and so there is no rule in our language about their precise application. There is no sharp line between a hearty eater and an average one, between an absent-minded person and a normal one, between a good swimmer and a fair one. This is what is meant by saying that these terms, "hearty eater," "absent-minded," "good swimmer," are **vague.**

A vague word refers to a certain range of variation in quantity, number, or intensity. If the word marks any distinction at all, there are always some things to which it definitely applies, some things to which it definitely does not apply, and a twilight zone, or *area of doubt,* in between (but remember there is no sharp line between the area of doubt and the other areas, either). As Edmund Burke once said, "Though no man can draw a stroke between the confines of day and night, yet darkness and light are upon the whole tolerably distinguishable." A man who eats several pounds of meat at every meal is certainly a hearty eater (if not a glutton), and a man who eats only a few pieces of fruit and dry toast is certainly *not* a hearty eater. That much we know from the rules we follow in using this term. But what if he eats half a pound of ham for breakfast? Nine ounces? Ten ounces? You can give either answer: he is a hearty eater, or he is not. But you cannot claim that this is the same answer that other people who understand English must give.

Obviously, vagueness is quite different from ambiguity. When a statement is ambiguous, you have a choice between different senses of a word. When it is vague, there is no doubt about the sense, only the degree. And vagueness itself is a matter of degree; in some words the area of doubt is fairly small, in others it is quite large. "Tall tree" is vaguer than "tall man," because in the second case the area of doubt is a matter of inches, but in the first case it is a matter of feet.

When a vague comparative term is used to define a noncomparative term, the vagueness of the former becomes incorporated in the latter. For example, in 1960, the Court of Common Pleas of Dauphin County, Pennsylvania, declared that a law setting up a Motion Picture Control Board was in violation of the state constitution. Following the language of the United States Supreme Court in the *Roth* case (1957), the law referred to "contemporary community standards" in defining "obscene." But the court noted that Brigitte Bardot's film, *And God Created Woman,* had been seized by the district attorney in Philadelphia, whereas it did not create any excitement in Pittsburgh; this showed, said the Court, that Pennsylvania is not a "community." Perhaps the Court was right on this point. Or perhaps it would be better to say that "community" is unconstitutionally vague. For if a "community" is defined in part by similarity of moral standards, and no precise agreement has been reached on *how* similar they have to be to make a community, then "community" has some degree of vagueness. And if "obscene" is defined in terms of "community," then to that extent it, too, is vague. For our indecisiveness about what is a community will reappear when we try to determine what are the "community standards."

That does not necessarily mean, of course, that the terms are useless. Many crucial legal terms—the "excessive fines" and "excessive bail" and the "cruel and unusual punishments" prohibited by the Eighth Amendment, for example—are vague, yet highly useful. The trouble comes when we make illegitimate demands on them, and think there is a definite line when there is not. Borderline cases are bound to turn up, and the wider the area of doubt the more there will be. A civil-rights demonstrator, let us say, is arrested for "parading without a permit"—that is, demonstrating without police permission. Set aside the constitutional issues for the moment, and consider the question of bail. Suppose he is released after paying $25 bail; this is clearly not excessive. Suppose he is held on $30,000 bail; this is clearly excessive. But suppose his bond is set at $300 or $500. Then a dispute could arise: is it excessive or not? It may be that a search of similar cases in the past will show that a general and consistent practice has gradually been worked out in that community, so that, for practical purposes, the vagueness of "excessive" in this sort of context has been considerably reduced. Then an answer may be available. But suppose there are no precedents for such cases. Then there is no answer. The bail figure lies in the area of doubt, and we cannot say that it would be correct to apply the word "excessive" or to withhold it. Of course, sooner or later a court is going to have to settle the matter one way or the other. And the court will no doubt have *reasons* for settling it the way it does. But since there is no established usage to go by, the court will to some extent be establishing a new usage—a new rule about the meaning of "excessive bail."

One of the great things about vagueness is that, for special purposes, we can always reduce the area of doubt as much as we wish. If you want to define a hearty eater in exact terms, you can specify the number of ounces and types of food your hearty eater must eat. This does not guarantee that you will prevail upon other people to adopt your rule; but at least you will mean something exact, and others can see what you mean. In the same spirit, the state highway department may set precise standards for highway safety, if it wishes, in terms of number and severity of accidents per 100,000 passenger-miles. Since the nation became aware, in 1964, of our tremendous problem of poverty, and the fact that a huge and growing number of people are caught in a cycle of poverty—lack of education and skill, lack of mobility and incentive—from which they cannot break loose unaided, a great deal of thinking has gone into this problem—including the thinking reflected in the Economic Opportunity Act of 1964. What is poverty? "Poor" in ordinary usage is quite vague, but to cope with the problems of our society, it must be made more exact. The Council of Economic Advisers, in their January 1964 report, presented their definition of (a family's) poverty as *having less than a $3,000 annual income* (this figure has been raised somewhat as economic conditions have changed). According to this definition there were then 35 million Americans who were poor. But the aim was not to define "poor" broadly to make it cover a lot of people; the figure was set after a study of what is required to keep alive on a subsistence level. Other definitions have been offered for other purposes—by the United States Bureau of Labor Statistics, by Michael Harrington, and by others. For example, Herman Miller, a demographer in the Bureau of the Census, defines "poor" as "belonging to the bottom fifth of the income distribution."

It is important to bear in mind that decisions of this sort—by which a vague term is transformed, either temporarily or officially, into a more precise one—always involve some arbitrariness. You may be able to give a good reason why the line dividing poor and nonpoor should be somewhere around $3,000, but you cannot give a very good reason why it should be $3,000 rather than $2,999.25. When we have a continuous, or almost continuous, scale, from an income of one cent upward, the big differences are made up of many small differences, and any sharp line will separate things that are not really far apart. So it may seem wrong or queer to say that a man making $2,999.25 is poor, whereas one making $3,000.25 is not poor—especially when one consequence is that the first man, but not the second, will be eligible to be a poverty representative on the city-wide organization that administers the local antipoverty program financed by funds from the Office of Economic Opportunity. But this queerness has to be accepted—it is an inevitable consequence of drawing any line where differences of degree shade into one another (like saying that night begins at exactly 7:52:16 P.M.). And if we don't read out of our distinction more than we put into it, we will not get into trouble.

Yet this peculiarity that comes from imposing sharp edges on vague borders gives rise to an illegitimate form of argument that it is well to watch out for. This is the **black-or-white fallacy.** It is a subtle attempt to paralyze thinking about matters of degree by appealing to the arbitrariness of drawing lines. It has two forms.

The reasoning involved in the first form may be crudely stated in this way:

> A large difference of degree is made up of many small differences of degree.
>
> *Therefore,* a large difference of degree is not large after all.

Put in this form, the argument does not seem very plausible, but there are ways of giving it specious persuasiveness. A socialist might set up this argument:

> Everybody in the United States today—except for a few right-wingers who are living back in the nineteenth century—agrees that the government has to do some positive things to promote the welfare of its citizens—besides keeping civil order and handling diplomatic matters. No one wants to turn highway building over to private enterprise, or sell the Post Office to Du Pont. Since it is only a small step from federally sponsored roads to federal aid to education to universal scholarships for all students, to elimination of private universities, to elimination of all private enterprise—I can't see that there is any very great difference between what I advocate (namely, a socialized economy) and what everyone else advocates, namely, continuing the Post Office.

The logic of this argument (if such it may be called) is that since each of the differences is comparatively small, anyone who accepts any of the stages has no good reason for refusing to accept the whole thing.

And this is basically the same reasoning that is involved in the second form of the black-or-white fallacy, though it ends up with the opposite conclusion.

> A large difference of degree is made up of many small differences of degree.
>
> *Therefore,* the small difference of degree is really a large one after all.

This is the "slippery slope" argument; that once you set foot on the slide, you can have no good reason to stop at any point—since each point is only a tiny bit different from the one before—and so you are committed to going the whole way: *therefore,* don't take the first step. The antisocialist might use this form of argument in reply:

> The assumption underlying our fatal drift toward a socialist economy is that one can have a little bit of socialism—which is no more possible than having a slightly illegitimate baby or a slight case of murder. The society at the end of the road is regimented from top to bottom, according to a soulless master plan. We took the first step on that road the moment we allowed the government to go beyond its legitimate task of policing the streets and negotiating with other sovereign powers. Once you have a Post Office, it is easy to argue that a TVA project would hardly be any different, or a federally owned and operated communications satellite system, etc., etc. There's no logical stopping place; you are hooked.

The principle is that if no reason can be given for stopping at stage 4, after going to stage 3, then there can be no reason for not going to stage 10 once you have started stage 1. This is wholly fallacious, of course. But it may be convincing. A person who smokes one cigarette a day can easily convince himself that two couldn't hurt him, and after he gets to two, it may seem arbitrary to stop there. And wherever he stops, there will be some arbitrariness; that has to be accepted. There may not be a much better reason for stopping at two than for stopping at three, but there is a better reason for stopping at two rather than stopping at ten or twenty. Maybe there is an even better reason for stopping at none—but the black-or-white argument, by itself, doesn't prove this.

A Check-up Quiz Which of the following arguments commit the black-or-white fallacy?

1. In the past few days we have been reaping the whirlwind of the city government's failure to enforce the Condon-Wadlin law prohibiting municipal employees from striking. If we allow one

group of employees—the subway workers—to get away with a strike, what is to stop the others? Next it will be policemen, then firemen, then doctors in city hospitals, nurses, school teachers, water department employees. And if city employees, why not the Army, the Navy, and the Air Force?

2. In answer to the student committee that has asked the dean's office to allow a larger number of cuts per class each semester, I regret to say that as dean, on thinking this matter over, I realize that I can allow no cuts at all. Obviously it would wreck the educational enterprise if a student came to no classes at all; but if he were to come to only one class, that would not be significantly better. Thinking this through logically, we see that if I allow one cut, a student can claim that I ought to allow him two, and so on. It is nothing or all. I say it is nothing.

3. I was only trying to give my wife a compliment when I told her that her hat looked nice. Seems it was an old hat, and she rushed out and bought a couple of new ones, by way of reply. She was in such a hurry to do it that she spent the check that was supposed to go to the phone company this month, and forgot all about it. Next thing I knew the phone was turned off. Then my boss learned that I had not received an important call, and so had lost a valuable contract, so he fired me. Now I'm out of a job. Let it be a lesson to you: don't give compliments. One thing leads to another.

4. Once we get away from the old fallacious, mythical, and uninformed notions about race, and keep it clearly distinct from cultural, social, geographical, linguistic, and other differences between people, we see that the only really scientific concept of race is this: a race is a population which differs from other populations with regard to the frequency of one or more genes it possesses. But genes are tiny things, and it is arbitrary where we draw the line as to exactly what genes, or how many, people have to share in order to belong to the same race. Therefore there is no essential difference between one race and another; basically, we all belong to the *human* race.

5. If you admit that the President should be provided with an official residence, namely, the White House, then by the same token you must logically admit that the Vice President should also be provided with an official residence. For he is not adequately paid, either; he has to do a great deal of entertaining,

of both foreign and domestic notables. And certainly as long as we have a Vice President who is as active, and has as much responsibility, as Hubert Humphrey, he needs room for holding meetings of all sizes at any hour, day or night, and for putting up a large number of guests.

For Further Study L. Susan Stebbing, *Thinking to Some Purpose,* Ch. 12. Baltimore, Md.: Pelican Books, 1938.

OUTLINE-SUMMARY: chapter four

Seven distinguishable features of language can interfere with clear and cogent thinking. They may be placed under three heads:

A. Variability of meaning. A word that has one sense in certain contexts and a different sense in other contexts is said to have (1) *variable meaning* ("the key to the house"; "the key to the cypher"). A special case of variable meaning is (2) the fallacy of *equivocation,* which occurs when a word changes its sense in the course of an argument in such a way that the conclusion does not follow ("Jewels are hard; she is a jewel; therefore, she is hard").

B. Complexity of meaning. When a word has several distinguishable senses in the same context, all of which are relevant to the context, then it is said to have (3) *multiple meaning* (In "It is the East, and Juliet is the sun," the word "sun" means something that brings light, something that brings promise of a new life, something indescribably wonderful, and many other things). When the subtler senses of a word, or the complex syntax in which it appears, work to make the meaning difficult to disentangle, then the passage is said to be (4) *obscure* ("Dissemination of this directive is restricted to personnel directly concerned with the implementation thereof").

C. Indecisiveness of meaning. One word is more definite than another if the application of that word conveys more information (to know that something is a small bluebottle fly is more than to know that it is an insect). A word may be (5) too *indefinite* for some purposes. A word is (6) *ambiguous* in a certain context if it may have either (but not both) of two (or more) meanings in that context. *Semantical ambiguity* is uncertainty about which sense the word has (In "the Bible prohibits swearing," "swearing" can mean *taking an oath* or *speaking impiously or irreverently*); *syntactical ambiguity* is uncertainty about how the sentence elements are grammatically related ("the love of God" may be God's love of man or man's love of God). A word is (7) *vague* if it refers to a characteristic that objects can possess in some degree or quantity, and there is an area of doubt, that is, a range within which there is no rule that the word must either apply or not apply ("the immediate context of a word" is vague, in that whether it includes part of a sentence, or the adjoining sentences, or the adjoining paragraphs, is left open).

Comparative words (especially vague ones) and others defined in terms of them can be used to commit the *black-or-white fallacy,* which consists either (a) in illegitimately minimizing a large difference of degree, or (b) in exaggerating a small difference in degree, by appealing to the fact that any difference in degree is made up of minimal differences ("A miss is as good as a mile, because if you miss by one inch, you might as well miss by an inch and a quarter," and so forth).

Exercise 15

Examine the italicized words in the following pairs of sentences. Are the senses the same or different? Show the sameness or difference of sense by substituting synonymous expressions.

1. (a) He took his car to get it *fixed.*
   (b) He took the traffic ticket to get it *fixed.*
2. (a) He was walking along breathing the spring *air.*
   (b) He was walking along whistling a cheerful *air.*
3. (a) Platters *Served.*
   (b) Ladies *Served.*
4. (a) When he heard what had been said about him, he *exploded.*
   (b) When the bomb went off, he *exploded.*
5. (a) The more I *think of* that idea . . .
   (b) . . . the less I *think of* it.
6. (a) Historians have no *proof* that the Holy Grail existed.
   (b) The police have no *proof* that he committed the crime.
7. (a) The *vote* in the House of Representatives was close.
   (b) Some of the Representatives were elected by a very small *vote.*
8. (a) Jones had very little *money* in his pocket, . . .
   (b) . . . though he had a great deal of *money* in the bank.
9. (a) The burglars *entered* the house through the cellar.
   (b) The explorers *entered* the cave with the help of ropes.

10. (a) I wouldn't mind spending time with him if it weren't for his *politics*.
    (b) Everyone agrees that the President is a master of *politics*.

Exercise 16

In each of the following passages, rewrite the ambiguous part in two different ways to bring out the distinct senses involved.

1. Try our Austin-Leeds hand-shaped suits.
2. Last year, his wife left him in a cheerful frame of mind.
3. Sign: DOGS AND CHILDREN
DRIVE CAREFULLY
4. Beauticians and Ladies! Save your teeth and nails with one of our HANDY BOBBY PIN OPENERS. To get the correct size, fit a strip of paper around your index finger and mail it with $1.00 cash.
5. Mary had a little lamb.
6. Girl for Bundling. Progressive Laundry. 440 Oneida St.
7. Save time and cut fingers with a parsley mincer.
8. Purchasers of new cars will each receive an extra bonus of fifty gallons of high-test gasoline. Buyers of used cars will receive turkeys.
9. A planeload of smart setters are looking forward to one of the Ludwig get-togethers in October.
10. Your subscription will begin as soon as your membership is processed at our mailing house, and will continue until your expiration date.
11. Tourists Taken In.
12. On January 17, the meeting took place at the Vicarage, and there was a discussion on the nature of the Christian life led by the Vicar.
13. This is the world's most honored watch.
14. Dangerous Crossing! Beware of Trains Going Both Ways at Once!
15. You are judged by the company you keep.
16. There is no place like home.
17. Marv Pollow: the world's smallest Chevrolet dealer.

18. If you are not sure how to vote, see Lt. Hewitt, base Voting Officer.
19. In the kaleidoscope of our impressions we see the well-cared-for dogs of Japan, the temple with the 1,001 gilded statues of the Goddess of Mercy; the night we ate toasted bees, celery crisp, and the hundreds of little kids who were with us on a small steamer on the Inland Sea.
20. Eat anything with false teeth! Buy Brimms Plasti-liner.
21. For sale: one four-poster bed for antique lover.
22. The cigarette designed for men that women like.
23. While the Ross-Jannota wedding is taking place, more fashionable wedding guests will be gathering in the Church of the Holy Spirit in Lake Forest.
24. Flu shots will be available to all full-time students, members of the faculty, and employees.
25. The Henry Francis Du Pont Winterthur Museum—Reservations necessary except for last week in April through first four weeks in May for thirty rooms and the gardens only.
26. Building progressed over the weekend on the new home for the Lawton Parks family, whose Tallevast residence recently was destroyed by fire, thanks to the efforts of volunteer helpers.
27. If your firm is planning expansion you need a first-hand report on the possibilities in Northern Ireland. Everywhere else in the United Kingdom expansion plans are bedeviled by one or more of three great shortages—not enough money; not enough men; not enough space. Only Northern Ireland can offer you all three.
28. Save your trouble with an unqualified establishment in which you have little or no confidence. Let us take care of all your laundry and dry cleaning work.
29. PUPILS WITH MUMPS AND TWO OTHER DISEASES MAY ATTEND SCHOOL
30. In Salem, Ore., police looked for a burglar who broke into Mrs. Jeanne Hopkins' home, opened closets, ripped up linoleum between the living room and dining room, opened a can of varnish and varnished an old newspaper, and baked a fudge cake from a recipe on a Betty Crocker Mix box.
31. RED SPY IMPROVES AFTER SUICIDE TRY

32. BOLL WEEVIL PROSPECTS ARE STILL FAVORABLE
33. Two Hawaii National Guard helicopter pilots counted 29 of the big fish, but said there were many more, possibly as many as 30.
34. Eat at Gary's restaurant, where the good food is an unexpected pleasure.
35. The past year offered its usual assortment of undergraduate antics, the most publicized of which resulted from the congregating of a large group of students on the night of May 22–23. DeKalb County police, who responded by the dozen to a riot call, dubbed the affair a "panty raid" on a women's dormitory and fired tear gas and flares to stop it. Students (backed by their dean) said it was no such thing, and retaliated by hurling rocks and fruit.

Exercise 17

Analyze the equivocation in the following arguments; distinguish clearly the senses involved, and show how they shift in the course of the argument.

1. The income-tax rule is that we do not have to pay tax on voluntary contributions to socially valuable non-profit-making institutions. Now the federal government is socially valuable, and it certainly doesn't make a profit—and the income tax I pay is a contribution to it, which I pay willingly, and therefore voluntarily. Therefore, I think I should not be taxed on the money I pay in taxes, but only on what I would have left afterward.

2. As an employer I am compelled by law to pay a portion of the social security tax of my employees, and I submit that this feature of the law is unconstitutional; because involuntary servitude (investment of time) is unconstitutional, and since time is money, the forced investment of money (a portion of the tax levied upon another person) is involuntary servitude.

3. Apparently my recent public statement was misunderstood, and this letter will clarify my position. I said, and I still say, that the Civic Uplift Committee which has been formed to improve the financial, moral, physical, and all other aspects of our city, should be politically independent. The mayor should choose members who are free of political obligations or connections, so that they can break away from the domination of the machine that has dragged us down to where we are.

But what follows from this? Here is precisely why I am against the present C.U.C., the way it is set up. For the members have all been chosen by the mayor and therefore cannot be politically independent, since they owe their appointments to him and are evidently people he knows or has at least heard about.

4. The purpose of congressional investigations, such as the recent public hearing attacking the activities of various labor leaders, is to accuse people of crimes that there is not enough legally valid evidence to convict them of in a court, and thus blacken their reputations. But until a man has been legally convicted in a court, he is innocent. Therefore, the Committee's main purpose is to blacken the reputations of innocent people.

5. As far as I am concerned, we need not pay any particular attention to the principal of the school on educational matters, because I don't see that he has any authority in education. He doesn't even have enough authority to keep the boys and girls behaving quietly in the lunchroom, which is frequently a place of bedlam.

Exercise 18

In the following passages *B* and *C* are both replying to *A*'s assertion. See whether one or both of them is using one of *A*'s words in a different sense; if so, rewrite the reply so that the speaker no longer equivocates.

I

A: "Democracy is the greatest form of government, when it is working well, for it carries out the will of the people, or public opinion, as expressed through the ballot box, the lobby, the street demonstration, the newspaper, and the petition for redress of grievances."

B: "Democracy is impossible, for the people and the public are abstractions; strictly speaking, a people has no will, only an individual, and so there is nothing for democracy to carry out."

C: "The will of the people is a dangerous guide for a government; the people is a great beast, as Hamilton said, and only the educated élite are in a position to know what policies the government should follow."

II

A: "I think they made an excellent choice when they decided that the national intercollegiate debating topic for this year would be: 'Resolved: that the United States should not recognize Communist China.' This topic should be easily debatable."

B: "I am shocked to hear you say that. Surely we are all agreed that China should not be recognized, and this is by no means debatable."

C: "The topic is silly because the situation is clear. How can anyone fail to recognize a huge country of 800 million people? You have only to glance at a map to recognize that it is there."

III

A: "Gulick is a very original painter, both in his choice of beetles as subject matter and in his incessant use of pinwheel compositional patterns."

B: "I agree that he is original; but is he good?"

C: "Whether Gulick ever knew it or not, Haliboy was painting beetles before he was born, and the young Roarshack exhibited six pinwheel compositions in Paris in 1922. So how can Gulick be original?"

IV

A: "I believe the Supreme Court was right in declaring that our Constitution is based on the principle of equal representation: one man, one vote. Before the state legislatures were forced to reapportion the legislative districts, you had cases where a few hundred scattered people in one part of the state had the same amount of representation as hundreds of thousands of people in another part of the state."

B: "But how can you call it equal representation when the poor upright rural citizens can now be outvoted and dominated by the teeming masses of the cities?"

C: "How can you insist on equal representation, when it will mean that some occupational and geographical and ethnic groups will not be represented at all? And how can you claim that the Court's decision was constitutional, when the Constitution itself allows for two senators from each state, no matter how large or small?"

V

To the Editor: I wish to take issue with Marya Mannes in her review of the play *Advise and Consent*. Her statement is this: "Demagogues are reactionary simply because they react, and putting a 'liberal' cap on a McCarthy again makes no sense in human terms. A man like that can be a Communist—which Van Ackerman isn't—but by his very nature not a liberal." This is a foolish and nonrational statement. Many liberals react strongly to segregation, for example. Her implication that a "liberal" demagogue could not arise is ridiculous—demagogues can appear from any political segment. It is foolish for so many "liberals" to believe that "liberalism" may not produce its own fanatics and demagogues. This brings me to that disturbing phenomenon, the illiberal liberal. Many "liberals" of my acquaintance and observation are among the most intolerant, narrow-minded and bigoted people I have ever seen.

chapter five | SOME RESOURCES OF LANGUAGE

If words were like counters in a game, whose value could be fixed once and for all by the rules, we could easily learn to manage them successfully. We would still have to take care not to mistake one for another, or add them up incorrectly, but we would not have to worry about being fooled by them, for their value would be their face value, and it would always be the same. In actual fact, words are more like coins in a kingdom (happily, imaginary) with enormous and rapid cycles of inflation and deflation, plus arbitrary rulings by the monarch and fluctuations due to sudden sentimental attachments and violent aversions.

If meaning were a matter of clearly distinct and distinguishable senses and definite syntactical rules, it would not be too hard—though it would require some effort—to avoid troublesome ambiguities and equivocations and to achieve that degree of precision that the occasion demands. But this is not so. And the most challenging difficulties in using language well are imposed by these features of language that are among its greatest glories—its capacity for the most delicate shades of meaning and its capacity to condense and combine meanings into richly complicated discourse. This second characteristic has already been alluded to briefly in the preceding chapter: it was there called "multiple meaning."

We must now take a closer look at this aspect of language, and especially at one distinction that is very familiar and yet needs some thought to become clear. We often distinguish between what a discourse says "explicitly," what it comes right out with plainly and openly, and what it says "implicitly"—what it merely hints at, insinuates, "implies" (in the colloquial sense). We can speak of "levels of meaning" here, because the implicit meaning rests upon the explicit—we can't hint at anything unless we say *something* openly. When we read a news story or an article hastily, we may get the main sense, the gist of it; but unless we are sensitive to the implicit meanings, we may miss something of the greatest importance to us if we are seriously trying to form a rational opinion about what is to be done. And when we write for others, hurrying to get down the main points without paying attention to the implicit meanings of our own writing, we may find out later that we have said things we didn't "mean" to say at all, and wish we hadn't said.

The purpose of the present chapter, then, is to explore certain aspects of meaning more fully, and to make clear some distinctions that are useful to the reader and writer who is aware of the importance of what he reads or writes.

§15. connotation and metaphor

Up to this point, we have discussed meaning in general, and some aspects of its behavior, without attempting to see what meaning really is, in itself. To give a full account of "the meaning of 'meaning'" would take us into more technical matters than this book can accommodate; yet the word is so variable—not to say slippery—that some further account of it is certainly in order. Even without providing a philosophical analysis, we should be able to clarify some important points about meaning that have extremely wide practical applications.

A few preliminary cautions are called for. First, it will be tolerably plain from the start that we are concerned here with *linguistic meaning*—that is, with something pertaining to words and groups of words (not, for example, with such senses of the word as are operative in "The child's crankiness *means* that he is tired" and "He didn't *mean* to break it"). But second, the capacity of a term to mean something is to be distinguished from another important capacity of a term (at least, of many terms), namely, to serve as a name.

When we think of names, we think first of *proper names,* which are invented or adopted to refer to, to apply to—to be the name *of* —a single individual, whether person, place, collection, object, or event:

Geronimo
Selma, Alabama
Pike's Peak
Mariner IV
The Holy Roman Empire
The Whiskey Rebellion

Two individual things may be given the same proper name, as two American Indians may be named Geronimo. "Geronimo" is still a proper name, for in each case it is assigned to one individual, by legal or religious procedures. It is not assumed that the two Geronimos have anything in common besides their names. And anyone who uses the name as a proper name in certain conditions intends to use it to single out a particular person, not a group of people.

Besides proper names, there are common names, or general terms:

American Indian
town
mountain
space vehicle
empire
rebellion

We can speak of *an* American Indian, *a* rebellion—or of *this* and *that* Indian, the rebellion last year or the rebellion next year. These terms can be applied to several individual things, and so we can speak as we did in the earlier chapters of the *class* of American Indians, of towns, empires, rebellions, and say that these terms (whether singular or plural, grammatically speaking) *refer* to the members of these classes. It is convenient to have a special term to refer to this relationship between words and things—the naming relationship. Let us say that the term "space vehicle" **comprehends** such things as Mariner IV, Vostok V, Vanguard II, Tiros I, Lunik IV, Zond I, Explorer XXVI. And let us say that the class of these and similar things is the **comprehension** of the term "space vehicle." The comprehension of "mountain" includes many familiar objects with proper names like "Mt. Wilson," "Mt. Everest," "Mt. Washington," "Mt. Monadnock," "Mt. Vesuvius."

Reference, or naming, is a very important function of language, but it is not to be confused with meaning. We *can* say, if we like, without too much distortion of ordinary usage, that "mountain" means (among other things) Mt. Everest, but this may be confusing. It is better to use "refers to" or "includes in its comprehension," and preserve "meaning" for a quite different aspect of words: their relationship, not to things, but to characteristics of things.

This other important aspect of words appears when we consider how we know which individual things actually belong to the comprehension of a general term. Obviously not everything is a mountain or a space vehicle—some things are, some are not. Unless the comprehension is utterly fluid, and changes from moment to moment—like the list of who's "in" or "out" among the taste-makers—there must be rules of admission to separate the ins from the outs. And when we stop to think about it, there are indeed such rules, which we use all the time; and to impart these rules is precisely to teach someone the *meaning* of the word.

We would say, for example, "You can't call that a 'mountain' unless it rises higher than a hill above the surrounding terrain," or "It's not a space vehicle unless it travels beyond Earth's atmosphere." These rules declare that certain characteristics are *necessary conditions* which a thing must satisfy in order for the term in question to be correctly applied to it. Of course, you *can* call anything you like a "mountain." But you can't *correctly* call anything you like a mountain or a space vehicle or an empire. These **necessary characteristics** for the application of a term are the basic ingredients of its meaning, and the term's relationship to them deserves to be marked by a special term itself: we shall say that a term **designates** the necessary characteristics for its application, or that this set of characteristics is the **designation** of the term.

One qualification needs to be added here. Many words, as we have seen, have several senses, which may differ from one sort of context to another. These necessary characteristics come in sets, and each set is really a different sense of the term. Presumably "space vehicle" has not yet had time or opportunity to develop distinct sets of necessary characteristics, so we can say quite simply that it designates certain characteristics in all contexts. "Indian" has two clearly distinct comprehensions: (1) people descended from the non-Eskimo aborigines of North and South America; (2) people native to the country of India. Each of these comprehensions, as my descriptions already show, has its own rules of admission, and so "Indian" designates two sets of necessary characteristics: (1) being descended from non-Eskimo aborigines of North and South America; (2) being native to India. In some contexts, one set of characteristics will be regarded as indispensable for application of the term, in other contexts the other. This point should be borne in mind during our discussion, so that we need not remind ourselves of it continually. When a word is used in a certain context, we know at least part of what it means if we know its relevant designation—which of its standard senses belongs to that kind of context. To say, "That building is a *bank*," is to say, in part, that it is a place where money and securities are more or less safely stored, where deposits are received, and so forth. There are services that some banks offer and others don't—and these, of course, are not necessary conditions of being a bank. But there are certain things that a bank must do—such as accept money or valuables for deposit—or it could hardly be called a bank at all.

But in many contexts, the full meaning of a word is more than its designation. When something is called a "bank," other characteristics may be attributed to it: security, honesty, institutional stability, and so forth. These are not part of the designation, since a bank could still be a bank without them (it could be an insecure and dishonest and failing bank), but they are part of the full meaning of the word in that context.

Here is another mode of meaning. How does it come into existence? The full answer to this question would require a fairly elaborate analysis of several linguistic processes, but the chief ones can be presented quite simply.

We have seen that when a class of things is named by a general term there are always certain necessary characteristics of the class: the conditions for deserving to be called by that term. But there is always another set of nonnecessary characteristics closely associated with the necessary ones. These we shall call the **collateral characteristics** of the class. And these are of several sorts, which we can put together for our present purposes. Take the term "bank," as used in financial contexts. (1) There are characteristics that *most* banks have, so that when we think of a bank it is easy to think of these characteristics; for example, security. (2) There are characteristics that banks are generally *believed* to have. Even if banks were frequently failing, if the news could be suppressed so that most people still thought of banks as financially stable, financial stability would remain as one of the collateral characteristics of banks. (3) There are characteristics that banks are often *said* to have—at least, the best, or best-known, or biggest banks—and certain words are customarily used in making these assertions. Thus, for example, in discussing the chances that the bank will be burglarized we generally use the "bank," rather than synonymous or closely similar terms. We *can* say, "the local savings and loan association is safe," or "the local depository of funds is safe," and perhaps we sometimes do. Much more often, we say "the bank is safe," and so safety becomes one of the collateral characteristics of banks, but not necessarily of savings and loan associations.

Or consider the term "Great Dane." A lady who led the long and, in 1965, successful fight to have the Great Dane made the official dog of the Commonwealth of Pennsylvania pointed out, quite properly, that a Great Dane was a good friend of William Penn's and is pictured with him in the mural in the governor's reception room in Harrisburg; the breed is notable for its loyalty. She also argued that the state needed some official symbols with improved collateral characteristics: "The state flower (mountain laurel) is poisonous. The state tree (hemlock) grows twice as tall in West Virginia. And the state animal (deer) had to be imported from Michigan some years back."

The collateral characteristics of a term's comprehension make it possible for the term to take on contextual connotations, but in order for these characteristics to become connotations, they must be brought to life, or actualized. And the principal method by which this is done is *metaphor*.

Every metaphorical description can be thought of as consisting of two parts: there is a term that is used *literally*, to refer to the thing being described; and there is a predicate that is applied *metaphorically* to that thing. Though metaphors may be statements ("His mind was overtaxed") or phrases ("a fertile mind") or even single words ("brainwashed"), we shall take statements as the basic sort, for the purpose of our analysis. A phrase ("fertile mind") is metaphorical only if the corresponding statement is ("His mind is fertile"). And the essential character of metaphor appears most clearly in statements.

What is a **metaphorical statement,** then? It is a statement that has two features. First, if we consider only the designations of the terms involved, we see that it cannot be true, for it involves an impossibility—either a logical contradiction or a physical impossibility that is evident from the context. For example, it is logically impossible that a mind should be fertile, as far as the standard designation of "fertile" is concerned, for it is not a physical object, like topsoil. On the other hand, I suppose it is logically possible to remove a brain and literally wash it, but when someone alive and kicking is said to have been "brainwashed," we understand that his brain was not actually removed and replaced. (If the context does not allow us to assume this then we have no right to take "brainwashed" as a metaphor.)

Second, because the metaphorical statement is asserted, with apparent seriousness and sincerity, by someone who must be assumed to be aware of the absurdity of his statement on the level of designation, we are forced to look for another meaning. We therefore turn to the collateral characteristics of the predicate-term, and run through them to select those that can be applied without absurdity to the subject of the statement. One of the collateral characteristics of "washing," for example, is *removing an unwanted condition.* Since a brain can have conditions that someone wants removed, we take the original metaphorical statement to be asserting this (among other things).

The general rule, then, is this: a statement involving an impossibility on the level of designation may be understood as attributing to the things referred to by the subject any collateral characteristics of the predicate-class that are not ruled out by the context. In expressions like "blood bank," "eye bank," "soil bank," we cannot ascribe all the collateral characteristics of "bank" to the objects referred to, but we can select certain characteristics, and thus interpret the metaphors.

An interesting example of metaphorical interpretation is provided by the controversy that was stirred up some years ago over Sir Charles Snow's analysis of what he called "the two cultures"—that of the natural scientists and that of the literary humanists—and the obstacles to communication between them. Snow made the metaphorical statement that scientists "have the future in their bones." F. R. Leavis attacked this statement by saying that it "cannot be explained as a meaningful proposition." It is hard to know exactly how to take this comment. True, the statement is literally absurd—but that is true of any metaphorical statement. You can have marrow or calcium or strontium-90 in your bones, but not the past, present, or future. It is this very absurdity that compels us to look beyond the literal meaning (designation) to the collateral characteristics that might provide a metaphorical meaning. There is of course no guarantee that our search will be successful. If Snow had said that scientists have Christmas in their bones, or marginal utility, or cognitive dissonance, we might not be able to find any collateral characteristics that are relevant to scientists' bones. In that case, the alleged metaphorical statement would not be a metaphor at all, but nonsense.

That is not the case here. As Martin Green wrote in *The Kenyon Review* (1962):

> But surely the phrase means that scientists habitually deal in kinds of knowledge and power that become socially significant some twenty or fifty years later; so that what is the future for us is contemporary and familiar to them: and that this experience is fundamental in their intellectual life?

There may be more to Snow's statement than this—whenever we start to spell out the meanings packed into a metaphor, we have the feeling that there may be other, more subtle, ones that we have left out. But this at least is a partial interpretation of the metaphor.

In giving this interpretation, we need not assume, of course, that Snow was *right* in what he said. When we explicate a metaphorical statement by extracting from it a series of literal statements (as Green does in this example), we often begin by looking for *true* statements. And perhaps Leavis was thinking, not that Snow's metaphor said nothing at all, but that it said nothing he could accept. However, some, or even most, of what a metaphor says might be false. The point is that we can't be sure we know what is false and what is true until we make the meanings explicit.

Both the values and the dangers of metaphor are illustrated by this example. There are two great things about metaphorical statements. They are economical, in that they condense a good many statements into one; and that is what makes them so significant and exciting. They are also creative, in that they give us new meanings, and enlarge the capacities of our language to express subtle distinctions that till then we had no words for. That is why a well-chosen metaphor is likely to catch on and stay with us as part of the living language—it seems to meet a need that had been there, even if unfelt.

But there are two great dangers in metaphorical statements, on the other side of the same coin. Because of the very complexity of metaphor, its multiple meaning, it takes a good deal of skill to control. And unless you are able to keep your metaphors from running away with your meanings, it is wise to use them sparingly. When the Warren Commission published its report on the assassination of President Kennedy, it suggested that the FBI and the Secret

Service should communicate and collaborate more effectively. FBI Director J. Edgar Hoover sprang to the defense of his bureau with the comment that this was "Monday-morning quarterbacking." But that metaphor was a two-edged sword. It did cut one way, since Monday-morning quarterbacking is certainly easier than Saturday-afternoon quarterbacking. But the other important point about Monday-morning quarterbacking is that it is often a good deal better, since by that time it may be clear what should have been done. Thus the metaphor means that the Commission's report is more correct about the FBI than J. Edgar Hoover had been some months earlier. This was hardly what Mr. Hoover had in mind, but it is what he *said.*

Metaphor can run away not only with meanings; it can run away with thinking, too, when the figure of speech takes control, and the mind is guided by that, rather than by logical connections. A conservative writes:

> Today, big and complicated Government has a hand in everybody's business and another in every person's pocket. These hands are moved by relatively obscure people tucked away here and there throughout the fathomless mazes of Government's bulging bureaucracy. The brooding Government's omnipresence is an open invitation to those who wish to use one or more of Government's complicated processes for unfair advantage over their neighbors. Strings are pulled, leaks of information accomplished, investigations are launched, all to the irreparable damage of many people—but all according to law.

The (personified) Government has both hands occupied, while its bureaucracy bulges in fathomless mazes, and various string-pulling, information-leaking, and investigation-launching activities are going on. This picture does not clarify what is happening; anyone who thinks about taxation in terms of putting a hand in someone's pocket, or who describes legislating and lobbying in these simple figures of speech, is quite likely to see things in a distorted or over-simplified way. This is *picture-thinking* at its worst.

In a metaphorical statement, the characteristics actually meant by the predicate are its connotations in that context. As a word is used metaphorically in various contexts, more and more of its collateral characteristics become connotations in one context or another. They are brought to life, made actual. They belong, from then on (for at least a time) to what is simply called the "connotation" of the word. The **connotation** of a term consists of all those collateral characteristics that the term has meant in one context or another.

At a given time, then, a term that is used in ordinary speech has connected with it three sets of characteristics: (1) the necessary characteristics designated by the term, (2) the characteristics that belong to its connotation, and (3) other collateral characteristics of its comprehension that have not yet become connotations, because the term has not yet been used to mean these characteristics. But in a living language, shifts among these three categories are constantly going on; and metaphor plays one of the leading roles in this change of meaning. Consider, for example, the word "parasite." In Elizabethan English it designated the characteristic of being a person who depends on other people to support him. Its designation was like that of "sponger" today, or the British "spiv." In the eighteenth century, biologists took the term over metaphorically to apply to a certain relationship among organisms, such as worms living in a host body. But they did not keep the metaphor alive; they simply assigned a new designation to the term, by definition, and made it mean (in biological contexts) an organism that lives in or on another, robbing it of part of its food or consuming part of its tissues. This designation has become the standard one, and when we call a person a parasite today, we use the term metaphorically; its original designation is now its connotation.

It is metaphor that transforms collateral characteristics into connotations, but once a term acquires connotations, they are always on tap and ready to spring into life, and they add in subtle ways to the meaning of a statement, even when not particularly noticed. The importance of connotations comes out clearly when we compare close synonyms.

Some time ago, Mr. Hoover wrote a letter to a TV word-expert, in which he said, "I abhor the word 'cop' in reference to members of our profession." And one can make out a case for this point of view. Consider these three statements:

(1) J. Edgar Hoover is the nation's *chief law-enforcement officer.*

(2) J. Edgar Hoover is the nation's *leading policeman.*

(3) J. Edgar Hoover is the nation's *top cop.*

What are the necessary characteristics of a law-enforcement officer? Presumably, that he is employed by a government body to protect the public against crime and is permitted to use force to attain this end. I do not claim to have listed all the necessary characteristics, and there might be a dispute about some of the ones I have mentioned. (For example, suppose a man were not permitted to be armed or to make arrests, but only report crimes; would he be a law-enforcement officer? I think not.) Now, what are the necessary characteristics of a policeman? Of a cop? The answers seem to be the same as before. "Law-enforcement officer," "policeman," and "cop" apparently designate the very same characteristics. And it follows, of course, that they comprehend the same things: anybody who is any one of these three things must also be the others.

Do they then have the same meaning? Apparently Mr. Hoover did not think so—and he was surely right. "Law-enforcement officer" connotes dependability, being well-trained, being law-abiding. "Cop" connotes at least possible corruptibility, toughness, insensitivity, being of negligible social importance, and not being very bright (though he may have a heart of gold). We are not surprised to hear of a "crooked cop," but "crooked law-enforcement officer" seems almost self-contradictory (though it is not).

It is these connotations of words that are of such great value to the propagandist, whose work we shall study in the next section. Of all propagandists—those who use words or pictures to alter people's attitudes, preferences and actions by deliberately inducing false beliefs—the advertiser makes the most blatant use of them. In this way, he provides a kind of laboratory in which we see connotations clearly at work: we see how, having accepted a given term as far as its designation goes, we are expected to accept all that is connoted by it as well. And many of these connotations are not connotations of the word, but borrowed from other words with which that word is associated by similarity of sound.

Take the word "lager," for example. This word no doubt has connotations (or at least its comprehension has collateral characteristics that could become connotations). But when some brewers of lager beer are advised by their copywriters to avoid it like the plague, it is because their market psychologists tell them that to many people "lager" connotes slowness, tiredness, dizziness, laziness, lingering. A nail enamel called "Pineapple Yum-Yum" must be, on the other hand, irresistible to some ladies. And when the manufacturer of a new synthetic fiber chooses "Darlan" (rather than, say, "Merex," or "Dicuna"), it is because he hopes this word will conjure up visions of richness and elegance and enviability. The connotations at work here—and no doubt they *are* at work—do not arise directly from the collateral characteristics (the buyer who is moved to buy clothes made of Darlan doesn't know what the characteristics of that fiber may be). They arise from cross-references to other words, via common syllables. "Dar" in "Darlan" connects with "darling"; "lag" in "lager" with "lagging." The words of a living language develop multiple interrelations, and every common syllable carries with it some sense—however vague and faint—of allusion to other words.

A Check-up Quiz Here are five metaphors referring to events in recent history. Give three to five characteristics connoted by each metaphorical term in its context.

1. Adlai Stevenson said the Republican party was "dragged kicking and screaming into the twentieth century." What does this say about the Republican party?
2. In his famous *Life* interview, early in 1956, the late John Foster Dulles, secretary of state, said, "We walked to the brink of war and looked it in the face," thus (unintentionally) contributing a new word, "brinkmanship," to the language. What did his statement say about the United States' foreign policy?
3. Max Ascoli, in *The Reporter,* once referred to the United States during the Eisenhower administration as "taking a holiday from history." What does this mean?
4. Winston Churchill said to the House of Commons in 1953, "If there is not at the summit of the nations the will to win the greatest prize and the greatest honor offered to mankind, doom-laden responsibility will fall upon those who now possess the power to decide." The term "summit" came to be applied to conferences of heads of governments and chiefs of state. What does it connote?
5. If the newspaper says there is a "power vacuum" in a certain part of the world, what are we to understand about that part of the world?

For Further Study Porter G. Perrin, *Writer's Guide and Index to English,* 3rd ed., Chicago: Scott, Foresman & Company, 1959. Hugh R. Walpole, *Semantics,* Ch. 7. New York: W. W. Norton & Company, Inc., 1941. René Wellek and Austin Warren, *Theory of Literature,* 3rd ed., Ch. 15. New York: Harcourt, Brace & World, Inc., 1956.

§16. suggestion and slanting

We have distinguished two levels of meaning that can be found in many words and phrases: the level of explicit, more or less standard, sense, which is the designation of the term; and the level of implicit meaning, which is the connotation of the term. A parallel, though quite different, distinction can be made for sentences as a whole, and particularly for statements.

When you assert a statement, you show belief in it, and the primary function of assertion is to communicate belief (including, in the case of lies, ostensible or purported belief). But, our language being what it is, you can often show that you believe other things besides what your statement states. This feat is familiar in ordinary speech. For example, you can say, in a flat tone of voice: "The Republican candidate for mayor has refused to appoint a Human Relations Committee." If you stress the word "Republican," you manage to say something more: namely, that perhaps the Democratic candidate has not refused to appoint such a committee. If you stress the word "appoint," you suggest that, if elected, he probably will be willing to cooperate with such a committee if someone else sets it up. The difference in what is conveyed by the three assertions is not a difference in what they state, but in what they suggest. What an assertion **suggests** is what the speaker or writer shows that he probably believes, over and above what he states. Of course, he may not actually believe it—he may be trying to suggest something he knows to be false, or he may not even be aware of what he is suggesting. Nevertheless the suggestion is there if he *seems* to believe it—given the conventions governing English usage, and the assumption that he is sincere.

There are many such conventions, and correspondingly many ways in which suggestion can occur. Putting two statements close together, without a transition, may suggest that the events they describe are causally connected in some way: "Reverend Jimmy Dodds was the visiting preacher at First Baptist Church Sunday. Workmen were busy Monday putting a new roof on the parsonage." Modifying a noun with a noteworthy adjective may suggest that an important distinction is being made. For example, it is suggestion that makes it sound a little strange to speak of "successfully impersonating a lion" (Wolcott Gibbs once asked, in *The New Yorker*, "Has any actor ever *unsuccessfully* impersonated a lion?"). Or to call Edna Ferber "the world's greatest living American woman novelist," as the blurb on one of her paperback editions does, is to suggest that she is not so great after all, if you have to make so many qualifications to find a category for her—especially if, having limited the category to Americans, you have to make it seem more important by adding "world's."

A statement may be made in such a way as to show that something else is being assumed or presupposed; this presupposition is then part of what is said—though only by suggestion.

> GOVERNOR: "Well, it is very hard for me to understand why we are . . . holding them back and preventing them from operating in Cuba, ninety miles off our shore. And I hope it is not as a means or as an endeavor to placate or appease the Soviets."
>
> REPORTER: "Do you think it is?"
>
> GOVERNOR: "I hope it is not, I said."

This is a fine way to get across the suggestion that there is some reason to think the government may be trying to "placate or appease," without committing yourself to any overt statement at all. It is all done by presupposition: for to express a "hope" that something will not happen makes no sense except on the assumption that there is some danger of it. Imagine how you would feel if someone called you up one evening and said, "I *hope* your house will not be bombed."

One of the most valuable uses of suggestion is to indicate comparative importance, without having to spell it out. To put things in a list is always to suggest, at least mildly, that the order is significant—indeed, if we want to rule out this suggestion, we often have to state explicitly that the order is *not* significant, but merely random or alphabetical. When a person lists his emergency telephone numbers as "Doctor, TV Repairman, Fire, Police," we take this to suggest, though perhaps not strongly, that the first two have a somewhat higher priority than the last two—either in the number or desperateness of emergencies. On the other hand, when a series of terms occurs at the end of a sentence, the suggested emphasis rises from item to item. Hence the absurdity of the newspaper report of an attack on a nominee for the school board: "He accused Tudisco of insulting President Eisenhower, democracy, and *Time*."

Sometimes what is suggested is just what is *not* said. When, in the context at hand, it would be natural to say something if it is true, then to avoid saying it suggests that it is *not* true.

> REPORTER: "Is the World's Fair going to show a profit this year?"
>
> WORLD'S FAIR PRESIDENT ROBERT MOSES: "The contribution of this Fair to our times and our city in the end will be measured not by the clicking of turnstiles, but by the effect it has had on thinking people of all ages."

"Freely translated," remarked *Time*, "Moses was admitting that the Fair would never make any money."

Because suggestion comes in all degrees, from the most delicate hint to the most obvious insinuation, it is not always possible to be sure whether something is suggested, and a person with paranoid tendencies—or one who is merely hypersensitive—may find suggestions where in fact they do not exist, or may find them stronger than they are. When, in 1965, Cuba issued a postage stamp with Lincoln's picture on it, and the words, "You can fool all of the people some of the time, some of the people all of the time, but not all of the people all of the time," this was interpreted as a dig at United States foreign policy. Perhaps it was. A letter-writer protests to a national magazine,

> It is interesting to note how your socialistic magazine, like so many others of your ilk, can subtly twist the truth. For example, you quietly malign the House Committee on Un-American Activities by simply manipulating its wording to read House Un-American Activities Committee, thus dressing the Committee in subversive attire.

Perhaps to put "Un-American" before "Committee" carries some faint whiff of accusation—though it is hard to see how this would count very much in a context in which the activities of the committee were reported. A more extreme case is a newspaper report of a woman who had been screening school texts for un-American propaganda on behalf of the Citizens Committee on Education, in California.

> Mrs. Logan . . . said she recently read a geography textbook which told how certain areas of Russia had the same climate and topography as some sections of the United States and grew the same products.
>
> She said she resented the fact that the book didn't point out that even if all these things were the same, the way of life was different.

It is certainly too far-fetched to interpret the textbook as suggesting that because the topography is similar, everything else is, too. But to point out topographical similarities does suggest that American and Russian farmers face similar problems—and no doubt even this sympathetic suggestion was sternly disapproved by the Citizens Committee on Education.

The problem that suggestion poses to the reader or listener is part of the same problem we have been considering: he must be alert to what is being suggested, and able to grasp it clearly. When the matter is important, he may have to state what is suggested, so it is plain. This is what we have just been doing, to some extent, in considering various kinds of suggestion. "I hope the government's policy is not an endeavor to placate the Soviets" suggests that there is ground for suspecting that the policy *is* an endeavor to placate the Soviets. What was implicit in the original sentence has now been made explicit, so that it is open to critical inspection and logical testing.

The problem that suggestion poses to the writer or speaker is one of control. As critic and corrector of his own work, he must be able to see what in fact he *has* suggested, perhaps inadvertently. Perhaps it is what *ought* to be said; but if it is not, then it must somehow be canceled out. This may mean rearrangements or substitutions of syntax. For example, suppose you find that you have written this sentence:

> George Santayana was of Spanish birth and lineage, but, in consequence of his mother's first marriage, he was raised in Boston and became a professor of philosophy at Harvard.

The suggestion is that either his mother's first marriage, or the marriage plus his being raised in Boston, were direct causes of his becoming a Harvard professor of philosophy. In any short passage where so much information is to be packed in, it will not be easy to avoid *some* misleading suggestion, and the best procedure would be to separate some of these statements in the larger discourse of which this is (presumably) a part. One way of eliminating the undesirable suggestion—but does it introduce different and equally undesirable ones?—would be to write:

> George Santayana, professor of philosophy at Harvard from 1907 to 1939, was of Spanish birth and lineage, but in consequence of his mother's first marriage, he was raised in Boston.

When the matter is very important, the only safe plan is to aim at the plainest and most explicit language—where everything that is said is, so far as possible, said in overt statement, and nothing is left to interpretation. It may be a matter of war or peace in diplomacy; it may be a matter of life and death (or at least false hopes of life) in medicine. In one of his early reports on the Salk vaccine, after forty million inoculations, Dr. Jonas Salk said, "Inferences that the theoretical considerations were unsound or were not applicable . . . seem not to have been supported by time." As a piece of prose, this may be criticized on other grounds; it is offered here only as an example of extreme caution in making a statement. It does not avoid all suggestion, of course (for example, it suggests that there *were* such "inferences," and that the speaker has been testing them carefully); but it avoids any suggestion of overconfidence in the results of the test or of hasty generalization.

Suggestion is an immeasurably valuable resource of language—think of how tedious and exasperating it would be if everything we wanted to say had to be said explicitly. But it takes skill to deal with, too—and most of all when it is deliberately used to deceive. Morally speaking, deceptions may not be very different. But from a linguistic point of view, there is an important distinction between two methods of deception. The first is the plain falsehood, when what is stated is simply untrue: "Santayana died in 1939." The second is more subtle: the statement made is quite true, but what is suggested is false. In that case, we can't simply say that the assertion is false, because on one level it is *not* false; yet anyone who accepted all that it says would be led to believe a falsehood. It is not false, but *misleading*. Take misleading advertising, for example. I have seen a full-page advertisement of portable television sets with a large picture, under which, in boldface sixteen-point type, it says:

Your "second set"—a G-E 14-"incher" (dia. meas.)

That's "diagonal measure" in the tiny type—that is, distance between opposite corners of the screen. The advertisement is not false, strictly, because it does admit at least one of the dimensions of the set. But by selecting this curious dimension, and whispering it in the smallest possible way, it probably leads many readers into thinking the picture is fourteen inches wide, instead of about twelve.

It is convenient to think of all the meanings of a piece of discourse as being on three levels, from the most explicit to the least explicit. A certain college newspaper, announcing a forthcoming talk on hallucinogenic drugs by Richard Alpert, former professor of psychology and education at Harvard, filled in some background this way: "Dr. Alpert was dismissed from Harvard for expanding the consciousness of an undergraduate." The knowledgeable reader understood several things from this. On level 1, it states that the cause of Mr. Alpert's dismissal was an event having the characteristics *designated* by "expanding the consciousness of an undergraduate"—namely, that he allegedly gave illegal hallucinogenic drugs to an undergraduate. On level 2, it states that this event had some characteristics *connoted* by "expanding the consciousness of an undergraduate"—namely, that the drugs opened up new areas of experience, which were beneficial and knowledge-giving, and so forth. On level 3, it suggests that Harvard University is opposed to allowing undergraduates to have beneficial and cognitively rich experiences. It is, in fact, an excellent example of what I shall call "slanting." When a discourse is true on one level, but false on a higher level, and it carries the suggestion that because it is true on one level, it is also true on the higher level, then we shall say that that discourse is **slanted.**

From reading the discourse alone, you can't tell for sure that it is slanted, unless you happen to know the facts independently. If you compare two discourses, you can see that at least one of them is slanted. For example, in a news story in January 1946, *Time* reported that "the President [Mr. Truman] eased his croniest crony, George E. Allen, into the Board of Directors of Reconstruction Finance Corporation," and in August of that year, *Time* also contributed the factual report that "George is all the more remarkable because, to the naked eye, he is a clown." Words like "eased" and "crony" and "clown" are, of course, full of connotation, and with highly colored language like that, you have the right to suspect some tampering with the truth, some slanting via connotations. But it is conceivable that this is the exact truth, connotations and all. If, however, you pick up a *Time* issue in December 1954, and read that "the President [Mr. Eisenhower] . . . chatted quietly with . . . golfing companion George E. Allen, Washington lawyer and friend of Presidents," you get a somewhat different view of Mr. Allen. There is no contradiction on the level of designation—the facts that he was appointed by Truman and played golf with Eisenhower. But on the level of connotation, we now have terms like "chatted quietly," "Washington lawyer," and "friend of Presidents." And on the level of suggestion, we no longer get the impression of an incompetent being put over out of sheer pull, but of a capable person being consulted by an eminent chief of state.

In this example, we know that there must be slanting somewhere, because—unless we assume that the man in question changed his personality completely—the two passages conflict on levels 2 and 3. But we do not know from them alone which passage is slanted, or whether indeed they are both slanted in different directions.

There are numerous techniques of slanting, and it would perhaps be impossible to catalog them all. But they all involve one or both of two fundamental techniques. A slanted discourse is designed to nudge the reader toward a certain point of view; it is slanted toward a conclusion. It creates a general impression of the subject—of a man, of a proposal, of an action—that you are expected to accept because there is enough truth there, on the basic level of meaning, to make it all plausible. One way of getting you to accept the slant is by *selection* of facts—choosing certain ones and omitting others that are pertinent (as the college newspaper neglected to point out that the distribution of drugs was illegal). The second technique of slanting is *distortion* of facts by manipulating their arrangement so as to suggest relationships that do not in fact hold (as the college newspaper suggested that it was the "expansion of consciousness" that the Harvard University administration objected to, rather than, say, possible effects on health).

Examples of these two techniques are not hard to find if you happen to have the relevant information—of course, the newspaper editorial, or news item, doesn't tell you what it has left out. Consider selection first. Does Delaware County rank high among "open air" areas? One newspaper story says it does, and points out that within a one-hour drive from the county seat there are 2,440 square miles of open country; and within a two-hour drive, 13,200 square miles. What it doesn't say is that nearly all this land is privately owned. The county itself owns 438 acres of recreation land, and the other 2,600 acres of open space within the county exist only as a possibility that something may conceivably be done to preserve them before the developers buy them up. One of the most amazing cases of omission and playing down of information was the end of the federal government's suit against 29 electrical companies, which were fined nearly 2 million dollars in December 1960. This was the largest criminal antitrust prosecution in our history, and it revealed amazing lengths to which the officials had gone to conceal price fixing and market allocating that cost the public millions of dollars in supposedly competitive bids for large electrical equipment. But of 22 large newspapers studied (many of them among the best in the country), only 4 put the story on page one, and some newspapers omitted any reference to it whatsoever; the same was true of the newsmagazines, which were content with a brief report or none at all.

Distortion is achieved by juxtapositions and orderings that suggest more than can be proved. You may read in a magazine, for example, something of this sort:

> The bill now before the House Committee is a multimillion dollar scheme to provide government hospitalization, surgical and nursing services to some thirteen million social-security recipients, and others. While the contents of this measure cannot be labeled as in any way similar to the New Zealand socialized medicine program, it is interesting that the latter is known as "socialized hypochondria," on account of the ever-growing number of New Zealanders who march off

> to the physician at the slightest sign of a pain or pimple, pick up a prescription, then dash off to the nearest pharmaceutical house for "free" pills, ointments, and nose drops.

If the proposed plan is not at all like the New Zealand plan, of what relevance is all this (probably slanted) description of the latter? Only to plant the suggestion that that is where we are bound to wind up—in "socialized hypochondria." Newspapers again are sometimes adept at this kind of insinuated connection. So much emphasis has been given in recent years to accusations of dishonesty against some labor leaders, with extensive coverage of some of the court trials, that many people believe that *most* labor-union leaders are dishonest. Many newspapers habitually play up labor corruption on front pages, link "union" and "racket" together so as to establish the impression of a deep and necessary connection, and headline their news stories about labor problems in larger type and more vigorously connotative language: "Barden Bill Hits 'Union Tyranny,'" "Seek Underworld Link with Hoffa," and so forth. In many years the *New York Times Index* lists almost as many news items concerning racketeering and communism in labor unions as items concerning all other activities of labor—but no doubt such activities as giving to charity, setting up retraining and education programs, building hospitals, and so forth, are not exciting news.

What can we do? We can't write our own news, and we can't take everything we read to be exactly as it claims to be. The first thing is to get the total impression of the discourse, its angle of vision. The second thing is to distinguish: to see what is stated and what is suggested, what conveyed through designation and what conveyed through connotation. The third thing is to compare the discourse with other versions of the situation, looking for omissions and distortions. Then you have at least some chance to sort out truth from falsity, and to make up your own mind about the situation, instead of allowing someone else to make it up for you.

A Check-up Quiz Read the following account of a series of events, and assume that it is accurate and fair. The statements that follow it are about the same series of events. In the light of what the passage says, say which statements are slanted toward the students and which are slanted toward the president, and whether the slanting is done by connotation or suggestion or both.

At the Spring Convocation of Rheingold College (liberal-arts, coeducational, 1,000 students), President Ballantine congratulated his student body for its "disciplined, mature, heartwarming, and cooperative" deportment during the past year, in avoiding all forms of student demonstrations, while other campuses were rife with protest activity. "I am glad you like everything the way it is here," he said.

That evening, 5 students met at the local taproom and formed the Organization for Inspiring New Knowledge (OINK). The following day they sent out invitations to all students to join, and nailed a list of 96 demands on the door of the Administration building. Among them were the following requests: that the ban on student cars be ended; that the library be kept open till 11:00 P.M.; that men and women be permitted to visit each other in their rooms till 2:00 A.M.; that the drinking fountain in front of Founder's Hall be repaired; that the infirmary stock psychodelic drugs; and that the book store stock Batman comics. When an interviewer on the college radio station asked the president his response to these demands, he replied, "Ho, ho." That night, 23 students from OINK staged an all-night sit-in at the president's office. The following morning, when they blocked his entrance, the president became angry and had them arrested for trespassing and disorderly conduct. They were found guilty in magistrates court, and the cases are now on appeal.

1. PREXY'S BONER SPARKS STUDENT PROTEST
2. The plot was hatched by five beery students. . . .
3. Students demanded longer library hours and a broadening of stock in the campus book store. . . .
4. A short-lived movement for greater student freedom ended up in the magistrate's court this morning. . . .
5. OINK IS LATEST STUDENT INTEREST; GOES MARTIN LUTHER ONE BETTER
6. When the President laughed at their detailed requests, the officers of OINK staged an all-night vigil before his office door. . . .
7. The local flatfeet lost no time in hauling away the students who were interfering with the business of the college. . . .
8. The peremptory demands for a freer sex life, drugs, cars, and comic books, were met by a firm "NO" from constituted authority. . . .

9. Less than 2½ per cent of the students responded to OINK's call for support. . . .
10. Spring came to Rheingold College, and with it the first protest movement in the history of the educational institution. . . .

For Further Study Margaret M. Bryant and Janet R. Aiken, *Psychology of English,* Ch. 18. New York: Columbia University Press, 1940. Richard D. Altick, *Preface to Critical Reading,* 4th ed., Ch. 6. New York: Holt, Rinehart & Winston, Inc., 1960.

§17. emotive language

No account of the resources of language, however sketchy, would be balanced if it did not include some discussion of language and emotion. Poets and orators have always known that it is possible to move people by words—to make them weep or take to the streets. And though the works of those old-fashioned word-wielders may not be surpassed in beauty or wisdom, they are surpassed in mass effect by the techniques of the modern scientific image-maker and mind-manipulator. From the phony charity that takes a name made up of appealing words (like "disabled," "American," "veteran") and collects millions of dollars a year—only 10 per cent of which may actually be used to help any veterans—down to the Lollipop Foundation of America, which provides lollipops for children in hospitals, the magic of words is taken as the key to success. Who could turn down anything associated with veterans or with lollipops?

Emotions may be aroused in a straightforward manner, simply by inducing true beliefs: hope, by the confident expectation that present injustices will soon be remedied; anger, by the discovery that that hope has been cruelly torpedoed by political powers. But emotions may also be aroused, in a subtler way, merely by the utterance of certain words and phrases. It is this capacity of a term to arouse emotions, or feelings, that we shall call the **emotive force** of the term. "Disabled veteran" inclines us to feel some degree of pity; "swindler," some degree of contempt. These are fairly widespread responses. Where the emotions vary from group to group, from place to place, we may have to speak of the emotive force of a term as relative to a particular audience. "Human relations commission," for example, may evoke feelings of good will, hope, and satisfaction among middle-class people in a suburb; but the same term may evoke impatience, disgust, and despair among civil-rights workers who have come to believe that the commission cannot accomplish anything in the way of removing the obstacles to their progress.

We can describe the emotion evoked by a term as having a certain *quality:* alarm, disappointment, joyful expectation. We can also describe it as having a certain *direction* along an axis of approval–disapproval. A *laudatory term* evokes a positive, favorable feeling toward the things within its comprehension: "maestro," "star," "dialogue," "freedom." A *derogatory term* evokes a negative, unfavorable feeling: "drag," "drip," "alienation," "mess." In between, there are more or less *neutral terms,* not associated with any very distinct attitude: "electron," "certiorari," "economic strata," "meeting." True, neutrality is a hard thing to be quite sure of—except with technical terms that are never used in highly emotional contexts. For almost any term, however plain and simple, may be given emotive force by management of its context.

The emotive force of a term, whether positive or negative, depends upon its meaning. This may not be obvious at first, and it is worth careful attention. For example, two terms may have the same, or very nearly the same, comprehension—that is, apply to the same things. If they differ in emotive force, that may be because they differ in what they designate. A press agent, a publicist, and a public-relations counselor are the same thing, in one sense—namely, that anyone who can correctly be called by any one of these terms can also be correctly called by the other. (I'm not sure of this, but suppose it is true.) Still, the difference in their emotive force (the third one being considerably more honorific than the first one) is due to the fact that they designate different characteristics. Even if every automobile-worker payment plan that the General Motors management called "guaranteed annual wage" were also called "supplementary employment benefits" by the union management, and vice versa, the two terms would not have the same designation. And if one is somewhat more derogatory than the other, the explanation lies there. "I am giving the matter due consideration; you are certainly taking your time about it; he is stalling"—so says the emotive verb conjugator. But they don't mean the same thing.

The more interesting and deceptive cases of emotive force are those that depend not upon the designation of a term, but upon its connotations. Presumably "Asian" and "Asiatic" designate the same characteristics, but the State Department uses the former, never the latter (except that the latter once slipped into one of President Eisenhower's State of the Union messages). A few years ago an Indian diplomat explained the difference in emotive force—"Asiatic" sets an Asian's teeth on edge because "It so often in the past preceded the word 'hordes.'" The word "Negro" has a negative emotive force for some Negroes—there have been proposals to substitute unemotive terms like "Afroamerican." But the connotations that give "Negro" this negative force, though they have a long history going back to the word applied by the early Portuguese slave traders, are not very much alive in many other circles, and consequently the word can be used fairly neutrally.

This word illustrates the dependence of emotive force on connotation; for as the connotations change, so does the emotive force. The same thing has happened with other group words: "Quaker" and "Methodist" began as terms of contempt, but when the groups they comprehend came to be accepted as respectable and equal members of the community, the connotations of oddness and ridiculousness were lost, and these groups now apply the words to themselves, even with affection. Other words have gone up and down. "Drug store" is now a rather bad word, because of the connotations of the word "drug" due to its frequent connection with narcotics addiction; pharmacists tend to avoid it. "Lobbyist" is losing much of the intensity of its negative emotive force, as lobbying becomes more of an accepted and to some extent regulated activity. Whereas Will Rogers could say that "A lobbyist is a person that is supposed to help a politician make up his mind—not only to help him but pay him," the usual way of describing his activities now is in terms of the soft sell, education, information, advising. On the other hand, some of the euphemisms that have been chosen to refer as neutrally as possible to the poor and underprivileged can hardly be kept from acquiring unfavorable connotations. Not long ago, "culturally deprived children" was regarded as a neutral description (designed to replace "underprivileged children"), and was even carefully defined ("children whose experiences, generally speaking, have been limited to their immediate environment"). But within a few years, according to a directive in the New York City school system, it was felt that "culturally deprived" was too insulting to use any more.

The trouble with emotive words—that is, words with marked emotive force—is that they get in the way of reasonable and responsible discussion. Because they carry with them implicit judgments of approbation or disapprobation, they often beg the very question at issue. They are too hot to handle. A trivial example is provided by a hearing a few years ago on an application to bring back "clean, wholesome burlesque." Although the applicant insisted that his show would be a burlesque in the strict sense, as defined in the dictionary, others could not get away from the connotations of the word and the disapproval it aroused in them. There was a logical stalemate. The applicant, of course, wanted the word "burlesque" precisely for its connotations, and the *approval* they would arouse among his potential clientele. But as long as he insisted on appropriating the term, he had no hope of getting his permit, since the emotive effect worked both ways. The only way there could be any real discussion of the merits of the application would be by substituting a neutral term. "All right, let's call it a 'satirical revue,'" they might say—and then they could get on with the discussion. Of course, "satirical revue" does not have exactly the same meaning as "burlesque," but it might be close enough for the purpose at hand.

Consider how another dialogue might be thrown off the track or held up by the introduction of an emotive term.

> *A:* "It is dangerous to rely on counting untrained noses to form basic policies today. I believe our only hope is to develop human reason among the scientific élite to the point where it is able to cope with the enormous complexity of our problems. I gather that you disagree with this. Are you, then, an anti-intellectual?"

Now, "anti-intellectual" is a rather derogatory term. And *B* is put on the spot. If he says No, he will seem to be agreeing with *A*'s opinion about the scientific élite; but *B* does not agree with this. If he says Yes, he will be accepting the term "anti-intellectual," and in effect showing disapproval of his own view. In this frustrating predicament, it would not be surprising if he lashed out with a counter-emotive term of his own:

> *B:* "Well, I certainly don't go along with any such egghead notion as yours."

But this, of course, doesn't advance the discussion.

What can *B* do? He can propose a more neutral term to be used by both sides in the dispute, without committing anyone to any attitude.

> *B:* "Let's rather say that I don't believe that the problems of the world should be left up to scientific experts. Would you be willing to call me an 'opposer of scientific élites'?"

If both of them are satisfied with this term, they can get down to the real business at hand, which is to decide which of the two points of view is true. As soon as name-calling creeps into the discussion and feelings are stirred, there is always the risk that the direction of the argument will be lost and the conclusion never reached. This does not mean that you can't argue rationally if you care deeply about a subject. If that were so, we would be in a hopeless predicament, for the problems that it is most important for us to think clearly and rationally about are often those that generate the most violent feelings. The task of the straight thinker is not to suppress his emotions, but to make sure that they don't get in the way of the argument. That is why language is important. For when the conflicts of feeling are brought into the dispute through the emotive force of the key terms in which the arguments are carried forward, it is difficult for the parties in the dispute to tell whether they are making logically good points or not. So long as they find themselves using language that expresses their own feelings, they may think they are spinning out sound deductive and inductive arguments, but their critical faculties are so drugged by the feelings implicit in their language that they are in poor shape to tell a strong argument from a weak one.

There are two main ways in which strong feelings affect thinking, and they lead to two broad kinds of fallacious argument.

In the first place, feelings can narrow attention. They can limit the scope of the reasoning: the range of evidence taken into account, the number of possible hypotheses to be considered, the potential sources of new data. When feelings are aroused in a dispute in such a way as to lead one or both of the disputants to leave out of account some of the relevant facts, we shall call this the fallacy of **oversimplification.**

The oversimplifier, or "capsule thinker," may take advantage of other fallacies that we have noted—for example, the black-or-white fallacy or the argument from analogy. He is often recognizable by his breezy and confident manner, and certain phrases like, "What it all boils down to is . . ."; "To put it in a nutshell. . . ." Of course, it is conceivable that the truth does boil down to something, or fit into a nutshell, but if the subject is a complex social problem on which intelligent people have different opinions, the odds are that we are being invited to accept a conclusion before we have seen all the facts that have an important bearing on the issue. Thus, the oversimplifier may defend the policy of forcing Indians off the reservations without adequate preparation to cope with the problems of economic competition, by saying, "We are only setting them free—that is the whole story." Or he may attack the encroachments of the "welfare state" on our lives by saying that the matter can be brought down to a few simple questions:

> Is it really true that Henry Ford II and John Hay Whitney need social security? Is is really true that we require the solicitude of our congressman when he mails us those government pamphlets about tasty kitchen recipes or the way to pin the baby's diaper? Is it really true that the grain grown on the late Colonel Robert R. McCormick's farm at Wheaton, Illinois, needs price supports?

An issue of *Free Student,* reporting on the sentences handed out by Judge Crittenden to those who were arrested at the sit-ins at the University of California at Berkeley quoted one student as saying: "The courts, like the university, are an instrument of the same system that is murdering the people of Vietnam and smothering the self-determination of the people of the Dominican Republic." "System" is always a good word for oversimplification; it conjures up a unified organization lurking behind the scenes, and it doesn't require any detailed proof of an actual connection. It is conceivable that the President of the United States and the Pentagon, who certainly had something to do with Vietnam, ordered that the students should be given stiff sentences (unless they promised to avoid civil disobedience for one or two years). But if it weren't for the sinister emotive force of "system," surely people on all sides of these issues—those for and against the escalation of war in Vietnam, those who thought the Dominican invasion a stroke of genius and those who thought it a disaster, those who supported and those who condemned the Berkeley sit-ins—could agree that all these are separate questions, which ought to be considered on their own merits, not lumped together.

In the second place, feelings can shift attention. If we feel similarly about two things that are really distinct, we may find it that much harder to keep them distinct in our minds, and to remember that the facts that bear on one have no bearing or little bearing on the other. Then it is easy for one party in the dispute, whether knowingly or unknowingly, to slip from the point at issue to other points that are not at issue, to drag in ideas that only confuse the logical course of the argument. When feelings are aroused in a dispute, in such a way as to lead one or both of the disputants to bring into the discussion facts (or supposed facts) that are not relevant to the issue, we shall call this the fallacy of **distraction.**

This kind of "grasshopper thinking," which leaps about according to emotional inclination rather than following the logical trail of the argument, can also be illustrated by the example just given. For, besides seeming to reduce a variety of complex matters to a single "system," the remark quoted also may be avoiding the point. Presumably the speaker was explaining why he felt that the judge's sentences were unjust, and why he would not accept probation. He may have been perfectly right on both counts; but what *reason* did he give? That the government was doing the wrong thing in Vietnam and in the Dominican Republic. The logical question is whether this is a relevant reason. Conceivably it is, but no connection is shown here. He is against both, and he applies the same emotive term to both. If he succeeds in getting us to feel a vague suspicion about both, we are that much more prepared to think that there must be some deep underlying connection. If we are already strongly opposed to the President's actions elsewhere, we may be led to transfer some of that opposition to the judge handing down his sentence, without questioning too closely whether it follows that the judge must be wrong if the President was.

The grasshopper thinker is sometimes seen at his best in the newspaper column, where the commentator shows his learning and wisdom by comparing recent events with earlier ones, and if necessary bringing in little homey examples to shed light on the situation. Observe him at work here:

> After supper, when the dishes and homework are done, and happy peaceful quiet descends on the family, the children begin playing their games. Mother and Dad look on benignly, over the tops of their newspapers. Suddenly angry, tearful cries ring out: "He cheated," "She won't play fair," "They're changing the rules on me." Now civilized society requires a set of rules, and they must be applied impartially. Business depends on it, above all. So when we see the current attempt in the House of Representatives to change the Rules Committee by adding additional personnel, to so-called "liberalize" it, we can only deplore what is happening. Chairman Howard W. Smith, that stern steward of the Rules Committee, is attacked as arbitrary and high-handed. But remember the court-packing plan of President Roosevelt which failed when the native fairness and good will of the American people rose up against it. There is nothing Americans hate worse than a prejudiced umpire.

If it is not too much of an oversimplification, we might outline this argument as follows:

Children should play fair.

President Roosevelt's attempt to enlarge the Supreme Court so he could appoint some new judges was unsuccessful.

> Baseball umpires should be impartial.
> *Therefore,* the proposal to enlarge the Rules Committee is wrong.

Nobody in a calm mind would regard this as a convincing argument; what has impartial baseball umpiring got to do with the Rules Committee's having or not having more members? The principle involved in Roosevelt's case was quite different from that involved in the House of Representatives. But the point of bringing in these other matters, of course, is not to give a good argument, but to make it look as though a good argument has been given. It works, if it works at all, only by arousing the reader's emotions to a pitch of indignation at which he is unable to see clearly that the reasons don't support the conclusion; it is enough that he is against the other things, so he is willing to be against any attempt to cut down the authority of Representative Smith.

As these examples show, the techniques of oversimplifying and of distracting require the arousal of emotion in order to work. There are indefinitely many varieties of maneuver here; but four of them are so common they are worth special mention. I shall call them emotive devices—by which I mean the manipulation of emotions as a means of effecting oversimplification or distraction.

First, there is *the appeal to emotion.* This device involves the use of emotive language, together (generally) with some reliance on suggestion to hint at connections that we might be skeptical about if they were brought out in the open. Many different emotions can be appealed to. Very often it is fear. Of course, there is nothing inherently wrong about spreading an alarm—when there is something to be alarmed about, and when the amount of alarm is proportional to the danger, and when the manner of giving the alarm is such as to evoke rational action rather than blind panic and confused terror. For example, not long ago there was considerable discussion about the desirability of stricter controls over the purchase of guns—since anyone could buy, through the mails, powerful rifles and pistols, even cannon. There are serious reasons to be offered on both sides; and the issue is by no means trivial. But some of the arguments relied on appeals to emotion—and various emotions can be brought into play. For example, fear:

> When I think of my child walking home from school, all I can think of is some young punk, with his mail-order rifle, and telescopic sight and silencer, sniping from the rooftop, just for kicks. I demand that everybody who owns a rifle be registered and fingerprinted, and a record kept of the markings of bullets fired from that gun.

Or sympathy and pride:

> Here is the honest sportsman, who is trained to respect a gun, who knows it is for sport and for saving lives, not to destroy. He is the last of a dying breed of outdoorsmen, a tradition that goes back to our great frontier. Do you mean that this responsible sportsman should be treated like a common criminal and deprived of his Constitutional freedom to bear arms?

Second, there is *flattery*. The audience that is feeling good about itself (and indirectly about the flatterer) has its critical guard down. Says one school board member to another:

> Frankly, ladies and gentlemen, I am tired of hearing the opinions of these educators, professors, psychologists, and the lot: you are solid citizens, successful in the great world of business and finance, elected by the respect and affection of the people in this village, and you have the wisdom to establish the kind of educational policy that you want your children to have.

After that, they may be ready to swallow the policy the speaker is about to commend—despite the opposition of experts.

Third, there is *the appeal to illegitimate authority*. To appeal to authority is to cite as a reason for accepting a statement the fact that a certain person already believes that statement—the other premise (which may be merely suggested) being that the alleged authority really *is* an authority on matters of the sort in question. It is not hard to specify the general requirements of an authority, but it may be very difficult to tell when you have got one. A person is an authority on a given field when (a) he is in a position to have obtained the facts he claims to know, (b) he is qualified, by training and native ability, to draw sound inferences from those facts, and (c) he is free from relevant bias—that is, from prejudices and attachments that would prevent him from drawing rational conclusions or from communicating them fully and truthfully to others. But if someone is cited as an authority who fails to qualify on one or more of these counts, then the fact that *he* believes the conclusion to be true does not add any probability that it is true.

Thus suppose the dispute is over radical new proposals for clearing up our enormous traffic problems—for example, road pricing. On this system, a toll is charged for the use of roads and city streets, which is collected by some easy automatic system; the price is highest during rush hours, to encourage commuters to use public transportation; and the money would replace registration fees and fuel taxes. Would this system be practical? Economical? Fair?

Effective? In any extended discussion, many kinds of question would be raised, and many different experts would have to be consulted. Certainly it would be in order to say, "So-and-so has made a special study of commuting patterns, and he says that our traffic will become intolerable unless we find an alternative plan," or "So-and-so is an electronics expert, and he claims that a simple collection and billing system would be feasible." The authority here can be taken to be legitimate. At the other extreme, it would obviously be silly to say that the plan is opposed by the President of the American Philosophical Association or Mrs. America of 1962. In between, it may be hard to decide. Does seeing violence on television tend to encourage juvenile delinquency? In the first place, it may be that no one is really an expert on this subject—if research has not yet gone far enough. That won't keep a lot of people from appearing as experts. Suppose the argument runs, "Mrs. J. K. S., Juvenile Court judge, says that in her opinion much juvenile delinquency, with which she deals every day, is due to violence on TV." Is Judge S. an authority? She must be on *some* aspects of juvenile delinquency, but what about its *causes*? In such a case as this, we can only warn ourselves that appeal to authority is of no avail unless some evidence is already at hand, or is immediately supplied, to show that the authority is genuine—*in that field.* Otherwise, we may fall prey to the illusion that because someone is an authority in one area, he must be an authority in some other area, as well.

To show that an alleged authority is *not* one eliminates that part of the supposed reason supporting a conclusion, but it does not prove that the conclusion is false. This is the confusion involved in the fourth emotive device: the *ad hominem argument.* Obviously, in a dispute, it is one thing to talk about the conclusion at issue, and another thing to talk about the people who are disputing—their motives, ancestry, or whatever. This is a form of distraction, for then attention is no longer directed to the matter at hand (*ad rem*), but to the person (*ad hominem*). Of course, when the question at issue concerns precisely the legitimacy of an alleged authority, it will be relevant to point out evidences of his bias.

> There is evidence that Mr. So-and-so is uninformed about the subject.
> *Therefore* (probably), Mr. So-and-so's testimony should not be accepted.

The ad hominem argument goes beyond this; its schematic form is:

> We know something discreditable about Mr. So-and-so.
> *Therefore* (probably), his assertion is untrue.

Here is a concrete example:

> I am distressed to hear the United States condemning Portugal's attempt to pacify the people under its colonial rule in Angola, or condemning Sir Roy Wilensky because he wants power to keep order among the tribes in Rhodesia. After all, don't forget what the United States did to the Indians. When we cast off British colonial rule, it was not because we objected to the way the British were treating the native American Indians here. Not at all. We merely wanted a free hand so we could mistreat the Indians in our own fashion, without interference from abroad. And this is exactly what the Portuguese government and Sir Roy are asking.

Now, if the issue here is whether or not the present colonial powers are justified in their treatment of the Africans under their rule, this passage is of course completely beside the point—for it offers no reason to justify them. What it does do is attack American spokesmen for being ignorant of their own history; and what it implies is that they are therefore wrong in what they say, so that the Portuguese and Wilensky are right. If the writer were only arguing that we should be charitable, and not so smug, he would have made his point. But the question was not the smugness of the Americans; rather it was the legitimacy of certain colonial policies.

This kind of distraction can be very effective, especially when, as in this case, it appeals to emotions of the finest sort—namely, moral indignation. The appeal is hard to respond to effectively. If you say, "Oh, dear, yes, didn't we treat the Indians badly—aren't we *still* treating the Indians badly?" then the writer has succeeded very well. For he has gotten the Portuguese and Wilensky off the hook, and changed the subject completely. On the other hand, you may be tempted to say, "Well, I don't think we treated the Indians that badly—and anyway, that was a long time ago, and people have learned since then that colonialism is bad." This is more relevant, but it, too, will be the wrong reply, if it diverts the discussion to the subject of American history. If you say, firmly, "Don't change the subject. We can talk about American Indians later; right now, I repeat that . . . ," this may seem somewhat cold-blooded, but it is the only proper response—from a logical point of view. You see the trap, and refuse to get caught.

A Check-up Quiz In each of the following pairs, one term is laudatory, one derogatory. For each pair, find a term (which may be a long one) that has a closely similar designation but is fairly neutral.

1. civil-rights demonstration . . . protest agitation
2. governmental leadership . . . power structure
3. enterprising . . . opportunistic
4. victimized by one's trusting nature . . . played for a sucker
5. interesting high-school athletes in coming to that college . . . recruiting muscle-men for the team
6. driving along at a pretty good clip . . . speeding recklessly
7. questioning the feasibility of winning . . . defeatist
8. unassertive person . . . doormat
9. plan . . . scheme
10. earthy . . . gross and unrefined

For Further Study Hugh R. Walpole, *Semantics,* Ch. 2. New York: W. W. Norton & Company, Inc., 1941. L. Susan Stebbing, *Thinking to Some Purpose,* Chs. 3, 4, 5, 6, 8, 13. Baltimore, Md.: Pelican Books, 1938. Robert H. Thouless, *Straight and Crooked Thinking,* Chs. 3, 5, 6, 7, 11. New York: Simon and Schuster, Inc., 1932.

OUTLINE-SUMMARY: chapter five

A common name, or general term, *comprehends* a class of individuals (as "college" comprehends Mt. Holyoke College, Grinnell College, San Jose State College, etc.); it *designates* a set of characteristics which are necessary conditions for belonging to its comprehension (since an institution cannot correctly be called a "college" unless it teaches something, the characteristic *teaching* is part of the designation of "college").

The *collateral characteristics* of the comprehension of a term are characteristics that all or most of the objects in its comprehension have, or are widely believed or frequently said to have (as dangerousness, sneakiness, and so forth, are associated with copperheads). A *metaphorical statement* ("This man is a copperhead") states an impossibility in the literal sense, and hence must be false on the level of designation (a human being cannot be a snake); to interpret it, we look for collateral characteristics of the predicate-class that can be attributed without absurdity to members of the subject-class (as a man *can* be dangerous, and so forth). The *connotations* of a term are those collateral characteristics that have been made a part of the meaning of the term by the metaphorical use of that term in previous contexts.

Besides what it states, a statement may also *suggest* that certain things are true, by showing that they are probably believed by the speaker ("I won't go if *he* drives" suggests—but does not state—that I probably *will* go if someone else drives). When a discourse is true as far as the designations of its terms go, but false in respect to what they connote, or if it is true in what it states but false in what it suggests, then it is *slanted.* A slanted discourse, whether composed deliberately or unwittingly, is misleading. The techniques of slanting can be classified as *selection* (giving a one-sided impression by leaving out an important part of the picture) and *distortion* (giving the wrong impression by juxtaposing things in a suggestive way).

The *emotive force* of a term is its capacity to arouse emotions, and this force may be either positive ("immense scholarship" is laudatory) or negative ("academic pedantry" is derogatory) or neutral ("displaying considerable learning and use of scholarly methods"). Since the emotive force of a term is dependent on its meaning (both its designation and its connotation), when we substitute a neutral term for an emotive term (that is, one with marked emotive force), it is never an exact synonym, but it may be sufficiently close in relevant respects to take its place in a particular discussion, where it will be less likely to interfere with the reasoning. Emotions get in the way of a dispute by *oversimplifying* the issue, that is, leading the disputants to leave relevant facts out of account, or by *distracting* them from the point, that is, leading them to bring in irrelevant facts. Certain *emotive devices* are common: (1) appeal to emotion, such as pity and anger; (2) flattery of the audience; (3) the appeal to illegitimate authority; (4) the ad hominem argument.

Exercise 19

In each of the following pairs of statements, either the same word is used metaphorically in two different contexts or similar metaphors are used in the same context. In each case, point out some differences of meaning between the two metaphors.

1. (a) The administration has a *blueprint* for socializing America.
   (b) The administration has placed the socializing of America on its *agenda.*
2. (a) We have declared a *war* on poverty.
   (b) We have decided to effect a final *cure* of poverty.
3. (a) Our church has launched a *Five-Year Plan* for memberships.
   (b) Our church has launched a *Sixty-Month Plan* for memberships.

4. (a) His bill to require beer to be labeled as dangerous to health was *throttled* in the committee.
   (b) The movement to protest denial of voter registration rights was launched last year, but it was soon *throttled.*
5. (a) The *tentacles* of the opium rings worm their way throughout the world.
   (b) The *tentacles* of Interpol, in its constant battle with the opium trade, reach out around the world.
6. (a) The impressive victory for the federal highway program was *engineered* by the trucking and tire-manufacturer lobbies.
   (b) The impressive victory for the federal highway program was *bulldozed* by the trucking and tire-manufacturer lobbies.
7. (a) By ordering the Reserves into a state of readiness, the President flexed the nation's *muscle.*
   (b) The brains of VISTA (Volunteers in Service to America) are in Washington, D.C., but its *muscle* is the thousands of dedicated workers out in the field.
8. Senator Ashurst: "I appreciate your congratulations on my 'seeing the light' with regard to the new bill. The truth is
   (a) I didn't see the light;
   (b) I felt the heat."
9. (a) Mrs. Belmont: "I hear you told everyone at Oelrich's last night that I look like a frog."
   (b) Mrs. Stuyvesant Fish: "A toad, my dear, a toad."

Exercise 20

State explicitly what is suggested by each of the following:

1. Invitation to join a fencing club: "Join us now. New blood always welcome."
2. Kahlil Gibran returned to his beloved Becharri only after his death in 1931.
3. Caryl Chessman went to the chair today, unrepentant and an avowed agnostic.
4. The 49'ers were solid in their praise for Albert when they heard he was quitting.
5. The FBI described Beausoleil as "extremely dangerous." It said he likes to roller skate and play Chinese checkers.

6. Mr. Hill, self-styled "Boss of Britain's Underworld," said he wrote his autobiography "to open the public mind to the difficulties facing the young criminal."
7. Advertisement: "Smoke Dukes, with the Filtroid Filter, which takes out more tars, and more worries, than any other filter."
8. Radioactive readings have been abnormally—but not unusually—high in Los Angeles the past week.
9. "We've trained our dog to watch the TV for us" [Walt Kelly].
10. The only sound and proper course is for the administration to return to conservative financing, fiscal solvency, and governmental economy. Otherwise, it is clear that our largest campaign contributors will not support us.
11. If we don't get out of here soon, we won't get out at all.
12. The objectives of our organization will be to restore a spirit of patriotism throughout the country and fight the all-digit telephone number.
13. MORTUARY SUES MAN WHO CAME BACK AFTER FUNERAL
14. DOCTOR URGES PARENTS REDUCE CHILD POISONING
15. MAN TREATED, DROPPED INTO 10-FOOT HOLE
16. FORMER FBI MAN IN JERSEY PULPIT
    Called by Old Hackensack Church, He Plans to Fight Crime at its Source
17. 3 THUGS BEAT TRUCKER SENSELESS FOR PALTRY $7
18. The *Times Herald* will not be published on Independence Day, Saturday, July 4. Our wish is that our readers will enjoy this holiday safely and sanely.
19. Hiking is healthy, provided you are alert against footfaults, poison ivy, sunstroke, heat exhaustion, poisonous snakes, rock slides, polluted water, and badly fitting shoes, the Greater New York Safety Council announced recently.
20. The friends of Reverend Stuart Woods will be sorry to hear that he is in the St. Catherine's General Hospital recovering from a sudden operation.
21. Col. Parrish credits this experience, along with a preceding ten years of teaching in the public school systems of Bedford and Glenwood, Iowa, and Grand Junction, Colorado, in addition to

assignments in Iowa State institutions for feeble-minded children, as invaluable in her subsequent duties in the Army.

22. These are the animals city kids long to see. . . . This may be zoological heresy, but it would be refreshing and more instructive than a dozen monkeys. Should our youngsters grow up to be delinquents without ever having seen a cow?
23. At the May meeting of the Greenville Home Demonstration Club, Mrs. C. C. Hedrick gave a review of the book *Naked Came I,* by David Weiss. Mrs. O. S. Mann and Mrs. J. R. Johnson gave demonstrations.
24. Naturally you don't want to run over and kill an animal, but remember that human lives (including your own) are more valuable than those of animals. If you are forced to choose between hitting a small animal and risking human lives, then hit the animal. However, don't tackle too big a beast. Hitting a cow or horse or a hog may seriously damage your vehicle or even upset it [War Department Technical Manual 21–305].
25. "We got up every morning at sunrise," said Mrs. Croneis, remembering her trip with a scrapbook full of snapshots. "For breakfast we would have freshly caught fish, delicious little river shrimp, papaya (a delicate jungle fruit), and little surprises. The cook was a head-hunter, but he never failed to provide excellent food."

Exercise 21

Read the following newsmagazine reports very carefully and discuss the questions below.

A.

DRIVE FOR SAFETY [1]

The junior United States Senator from New York leaned over the hearing-room table and spoke harshly to the head of the largest manufacturing company in the world. Said Bobby Kennedy to General Motors Board Chairman Frederic Donner: "How can you appear before this committee and not even know about *that*?"

What seemed to upset Kennedy was that none of the top G.M. executives who appeared last week before a Senate Government Operations subcommittee investigating auto safety had ever seen a

[1] Reprinted by permission from *Time,* July 23, 1965.

Cornell University survey that critically compared G.M.'s door-hinge design with others. In auto collisions, Cornell reported, 5.1 per cent of G.M. cars lost their doors, compared to 0.8 per cent of Chrysler and 0.6 per cent of Ford cars. No one was sure how Kennedy could have expected G.M.'s highest policymakers to know the details of a relatively obscure report,* but his questioning typified the hostile, guilty-until-proven-innocent atmosphere of the hearings. The auto executives were placed in a bad light by other committee questions. Donner, for instance, could not tell Kennedy precisely how much G.M. spends for safety. G.M. at week's end estimated that the 1964 expenditure had been $124 million.

Force-Feeding. The major contention of the Senate subcommittee was that the auto men, with little loss in profits, could make cars safer, reduce the highway death toll that this year will be about 50,000. The hearings were called to consider several bills, some of which would force the companies to build safety devices into cars. Industry leaders argued that they have already done much, and are doing more to increase safety, but that consumers are unwilling to pay for safety features. "If we were to force on people things that they are not prepared to buy," said Donner, "we would face a customer revolt."

The auto men had some imaginative proposals of their own. American Motors President Roy Abernethy suggested that the industry "force-feed" safety to the public by including effective if still unpopular safety items as "delete options"—that is, standard equipment unless the customer specifically asks to have them removed. He also proposed uniform, nationwide traffic laws.

Latching the Door. Donner announced a $1 million G.M. grant to M.I.T. for a four-year study of traffic safety. Chrysler Vice President Harry Chesebrough disclosed that his company's 1966 models will have a new door latch that will substantially reduce the chances of car doors opening in an accident; he also called for the creation of a federal automobile center to coordinate safety programs. All the executives promised that their 1966 models would have many of the safety devices that the government has begun to require on its own cars.

For all their acrimony, the hearings may well serve the worthwhile purpose of arousing concern on the part of companies, consumers and government agencies. Since the Senate subcommittee began investigat-

---

* The company later said that the figures were misleading, that the study involved old as well as new cars, and that G.M. door hinges for the 1959–65 model years "more than satisfy 1967 [federal] requirements."

ing in March, New York State has named a board to build a prototype safety-car, Maryland has tightened its standards for tires, and other states have begun to consider stricter safety rules. A recent nationwide poll shows that traffic safety is now one of the half-dozen problems Americans worry about most.

B.

Auto Safety: Who Will Take the Lead? [2]

One mid-September day in 1899, Henry H. Bliss, a New York City real-estate dealer, stepped off a trolley car near Central Park right into the path of an oncoming horseless carriage. Bliss thus went down in history as the first known victim of a United States automobile traffic accident. But he has since been joined by 1.5 million other Americans —a tragic toll that exceeds the nation's combined casualties in both world wars. Last year alone, auto-traffic fatalities amounted to a record 47,700, and, at the rate automobiles are multiplying and colliding, experts fear the total may double within the next two decades.

The automobile not only kills more Americans than any other form of mass transportation, it is the only form that is not regulated to some degree by federal safety controls (though there are state and local regulations). With alarm about traffic deaths mounting, however, government controls may soon be on the way. Democratic Senator Abraham A. Ribicoff of Connecticut last week convened the Senate subcommittee on executive reorganization with the avowed intent of finding out what role Washington might play in helping to reduce the increasing auto carnage. And he started out by importing some of Detroit's highest-powered auto executives as witnesses and subjecting them to a tactful, but skeptical, grilling about how devoted they are to promoting safety and how safe their cars are.

Driver Failure. All the auto men, ticking off the safety provisions that their companies build into their models, voiced their continuing concern over the rising total of traffic fatalities. "No consideration," General Motors Corp. Chairman Frederic G. Donner declared, "is more important to us than safety." The executives also attributed most accidents to driver failure. "More than 85 per cent of [auto accidents] involve the attitude, behavior, and judgment of the human being behind the wheel," American Motors Corp. President Roy Abernethy asserted.

---

[2] Reprinted by permission. Copyright, *Newsweek, Inc.*, July 26, 1965.

Ribicoff, while admitting that this was so, nevertheless sharply scolded the auto makers for failing to introduce more new safety features on their own initiative. Most of those that will appear on 1966 models (including rear seat belts, padded instrument panels and recessed door latches) have already been made required equipment for the cars that the federal government will buy from the industry starting with the 1967 model year. "Should the automobile industry always be lagging behind," Ribicoff chided, "waiting for somebody to tell them something has to be done? It would seem to me that if the automobile industry took the initiative and took the lead, you wouldn't have to have hearings like this."

For years, the industry has fended off this charge by contending that the public is reluctant to accept new safety devices. Donner, noting that both directional signals and safety belts were slow to catch on after they were introduced, argued that "if we were to force on people things they are not prepared to buy, we would face a consumer revolt."

Donner insisted that G.M. was, nonetheless, still pushing hard on promoting safety. He announced that the company is donating $1 million to the Massachusetts Institute of Technology to help finance a research program on auto safety. But, along with Chrysler Corp. Vice President Harry E. Chesebrough, Donner was unable to cite many specifics about company safety programs and costs under bristling interrogation by Senator Robert F. Kennedy, who often attacked like a prosecuting attorney.

Criticism. When Donner and G. M. President James M. Roche reported they were unfamiliar with a Cornell University study that showed the doors of G.M. cars tore off more easily in accidents than those of competitive makes, Kennedy snapped: "I'm shocked. This important study has been made. It's important to your company and the safety of drivers. Yet the top executives of the company don't know of the findings." One particularly acid exchange with Donner and Roche followed after Kennedy asked how much it was costing G.M. to contribute to outside safety programs:

DONNER: This, sir, isn't a matter of cost.

KENNEDY: I know the cost may not be of concern to you. But it is to me.

ROCHE: G.M. spent about $1,250,000 on aspects of safety.

KENNEDY: What was the profit of General Motors last year?

ROCHE: $1.7 billion.

KENNEDY: With your profits of $1.7 billion, I can't believe that

General Motors couldn't afford to have a detailed study of accident and safety features. If you took the initiative and invested some of your money, we'd do very well.

For G.M. auto safety also was at issue last week in a San Jose, California, County Court, where the giant auto maker was defending itself against one of an estimated fifty legal claims that have been filed by owners of its Corvair automobile. The claimants are all seeking damages for accidents stemming from the allegedly unstable design of the rear-engine Corvair, mainly the 1960 to 1963 models.

Stiff Questioning. At the San Jose trial of a $400,000 damage suit brought by a 39-year-old divorcee whose fiancé and daughter were killed in the crack-up of a 1960 Corvair, G.M. produced a witness every bit as impressive as the corporate brass who paraded before the Ribicoff subcommittee. Retired British racing star Stirling Moss appeared in the witness box (standing, in accordance with British legal tradition) to defend the Corvair's driving characteristics. The car, Moss maintained, was not inherently unstable "unless a driver got into a turning position requiring that he be very professional or very, very foolish." Moss added that design alterations made in the 1964 and 1965 Corvairs were not corrections of the alleged instability but simply the fruit of engineering progress.

Chrysler, too, encountered stiff questioning about the mechanical soundness of some of its cars at the Ribicoff hearings. Vice President Chesebrough admitted that certain 1965 Chryslers, Dodges, and Plymouth Furys had been sold with steering mechanisms that might break away from their moorings under stress unless they were rewelded. He testified that dealers were notified—but that the car owners weren't.

KENNEDY: Why weren't the owners notified?

CHESEBROUGH: The probability (of steering failure) was so remote that we didn't think it was important.

KENNEDY: . . . I'm shocked. How many of these people had accidents?

CHESEBROUGH: None.

KENNEDY: Did you write to them?

CHESEBROUGH: No.

KENNEDY: Then how did you know they didn't have accidents?

CHESEBROUGH: We didn't.

KENNEDY: Again I'm shocked.

There were implications for the auto industry in the actions of state governments last week. In California, Governor Edmund G. (Pat) Brown signed a new smog-control law making it mandatory for all cars in the state to be equipped with exhaust control devices. And in New York, Governor Nelson Rockefeller gave his approval to an appropriation of $100,000 for a study on whether it is feasible to develop a car with maximum safety features.

As the Senate hearings recessed with only Ford Motor Co. President Arjay Miller to be heard this week, Ribicoff seemed to have achieved one major breakthrough. Whereas the auto makers have gone their separate ways on safety in the past, they now appeared agreeable to a concerted attack on the problem. Chrysler suggested setting up a federally financed automobile-safety center to study such neglected subjects as accident causes and stricter driver licensing. All the executives, moreover, agreed to begin looking into a coordinated, industry-wide program to engineer more safety features into new cars. "I can assure you," G.M.'s Donner told Ribicoff, "that we'll sit down and talk this over." True to their word, autodom's top leaders—including Donner, Chrysler Chairman Lynn Townsend, and Ford Chairman Henry Ford II—arranged an industry summit meeting for this week to compose a new safety policy.

1. Describe the general impression given by each of these reports, especially the attitude toward (a) the automobile industry, (b) Senator Kennedy, and (c) the problem of automobile safety.
2. Find pairs of approximately synonymous terms, one from each article, and explain how the differences in meaning (designation or connotation) contribute to the general impression.
3. Find statements that are given in *A* but not in *B*, or in *B* but not in *A*, and show how they lead to different suggestions.
4. Analyze differences in order and position of facts that are given in both *A* and *B*, and show how these differences suggest different things.
5. To what extent, by combining and comparing the reports, can you reach a tentative judgment as to which report is probably more nearly correct?

Exercise 22

Label the emotive devices in the following passages, and say whether each is used for oversimplification or distraction.

1. The calamity howlers are in evidence on all sides. They cry out with fervor the minute anyone mentions any change in the Tennessee Valley Authority. These peddlers of gloom are fighting this proposed

contract. They say this contract means "dismemberment of TVA." They go so far as to say that TVA is being, quote, "cut to pieces." What an oversimplification! Remember that Lord Action said, "Absolute power corrupts absolutely." We must save TVA from that peril.

2. I have heard a spokesman for the opposing party come right out in public and admit that when the Soviets got the first sputnik up before our space vehicles, they were ahead of us. This is part and parcel of the kind of negative thinking that everything they do is right, and everything we do is wrong. That is rotgut thinking. There is no other name for it.

3. When I ran for City Council last time, I ran on a platform of Clean Politics, Clean Streets, Clean Desks, and Clean Living. Now my opponents charge that in the past few years there has been a liquor-license scandal, and that the streets are no cleaner than before. Well! I hope it is understood by everyone that I don't have the kind of time that my opponent has to go around looking for trash in the streets—if I did that, I would be seriously handicapped in keeping the business of this great city humming. I don't know what makes him tick; I can only assume that he has launched a smear crusade against me.

4. The best suggestion offered in some time, in my opinion, for doing away with the social cost of crime is the system of reimbursing innocent victims of criminals. Too often we think of the past, not the future—how to revenge ourselves on the criminal, not what we can do, as a society, to make the crime less of a crime by alleviating its hardships. Think of the man, wounded by a gun fired by a robber, who has no money for hospitalization, who cannot afford to lose several days' pay, whose children are in the streets begging, while, through no fault of his own, he lies in the hospital. Isn't that picture enough to convince you? Surely we can afford it; it is humane; what else is there to consider?

5. Beauty! Irreplaceable beauty! What more precious gift does nature bestow, which man is duty-bound to preserve as long as possible! For a paltry increase in his ease and comfort, and the convenience of some bureaucratic power that rides roughshod over everything, beauty is tossed away. That's what's happening right now, before our very eyes—the Atomic Energy Commission insisting on putting a high-level high-power line through the quiet little village of Woodside, California, which has carefully preserved and enhanced its natural beauty. The line is an aesthetic affront. The AEC is insisting on

having its own way, with its usual imperiousness. The recent letter by Dr. Wolfgang Panofsky, defending the AEC, contained many inaccuracies, and obviously showed an inclination to discard all human values in the search for ultimate particles. Well, let Dr. Panofsky go back to his particles and leave aesthetics alone. He's no authority on beauty. And as a physicist, his bias is clear; obviously he wants the scientists to have a free hand, no matter what.

Exercise 23

Study carefully, and explain, the feelings aroused in the following passages, and the way emotive devices are used for oversimplification and distraction.

1. UNITED STATES STUDENTS: NOT ALL EGGHEADS

If you've lost faith in American youth and believe that any boy or girl who goes to college will quickly be trained by the first left-wing professor he meets to start undermining America and join any and all silly front groups—then have cheer. It isn't as bad as all that, even if it seems so sometimes.

Here's the Student Committee for Congressional Autonomy, recently formed by students at Northwestern University—a national organization of college students to defend the investigating power of Congress.

These college students timed their first major pronouncement to coincide with the opening of Congress, when Representative James Roosevelt (California) was expected to call again for the abolition of the House Un-American Activities Committee—a longtime aim of the Communist party U.S.A. and a lot of other people who aren't quite as savvy as the young men at Northwestern.

The students don't like Representative Roosevelt's idea at all, and aren't afraid to say so in spite of the enormous egghead pressure against them.

In a letter to Congress, released on January 3, the student organization asked all senators and representatives to sink the expected bill, and to join in the fight "to protect the autonomous right of Congress to inform itself and the American public of the persons and practices which would corrupt and destroy our way of life. . . ."

Their group charged that numerous organizations which oppose many congressional investigations are "weakening the investigatory power by corrupting the conditions which are essential to its effective and responsible use." These groups severely "distort certain provisions of the Constitution and totally ignore the necessity for Congress to search out the facts" in order to justify their opposition to congressional committees. . . .

Said John Kolbe, a member of the Northwestern Student Senate: "The central issue has now become whether or not Congress will continue to investigate matters free of the arbitrary controls with which its opponents seek to shackle it. It is no longer an attack on one or two committees. They have declared war on both the Congressional prerogative to inform itself and on the people's 'right to know.' By properly serving a public educative function, we hope to bring an end to that war" [reprinted by permission from *American Legion Magazine,* February 1961].

2. Jesus approved Mary's act of devotion when she anointed Him with "precious ointment," but Judas condemned it as a waste of money which should have been "given to the poor." Jesus could hardly have been charged with neglecting the poor, but He wished to protect aesthetic values, sentiment, and human dignity in death. So He praised Mary's act: "She did it for my burial."

This incident is relevant to a furor about the American funeral customs which has been created by Jessica Mitford's book, *The American Way of Death.* Also pertinent are some facts about Jessica Mitford Treuhaft, which were reported in the November 5, 1963, issue of *National Review.* Several people "under oath before legally constituted agencies of both federal and state governments" have identified Jessica Mitford as a member of the Communist party. In fact, according to the *National Review,* both Mr. and Mrs. Treuhaft have a long record of Communist activities.

Jessica Mitford's Communist connections are pertinent because they place her book in perspective as a part of the left-wing drive against private enterprise in general and—in this case—against Christian funeral customs in particular.

Although much fanfare is associated with the burial of Communist party leaders, wherever communism has gone it has tried to destroy Christian burial customs. Since communism and Christianity are diametrically opposed in their estimation of man, this is not surprising. If man is no more than a dog, as the Communists assert, he should be buried like a dog without ceremony.

Using the customary left-wing tactic of raising wrong issues to obscure the real issues, Jessica Mitford accuses funeral directors of taking advantage of the grief of the bereaved to sell them caskets that they cannot afford and services they do not need.

Since funeral directors are human beings, no doubt there are some who are guilty of Jessica Mitford's charges, but throughout my years in the active ministry, during which time I conducted hundreds of funerals, I never met an unscrupulous funeral director, who in my opinion took advantage of the grief of the bereaved. . . .

Those who attack embalming as an unnecessary expense should investigate the history of the practice. Formerly, funeral directors packed the deceased in ice to preserve the body between the time of death and burial. Most people welcomed chemical embalming as an improvement, but perhaps the critics would prefer to return to the ice pack. . . .

However, all these questions are not the real issue. Jessica Mitford, and others like her, avoid the real issue: the freedom of those purchasing the funeral service. The living—and the dead through their previously expressed wishes—should be free to have the funeral director of their choice and the kind of funeral they wish, whether expensive or inexpensive, simple or elaborate, religious or secular. It is this freedom of choice that communism, and its socialistic counterpart, seek to destroy . . . [from an article by Rev. Irving E. Howard in *Christian Economics,* December 10, 1963; reprinted by permission].

3A. Erasing the Taint of Loyalty

Dutifully reacting to the expressed displeasure of hundreds of prominent educators, the United States Senate has tinkered with the loyalty provisions of the education act under which federal loans are made to students.

The ironic effect is to put more teeth into the legislation. The educators, and the immature college boys who have to believe everything they say, regarded the present provision requiring an affidavit of loyalty to the government supplying the money as "insulting." Under Senate changes, the oath is not required. But any student who applies for a loan while a member of a subversive organization makes himself eligible for criminal penalties.

In the unlikely event that the House concurs in the changes this session, this may satisfy the 100 colleges which felt insulted, and encourage more students to sign up for federal assistance.

What the tinkering will not do is answer the question of why loyalty oaths are deemed so repugnant. Is it evil to be loyal to one's own team, or gauche to put it into writing? Or is there some kind of educated higher loyalty, of the sort shown by Dr. Klaus Fuchs? [*Philadelphia Evening Bulletin*].

B. Student Loyalty

The right-wing *National Review* misses few opportunities to cry out against government interference, but when the presidents of Harvard and Yale suggest that the federal government *is* interfering, and improperly so, with higher education by requiring students seeking a federal loan to file a loyalty affidavit, the *National Review* is appalled.

Yet what practical or moral good is served by demanding that a student swear that he "does not believe in, and is not a member of and does not support any organization that believes in or teaches the overthrow of the United States government by force or violence or by any illegal or unconstitutional methods"? As President Griswold of Yale said in an article in *The New York Times Magazine* last week, such affidavits are inherently futile as safeguards against disloyalty or as a means of inculcating loyalty, as well as being in Alexander Hamilton's words, "a subversion of one great principle of social security, to wit: That every man shall be presumed innocent until he is proved guilty."

A bill to delete the affidavit requirement from the National Defense Education Act will again be introduced in the Senate by John Kennedy and Joseph Clark and has a reasonable chance of being approved, for the initiative of Kennedy (Harvard '40) and Clark (Harvard '34) has the support not only of colleges and universities but of two influential former college presidents who could assure the amendment's adoption—Secretary Flemming and Mr. Eisenhower [*New Republic*].

chapter six | DEFINITION AND CONTROL OF MEANING

A price must be paid for the varied powers of language which we have been considering in the last two chapters: its powers to drive home a conviction forcefully, to distinguish delicate nuances of meaning, to suggest a wealth of ideas in a figure of speech, to arouse all sorts of emotion. For it is this very resourcefulness that sometimes makes language difficult to keep under control, so that it conveys exactly (no more, no less) the meaning that it is called upon to convey.

The simplest breakdowns in communication occur when we use words whose meanings are unknown to others—perhaps old forgotten words we have happened to pick up from reading some of the more playful poems of W. H. Auden (words like "etiolate," "infarcted," "macule," "coruscation"), or perhaps brand-new words that have just been invented for some notable purpose (like "ekistics," Constantin Doxiadis's term for the science of human settlements; or "cognitive dissonance," which psychologists have been using to refer to a conflict between incompatible beliefs or attitudes that a person holds at the same time, consciously or unconsciously). In these cases, it is not hard to put our finger on the source of the difficulty, and communication is resumed as soon as the meaning of the word is supplied.

More challenging breakdowns occur when clotted syntax and queer juxtapositions of terms lead to obscurity. We may have to tidy up the syntax, invert an inversion, or fill in a mysterious ellipsis—changing, for example, Browning's

> What may serve for sun, what still
> Wander a moon above me?

to "What may serve as a substitute for the sun? What may still wander above me as (or in place of) the moon?" We may have to find words whose connotations clash less discordantly, or whose relevant senses are less remote and archaic:

> an ocean's course
> From this our sea whose mere intestine pants
> Might seem at times sufficient to our wants.

If, for clarification, we tell ourselves that "intestine pants" may mean the limited motions of a comparatively small and domesticated sea, this substitution may sacrifice part of the full meaning—but only in order to make sure that the remainder, at least, is understood.

The most unfortunate breakdowns, from a logical point of view, are those that happen without notice, without anyone's fully realizing what has happened. And, as we have seen, the prime cause of this difficulty is ambiguity. Sometimes ambiguity merely puzzles, and leaves things up in the air—if both of the possible senses are obvious. More often, the reader seizes upon one of the possible senses without realizing that the other is there—although it happens that the other one was the only one the writer was aware of. Another source of the same sort of trouble is vagueness. For again, the reader or listener may not notice how vague the word is in that context; taking it to be more precise or less precise than it is, he may be led astray.

These troubles call for stricter controls over language. Take diplomatic communication, for example, where often the decision to use a particular word may be pondered for a long time. Suppose the secretary of state wants to state in a speech that the United States hopes for a gradual discontinuance of the cold war. Should he say that the prolongation of the cold war is "intolerable"? That may be taken to imply that the United States is about to take some positive step, though this is not in fact contemplated. Perhaps "vexing" or "onerous" would be better—or perhaps the connotations of these terms will also be misleading. Suppose the President calls the continuing division of Germany into two parts "abnormal." —Or suppose the State Department announces that we have a "vital" interest in a certain situation—will this mean that we are prepared to go to war to preserve that interest? In ordinary circumstances, perhaps, we seldom need to weigh words quite so carefully, or require of ourselves that degree of precision—yet when we realize how often, in all affairs of life, things go wrong, cooperation is lost, people are made miserable, because of misunderstanding, we can never take language lightly. To use it at all is to take on something of a responsibility.

Since ambiguity is relative to a context, one way of coping with it is by changing or enlarging the context. We have seen, in Chapter 4, how this contextual control can remove the ambiguity from a term or a piece of grammar. But some words are hard to pin down by even the most carefully constructed context. Large parts of the meaning may be made clear, but certain areas of doubtfulness may linger on. In that case, a more direct method is required for fixing and holding the meaning—it must be *elucidated.*

§18. defining your terms

When the occasion calls for elucidation of meaning, there are several ways of going about it. One of the commonest is *giving examples.* A person who doesn't understand a particular term is bound to get some notion of its meaning if he knows at least some things to which it applies.

There are two ways of giving examples. If we have an example on hand, available for inspection, we can produce it and actually point to it. What is an "apse"? Well, look at that church: notice how part of it projects from the building; that is an apse. What is "jazz"? Well, let me play you a record. If we have no examples to exhibit, then we have to cite them, rather than point. We might say, "Go and look at Christ Church for an example of an apse," or "Get hold of Count Basie's 'Take The A-Train' and play it for yourself." Citing examples is easier than producing them; but logically it amounts to the same thing, since the citation gives instructions for finding an example.

Whichever way examples are given, an important question may arise about their number and quality. It is clear that one example can tell a person something, but it can also be extremely misleading. When our inquirer sees a particular apse or hears a particular piece of jazz, he may experience many things that are irrelevant. He may notice that the apse is semicircular and think that this is a necessary condition for being an apse; he may be impressed by the speed of the piece on the recording, and think that speed is essential to jazz. On the other hand, he may notice that the apse has high windows, and think that any part of a building with high windows is an apse, even if it doesn't project; or he may be struck by the music's use of a certain blues scale, and think that any music based on that scale must be jazz.

One way to correct these misapprehensions, of course, is to give a number of examples. In some few cases, where the comprehension of the term is small, it might be possible to cite all its members. But even where the existing examples are few (as with species like the Arabian oryx, the white antelope of the desert, that is on the verge of extinction), remember that the comprehension of the term includes past and future individuals as well. Still, in many cases we can at least provide a number of examples of the comprehension. And the more varied the examples, the better: for when you see how many characteristics an object can leave out and still be an apse, you have a more distinct conception of how many characteristics it *cannot* leave out and still be an apse. With a comparatively simple concept, like *apse,* it doesn't take many examples to give a fairly good idea; with a concept like *jazz,* it would certainly be desirable to take into account a number of widely different examples before trying to decide what "jazz" means.

When we have only one example, or only a few examples, or for some other reason find it desirable to limit the number, then it becomes important to choose a *good* example. A good example, in this sense, is not necessarily *good*—a good example of jazz need not be jazz at its best—but rather a highly exemplary example, that is, an example that brings out the typical and salient features of jazz very sharply and plainly. Let us call such an ideal example a *paradigm.* It is easy to say what is *not* a paradigm; if you were giving an example of a whooping crane, to show what kind of bird it is, you wouldn't select one that was abnormally small, or deformed, or oddly colored. But no very final positive instructions can be given for choosing paradigms, except that they should exhibit fully the necessary conditions of membership in that class. What is a good example, we might ask, of connotation? Of moral turpitude? Of cognitive dissonance? Of peaceful revolution? Of pneumonia? In elucidating such terms as these, it may be of the utmost importance to find the right paradigm.

Examples can be enormously helpful in elucidating meanings; but they are seldom sufficient by themselves. Even to cite an example—even to make clear what we are pointing at when we point—we have to use words. An example of cognitive dissonance or moral turpitude or connotation will be a great deal more illuminating if we can comment on it and say what is crucial and what is irrelevant in it. Not long ago, the adjective "camp" came to be widely used among the avant-garde. It was something of a catch-all term, and when you asked people what it meant, the usual response was to give examples: the movie *Golddiggers of 1933,* Andy Warhol's eight-hour movie *Sleep,* pop art, feather boas, Batman comic books, Noel Coward—all were said to be "camp." With such a heterogeneous collection, it would be difficult for the uninitiated to discover what it is that they all have in common, but it seemed that what the camp experts found in them was something like "being so bad it's good," that is, being so vulgar, bizarre, tasteless, blatant, outrageous, or whatever, that it can (somehow) be enjoyed just for its sheer badness. I don't know whether this fuller elucidation actually cleared up the concept, but at least it helped to fix some meaning for the term. And without the verbal aids, the examples would be of limited help.

Verbal elucidation may take a number of forms. Sometimes we explain certain aspects of the *usage* of a term, without attempting to give its full meaning. We say, for example, that Priscilla is a girl's name; or that "migrate" is used for groups of people, but not for individual people; or that "Damn!" is an expletive generally evincing anger or annoyance. Sometimes it is helpful to say something about the *origin* of a term. The term "mundialization" has been coined for the effort to persuade political units to commit themselves to the principle of world federalism; the meaning is at least partly elucidated by pointing out that the term derives etymologically from the Latin "mundus" (world). To one who knows Greek, the word "triskidekaphobia" obviously means "fear of the number thirteen." This, of course, does not imply that etymology is always a safe guide to meaning; "camp" derives ultimately from Latin "campus" (field), but it doesn't follow that things that are camp are always connected with a field. Again, we may point out that a word is a portmanteau word that has been coined by piecing together others—that "Comsymp" combines the first syllables of "Communist" and "sympathizer," rather than "commendable" and "symptom."

But the most important kind of verbal elucidation is the *defini-*

tion. As we have already seen, the characteristics designated by a term (in a given context) are those characteristics that anything must have in order for the term to be correctly applied to them (in that context). And when two terms have the same designation (that is, necessary conditions) in a certain range of contexts, they are synonymous in those contexts. A **definition**, as this term is used in this book, is a rule of synonymy. It can be formulated in somewhat the way we might formulate the rules of a card game or the rules of a tennis tournament:

"Iamb" *to have the same designation as* "foot consisting of a short syllable followed by a long one."

This may be written more briefly with a colon:

"Iamb": "foot consisting of a short syllable followed by a long one."

There are several points to notice about this definition (which is offered as a paradigm, but is not expected to be self-explanatory). First, it consists of two parts, the term whose meaning is in question or in doubt and is to be elucidated (this is the **term to be defined**), and the term that is offered as synonymous with the first term and is assumed to be more familiar or more explicit (this is the **defining term**). The definition is not a statement about these two terms (the verb is in the infinitive), but gives a rule about the relationship of the two terms. A different definition would give a different rule, for example:

"Iamb": "syllogism one of whose premises is unstated."

Note that both the term to be defined and the defining term are put inside quotation marks. That is because the definition is not, strictly speaking, about *things*, but about *words* and their meanings. Definitions in dictionaries do not use quotation marks, but a different convention; they put the term to be defined in boldface type. Nor do they use a special symbol of synonymy, but simply list one or more defining terms after the term to be defined. A definition does not only elucidate the meaning of the term to be defined (if you are already familiar with the defining term); it is also a rule of substitution. Given any true statement containing either of these terms, the definition allows us to substitute the other. By our first definition, if we can say:

His verse contains nothing but *iambs*,

then we can say:

> His verse contains nothing but *feet consisting of a short syllable followed by a long one.*

By our second definition, if we can say:

> His first argument was a *syllogism one of whose premises is unstated,*

then we can say:

> His first argument was an *iamb.*

True, no one will know that these pairs of statements say the same thing unless he knows the relevant rule of synonymy, and in this case the first rule of synonymy is much more familiar than the second (which was only invented for this discussion). We will consider the importance of this distinction shortly. But at the moment, what is to be noted especially is that, because a definition is a rule of substitution as well as a rule of elucidation, the two terms in it must be put in parallel grammatical form, as far as possible, so that their substitutability is plain. It won't do to write a definition like

> "Unwitting": "when you don't know that something is true."

For then the substitution makes nonsense:

> The taxi driver was an *unwitting* accomplice in the burglary.
>
> The taxi driver was a *when you don't know that something is true* accomplice in the burglary.

We must not expect of a definition more than it can provide; bear in mind that a definition does not tell the whole story about the meaning of a term. Its job is to mark off the designation, or *a* designation; it says nothing about the connotation of the term. When we explicate a poem and bring out the richness of connotation and suggestion, we are elucidating meaning but we are not giving a definition—indeed, we must already know the relevant definitions before we begin to explicate. And this is why metaphorical terms cannot figure in definitions. For what the metaphor means, it means through its connotation, and it would be confusing to lay down a rule connecting the designation of a literal term to be defined with the connotation of a metaphorical defining term. That is what is wrong with a "definition" such as:

> "Faith": "the candle that lights the way through the gloom of skepticism."

This may (or may not) be an illuminating *description* of faith, but it is by no means a definition of the *word* "faith."

A rule of synonymy is like any other rule: you can either follow it or refuse to follow it, depending on your needs and purposes. It may be adopted by a large number of people, and become a general practice; or it may be employed briefly, for some special momentary purpose, as in a particular essay or act of Congress. Moreover—again as with any other rule—there are two ways in which a definition can be introduced into a discourse, and this distinction is an important one. We may introduce a definition in order to report or describe a rule of synonymy that is actually followed by some group of people: in that case, let us say we have a **definition report.** Or we may introduce a definition in order to propose or suggest a *new* rule we would like to follow ourselves, or like others to follow: in that case, let us say we have a **definition proposal.**

A dictionary, of course, does more than give definitions; its primary function is to give definition reports. When it defines "iamb," it says, in effect, that this is the way the term "iamb" is used by English-speaking people. Moreover, it may indicate the range of contexts in which a term is used in a certain sense (this is the *scope* of the definition): "heraldry," "medicine," "zoology," "architecture." Thus the definition report about "iamb" is a statement about the way this word is actually used in discourses on prosody. It says that among prosodists, such-and-such a rule is generally followed. And so the definition report may be put this way:

> "Iamb" (in prosody) *has the same designation as* "foot consisting of a short syllable followed by a long one."

This, of course, is a statement, and in fact a true one. Compare:

> "Iamb" (in logic) *has the same designation as* "syllogism one of whose premises is unstated."

This is also a statement, but it is false; at least, so far as I know, "iamb" has never been used by any logician to mean a syllogism with a suppressed premise.

For convenience, let us use the equal-sign as an abbreviation for "has the same designation as." Then the true definition report above can be written:

> "Iamb" (in prosody) = "foot consisting of a short syllable followed by a long one."

"Iamb" happens to be used only in prosody, so the scope of its definition does not need to be specified, as it would if the word were variable in meaning and meant something else to a carpenter, a mathematician, a sports-car enthusiast, or a surfer.

To report existing usage is one thing: to *change* existing usage quite another. Although we cannot say that "iamb" has an established meaning in logic, we could *give* it a meaning if it were convenient for our present purposes. For example, we could write:

> "Iamb" (in *Thinking Straight*) *shall have the same designation as* "syllogism one of whose premises is unstated."

Let us use a variant of the equal-sign as an abbreviation for "shall have the same designation as":

> "Iamb" (in *Thinking Straight*) ≈ "syllogism one of whose premises is unstated."

In this context, "shall" has the force of an imperative—it is like saying,

> *Let* "iamb" (in *Thinking Straight*) *have the same designation as* "syllogism one of whose premises is unstated."

This definition proposal does not merely present a rule, or describe its employment, but establishes it—at least in this book. The question is always open as to how far a writer can go in determining other people's usage. If an author declared that henceforth, in the usage of all logicians, "iamb" shall have this meaning, his commandment might fall flat—unless he happened to be an absolute dictator. For other logicians, even if they are fortunate enough to read his book, may feel that there is no need for this term (since they already have the term "enthymeme" for the same thing). Or they may believe that even if there is a need for *some* term, this one is not suitable. Sometimes it is better to coin a new term for a new concept (say, "one-legged syllogism" or "yllogism") than to give a new sense to a term that already has a fixed and familiar sense. Of course, if the definition proposal is found useful and appropriate, it may catch on—as other technical terms invented or adopted by earlier logicians have now become standard.

But an author has dominion over his own book, and if he stipulates that a particular term shall have a particular meaning, then his reader will either have to go along with him or abandon the book. Let us imagine that you came across this paragraph:

> The iamb can be troublesome, unless the missing ingredient is supplied, and this can always be done by applying the syllogistic rules to see what is necessary to transform the iamb into a valid argument.

The only way you could make sense out of this is to go along—however reluctantly—with the definition proposal that "In the present work 'iamb' shall have the same designation as 'syllogism one of whose premises is unstated.' " When you follow this rule, the paragraph is fine; without it, it is baffling. You can curse the author for introducing unnecessary technical terms, and you can resolve never to use this term in this sense in your own writing. But the freedom to introduce definition proposals is one of the prerogatives of authorship. Without it, as will be more evident later, many valuable words would have been lost to our language, and many discourses would be much longer and more confusing than they are.

A Check-up Quiz Which of the following sentences are definition reports? Which are definition proposals?

1. A landlord is a leech with property.
2. Capitalism is a social order in which the individual has the inherent right to own property and capital and the right to pass it on to his children and others.
3. To goof is to make a silly but not costly mistake.
4. In television, the hard sell is Dristan and drain your sinus cavities; the soft sell is Phil Silvers doing the Pontiac commercial.
5. A principle is a rule of inaction giving valid general reasons for not doing in specific instances what to unprincipled instinct would seem to be right.
6. A cyclone is called a "hurricane" in the West Indies, and it is called a "typhoon" around China and Japan.
7. In Mozart's time, the line between a "symphony" and a "divertimento" was not sharp, but divertimenti generally had more movements than symphonies (note the extra slow movement in K. 132).
8. Featherbedding is the bedding down of oneself with feathers taken coercively from others and with nothing whatever given in exchange.
9. Featherbedding is the practice of limiting work or output in order to provide more jobs and prevent unemployment.

10. What I call "jazz" is music that has (a) hot intonation, (b) polyrhythm, (c) polyphony.

For Further Study Hugh R. Walpole, *Semantics,* Ch. 6. New York: W. W. Norton & Company, Inc., 1941. Nicholas Rescher, *Introduction to Logic,* Ch. 3. New York: St. Martin's Press, Inc., 1964.

§19. testing a definition report

A definition report not only presents a rule of synonymy, but states that this rule has actually been adopted by a certain group of people for a certain range of discourses. It reports usage—and it may do so correctly or incorrectly. Our acceptance of that report may affect our own usage, and if it is incorrect, we may find ourselves failing to communicate. So it may be a matter of some importance to test the definition report ourselves.

Before we try to test a definition report, we must of course be clear about its scope. It may be a regional term:

> "Rug" (in United States conversations and writings) = "thick fabric used as floor covering."

But:

> "Rug" (in British conversation and writings) = "blanket" (in United States conversations and writings).

It may be a technical term of a science or art or craft:

> "Bus conductor" (in transportation) = "person who collects fares on buses."
>
> "Bus conductor" (in electrical engineering) = "electrical conductor forming a common junction between one or more incoming circuits and one or more outgoing circuits through which current is transferred with negligible loss over relatively short distances." (See the *Alcoa Aluminum Bus Conductor Handbook,* 1957.)

Once we settle the scope of a definition, we can proceed to test it. It is not hard to say what a complete definition of a term, in one of its senses, would be. The defining term would designate exactly the characteristics included in the designation of the term to be defined, no more, no less. Thus if the term to be defined is "aunt," the designation of this term, in its usual sense, can be broken down into two characteristics: (1) being a female, and (2) being related to someone in either of two ways: (a) by being the sister of a parent or (b) by being the wife of a parent's brother. (The second characteristic is a disjunctive one: being *either* a parent's sister *or* a parent's sister-in-law.) Characteristics (1) and (2) are not only necessary characteristics of the term "aunt," but also sufficient characteristics—together, they are enough to make an aunt an aunt.

When the term to be defined and the defining term actually have the same designation, then they have the same comprehension: all aunts, and only aunts, are females who are either a parent's sister or a parent's sister-in-law. It does not follow, of course, that if two terms have the same comprehension, then they necessarily have the same designation: compare "sizeable satellite of Earth (excluding the moon)" with "artificial object in elliptical orbit around earth." All the sizeable nonlunar satellites may be in fact artificial objects in elliptical orbits, and vice versa—but these two terms do not have the same designation. A comparison of the comprehensions of two terms gives us only a negative check on the correctness of a definition—but that check is useful, nevertheless.

Suppose we use a circle of circles to represent the comprehension of the term to be defined, and a circle of crosses to represent the comprehension of the defining term:

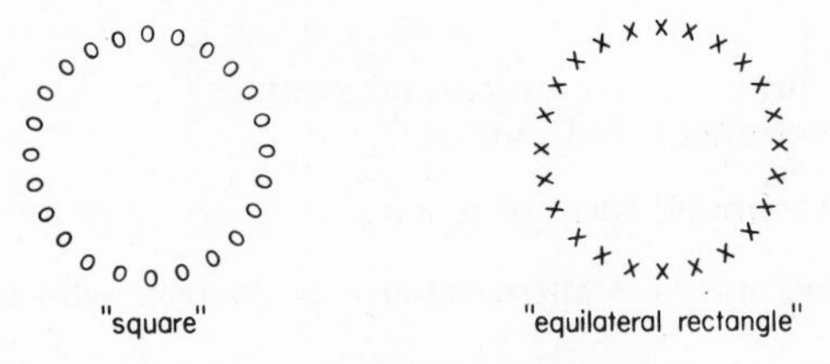

Then in a correct definition, the two circles will coincide:

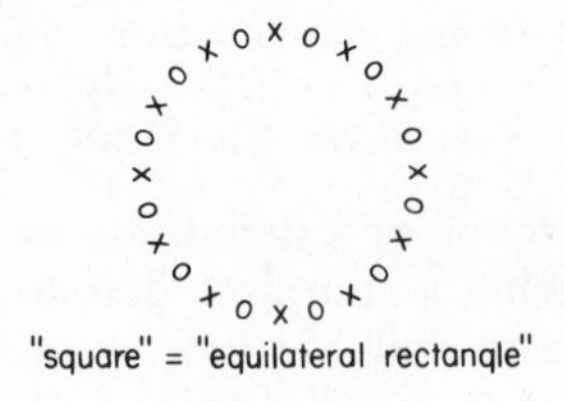

There are evidently two ways in which a definition report can go wrong. (1) If the comprehension of the defining term includes some things that are not in the comprehension of the term to be defined, then the definition is too *broad.* (2) If the comprehension of the defining term leaves out some things that *are* in the comprehension of the term to be defined, then the definition is too *narrow.* (As these two rules are stated here, a definition may be both too broad and too narrow.)

Suppose, for example, someone offers the following definition report of the term "compass," in one of its senses:

> "Compass" (in draftsman's language) = "device for describing a circle."

Is this correct? We first try to think whether there are, or could be, any devices for describing circles that would not be called compasses. For example, one can make a passable circle by tying a string to a pencil, fastening the string at some point, and moving the pencil around at the end of a string. Is this a compass? Would a draftsman call it a compass? Probably not—it is more like a substitute for one. Therefore, this definition is too broad; the defining term is too inclusive.

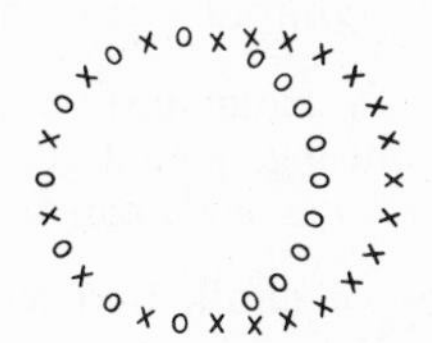

We repair an overinclusive definition by adding more restrictions to the defining term, so that it will mark out a smaller comprehension. Thus, we might try the following definition report instead:

> "Compass" (in draftsman's language) = "device for describing a circle, consisting of two straight legs joined at the top by a pivot."

Again, we ask: can we think of any actual or possible devices that would fit this description and yet not be a compass? It doesn't seem so. Therefore, the definition is at least not too broad. But now we must apply the second test: can we think of any compasses that do *not* fit this description? Well, there is the so-called "beam compass," in which the two legs are connected by a long bar, so that large circles can be drawn. Here the legs are straight, but they are not directly joined. This definition is too narrow; the defining term is too exclusive:

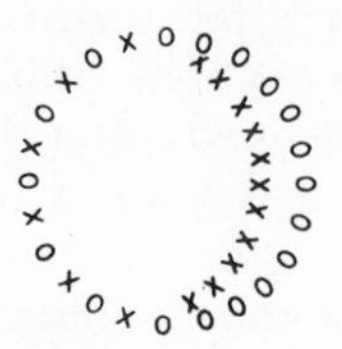

To correct this definition, we must relax the requirements set forth in the defining term, leave out the reference to being joined by a pivot. Nor does it seem essential that the legs should be straight. All the compasses we have ever seen may have straight legs, but suppose someone made an instrument that was exactly like a compass, and worked very well, except that the legs were bowed like a wishbone: would we call that a compass? Why not? Here we tread on the borders of the concept, and perhaps we should take care not to be dogmatic about it. It does seem that, as the word is generally used, a compass need not have absolutely straight legs—but it must have stiff legs, and they must be connected at one end. So perhaps we can be content with this definition report:

> "Compass" (in draftsman's language) = "device for describing a circle, consisting of two stiff legs joined at one end in such a way that the distance between the other ends can be adjusted."

(A wishbone with a piece of chalk tied to one leg can be used as a compass, but not being adjustable, it is not really a compass—or so it could be claimed.)

Of course, the example is somewhat artificial, since we would seldom need to be so fussy about a term like this one—though it is possible to imagine situations in which a decision about the exact definition might be crucial. Does a rocket missile fall under the accepted definition of "air weapon"? The Air Force has set some store by the claim that it does. Is a motorized wheelchair or golf cart a "motor vehicle"? It may make a considerable difference in the number of regulations that apply to it—concerning registration, periodic inspections, and whether it has to be equipped with a horn.

The two tests of a definition report also apply, of course, when we construct our own definition reports. Say that we are interested in the noun "executive." What is an executive? Or what does "executive" mean? These are two distinct questions, though they are connected. If we succeed in giving a definition report, we will answer the question about what "executive" means. Anyone who asks what an executive *is* may really be asking for a definition report. But he may be content with something less. At the very least, he is asking for some directions he can use in distinguishing executives from nonexecutives; he wants to be able to tell who is, and who is not, an executive—as far as the application of this term is fixed in general usage. Now, when we try to decide whether a given person is or is not an executive, we look for certain typical characteristics that mark the executive: let us call them *criteria* of executiveness, or criteria for the application of the term "executive." And we might well begin our search for a definition report by running over in our minds the criteria of executiveness.

One can think of quite a few. For example:

sitting behind a desk in an office
giving orders
receiving reports
being well dressed
being well paid
playing golf
having ulcers
having a secretary
administering the activities of a group of people
having name on door
having rug on floor

Any one of the characteristics might, in some circumstances, help you to tell whether someone was an executive or not; this is what is meant by calling them "criteria." But obviously if we picked out a handful of them for a defining term, we could easily wind up with a definition that is both too broad and too narrow:

"Executive" = "well-dressed person with ulcers who sits behind a desk."

The comprehensions of these terms do not coincide at all.

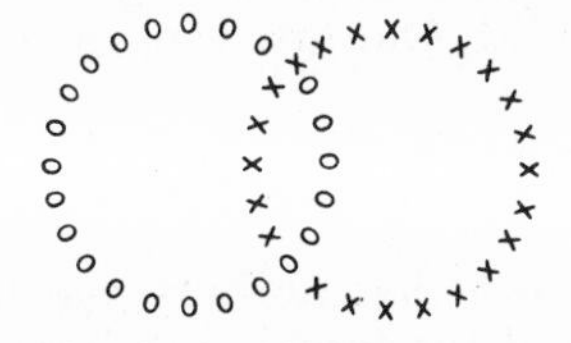

As we go down the list, we ask whether each criterion is necessary: whether a person without that characteristic could be called an "executive," whether it would seem odd or incorrect to call him that.

And most of these characteristics are clearly not necessary—a person can be an executive even if he is free of ulcers, dresses poorly, hates golf, and is secretaryless. But he can't be an executive unless he occupies a certain position in relation to some group of people who take orders from him; he can't be an executive without having the responsibility to direct certain of their activities and without having some power to see that his instructions are carried out. Is this still too broad? Would a teacher, a sergeant in the Marines, an intern in a hospital, be an executive according to this definition? A teacher is not an executive, because he belongs to an institution whose function is to teach; he becomes an administrator to the extent to which he gives up teaching himself and supervises others who teach, and he is an executive when his main activity is not teaching but administering. A sergeant is not an executive, because he not only orders marches, but goes on them. An intern is not an executive, because he is practicing medicine, whereas the hospital administrator only coordinates the activities of others. We might say, then, that an organization has a "primary function," which is performed by some of its members. With the help of that concept we can write:

> "Executive" = "person in an organization who does not perform the primary function of that organization, but has the responsibility of directing others in performing that function and the authority to exact compliance with his directions."

This may seem like a good deal of trouble to go to in clarifying the meaning of this term. But the effort is instructive if it brings out some of the difficulties in giving a definition report. Sometimes we can work our way through to a *complete definition,* in which the defining term lists all the necessary characteristics. Sometimes we have to be content with a *partial definition,* and this may be very helpful, as long as we realize its limitations. For example, if we were asked to define the term "compass," not in the draftsman's sense but in the explorer's sense, we might not be sure how many necessary conditions to list. Our first venture might be:

> "Compass" (in explorer's language) = "instrument for determining directions by means of a magnetized needle."

We might feel quite sure that nothing can correctly be called a compass (in this sense of the term) if it doesn't have a magnetized needle that indicates north, and thus provides some information about directions. Are there any other necessary characteristics? Does it have to be of a certain size, shape, or construction? We may not know how to answer these questions. So our definition as it stands may be too broad. Yet the information it gives is by no means useless, if we don't claim that it is a definition.

In that case, we may give valuable, though incomplete, information about the word, in two parts. We may say (1) that "compass" designates *at least* the following characteristics: being an instrument for determining directions by means of a magnetized needle. And we may add (2) that compasses are *usually* round, with a central pivot on which the needle can rotate freely; that they *generally* have the points of the compass marked out on their face; that they are *mostly* either small and made to carry in a pocket or large and fixed in position, as on a ship, and so forth. These words "usually," "generally," "mostly," which occur frequently in dictionaries, indicate that these characteristics are criteria for the term, without being necessary characteristics. Dictionary definitions of animal names often give several nonnecessary criteria:

> Lion, *n.* A large carnivorous mammal of the cat family, inhabiting sandy or rocky wastes of Africa and southern Asia.

Being a mammal, and being a member of the cat family, are necessary characteristics; but a dwarf lion, if one should be born, would still be a lion; and the lions that inhabit the Bronx Zoo are still lions.

To construct a definition report in the most orderly, and therefore the safest, way, then, we first consider the various criteria that come to mind when we use the term we are defining; we next try them out individually to select the necessary characteristics; and we build up the defining term piece by piece from these necessary characteristics. If we can satisfy ourselves at some stage that we have *all* the necessary characteristics, then we have the ingredients of a complete definition. And this is quite feasible for many of the words in our language, especially those used in special fields where there has been an incentive to fix their designations rather carefully. Many of our words in ordinary language—for example, "chair"—will not be susceptible of such a final definition. We may be quite sure that nothing can be a chair unless it has at least a fairly level surface at least wide enough to accommodate a person who sits on it. But that is not enough to make a chair. What else is needed? Different characteristics in different cases. When we call some objects "chairs," it is partly because we note that they have legs and backs; when we call other objects "chairs," despite the fact that they have no legs at all, it may be partly because they have backs; and if we call still other objects "chairs," though they have hardly any back to speak of, it is because they have legs and a wide seat. We know what the criteria are, but some of the main criteria do not seem to be really necessary; and this reflects a general looseness or variability of the term as it is actually used. As long as we remain lexicographers, limited to reporting prevailing usage, we can go no further. But, if we turn from recording meaning to making meaning—from definition reporting to definition proposing—there *is* something else we can do. We will consider this in the next section.

A Check-up Quiz Determine whether the following definitions are too broad or too narrow or both (or neither).

1. "House" = "instrument for providing shelter and living space on a continuing basis."
2. "Hole" = "cavity."
3. "Logic textbook" = "instrument for teaching logic."
4. "Barn" = "house for sheltering livestock and/or storing food."
5. "Dependent" = "person to whose support one makes a substantial contribution."
6. "Letter" = "written communication of more than a few sentences, sent through the mail."
7. "Square number" = "number that is the product of some other number multiplied by itself."
8. "Golf" = "game played with golf clubs and golf balls."
9. "Ounce" = "fraction of a quart."
10. "Typewriter" = "manually operated keyboard machine that prints letters by striking through an inked ribbon."

For Further Study Morris Cohen and Ernest Nagel, *An Introduction to Logic and Scientific Method,* Ch. 2, Sec. 2. New York: Harcourt, Brace & World, Inc., 1934. Roger Brown, *Words and Things,* "Introduction." New York: Free Press of Glencoe, Inc., 1958.

§20. the use and abuse of definitions

Although we sometimes do have occasion, when we are called upon to make ourselves understood, to offer complete or partial definition reports, it is seldom that we are *merely* interested in giving information about other people's customary verbal usage. Even if we report one of the senses of a word—for example, that "federal government" is sometimes used to mean a political system in which the powers to be exercised by the central government are specified and all residual powers are left to the regional governments—the aim is generally to single out that sense for special attention, to note (in case there might be ambiguity) that this is the sense in which we wish the term to be understood. When a definition occurs in the context of a serious exposition or argument—not at large, as in a dictionary—it is generally more than a report; it is also a producer of clarity (or unclarity, as the case may be).

This is even more obviously true of those definitions that are introduced as explicit proposals for new usage. A definition proposal may forestall ambiguity throughout a discourse by simply stipulating that only one sense is to be permitted; in effect, it says, "Never mind what the contexts may be from here on, or what other senses they might permit; in this essay, 'federal government' is to mean a central government that deals directly with individual people, not merely by way of the regional governments." A definition proposal may give a special precision to a term that remains vague in ordinary speech:

> "Unemployed person" ≈ "person who does not hold a regular full-time or part-time job and who demonstrably is hunting a job by applying at a state office or a factory, or by answering a want-ad."

This last clause, which the Department of Labor includes in its definition, diminishes the vagueness of "hunting for a job" (How hard is he hunting? How *recently* has he hunted?).

A definition proposal may borrow a familiar word (or part of one) and assign it a wholly new sense for which some word is needed. A good example is the word "destruct" in the astronaut's lingo, which means "the deliberate destruction of a rocket or space vehicle after it has been launched." Bergen Evans has commented interestingly upon this word, in *The New York Times Magazine:*

> This is a word needed in the most serious emergencies and in split-second urgency. It had, therefore, to be clear and unequivocal. It had to be a word not in common use lest its common meaning lead to some confusion. But it had to be sufficiently close to a common word to convey its meaning instantaneously. "Destruct" is a good coinage—though it has agitated many who feel that it is "bad English." How-

ever, it may engender bad English, since it is being used around the missile bases—I am told—as a synonym for "destroy." Thus a missileer's missus may say, "I've got to destruct all that stuff cluttering up the attic."

A definition proposal may introduce a new word for the new meaning that requires to be marked. Thus "cyborg" has been coined to refer to human beings who are benefited by nonliving devices that keep them comfortable, healthy, or even alive—such as the electric pacemaker for heart patients. And the word "snoof" has been brought forth (by an analogy with "deaf") to describe someone who is devoid of, or deficient in, the sense of smell.

A definition proposal, not being a statement about anything, is of course neither true nor false; it can't be refuted, and it can't be proved, for it is basically a decision to use a word one way rather than another for certain purposes in certain contexts. That does not make it immune to criticism, however. In the context of an argument in which certain premises are assumed or certain evidence is given, a definition proposal may carry with it important consequences. It makes a difference how you define "amateur" in sports, if you have a regulation by the Amateur Athletic Union that only amateurs can take part in the Olympics. It makes a difference, if you are working for conservation of natural resources, whether you define "conservation" narrowly as simply the preservation of areas from commercial development or more broadly as the allocation of areas (for commercial use, for recreation, or whatever) in such a way that their values will not be wasted. It made a great difference to the Tuscarora Indians of New York State in 1960, when the Supreme Court ruled that their land was not a "reservation" within the meaning of the "artificial" definition in the Federal Power Act, because the land was owned by the tribe, rather than held in trust by the federal government. For it meant that the New York Power Authority could seize the land on which they had lived since 1775 and use it for the Niagara Power Project. Definition proposals can have consequences.

And this is what makes them so valuable when they are properly used, and so harmful when they are misused. The troubles to which definition proposals (and, in some cases, definition reports) are susceptible are of various sorts. Much could be said about them, but we shall have to be satisfied with a fairly brief look here.

We may begin by noting that definitions, by their very nature, are not isolated pieces of language. If we define "*X*" in terms of "*Y*," we may take it for granted that the meaning of "*Y*" is already sufficiently understood. If it is not, we must supply a further definition of "*Y*." The official NCAA football rules lay down a large number of definition proposals at the start, for example:

"Catch" ≈ "act of establishing player-possession of a live ball in flight."

This technical sense of "catch" evidently presupposes a technical definition of "live ball," which is thoughtfully supplied:

"Live ball" ≈ "ball in play."

The term "in play" is not explicitly defined, but, its meaning is given by a set of rules that are presented later. Without those rules, the definitions would leave something to be desired, for the technical sense of "in play" cannot be understood from ordinary English usage. A little *Dictionary of Politics* that came out some years ago defines "McCarthyism" as "intolerance of liberalism"; but unhappily the dictionary does not define "liberalism," though this is a word that is certainly in need of some restriction upon its possible meanings.

In extended discourses, then, we are often faced with a set of definitions in which some build upon others; the more complex concepts are explained in terms of the simpler concepts that enter into them. If the set is logically worked out, some of the terms will be *basic* to it—that is, they will not be defined in that set, but their meaning will be taken for granted. The other terms will be defined by means of the basic terms. If, on the other hand, the writer does not decide definitely which of his terms are to be basic and which defined, his set can easily fall into one of the logical errors of definition, namely, *circularity*.

Circularity can occur in a single definition, though it is perhaps unlikely to fool anyone who looks at the definition carefully. One can say, truthfully, that "a man's liberty ends where another man's liberty begins"; but if this were to be put as a definition of "liberty"

"Liberty": "range of activity that does not interfere with the liberty of another,"

it would be quite useless. For no one who didn't already know what "liberty" meant would be enlightened by the definition; and anyone who did already know, wouldn't need it. There is a pretense at defining, but not the substance of it. A **circular definition** is one in which the whole of the term to be defined appears in the defining term. But we must not be in too much of a hurry to condemn a definition.

"Landscape" (in fine arts): "painting of a landscape."

Since the word "landscape" has two different senses here, we can say that there are really two different terms; the definition is somewhat puzzling, but not circular. And

"Psalmist": "writer or composer of psalms."

is not circular, providing "psalm" is defined without reference to "psalmist."

There is greater danger in a set of definitions, where the defining process can go around in a circle unnoticed—and the larger the circle, the more difficult it is to see what is going on. A little pamphlet called *Space Talk: A Down to Earth Glossary of Astronautical Terms,* published by one of the aviation companies, gives this definition on page 16:

REACTION ENGINE. An engine in which thrust is generated by expelling a stream of moving particles rearwards.

And this definition on page 18:

THRUST. The propelling force exerted in a reaction engine by its exhaust.

It seems that you have to know what "thrust" means before you can understand what "reaction engine" means, and also vice versa. When we substitute the defining terms for the terms to be defined, we find that each definition in the set becomes circular. For example, if we use the second definition to expand the first one, we get:

"Reaction engine" (in astronautics): "engine in which the *propelling force exerted in a reaction engine by its exhaust* is generated by expelling a stream of moving particles rearwards."

As a matter of fact, this substitution shows that the circularity in this little set could be avoided by some rewording, without losing any sense. We could write:

"Reaction engine": "engine in which the thrust is generated by expelling a stream of moving particles rearwards."

"Thrust": "propelling force exerted by exhaust."

A second, and less frequent, way in which definitions may go wrong is by leading into a contradiction. An **inconsistent definition** is one in which the defining term contains logically incompatible predicates.

"Squound": "round square."

An inconsistently defined term can have no application, since it is logically impossible for anything to belong to its comprehension. Such a definition is not likely to occur except through ignorance of the meaning of some word, or through a careless pursuit of grammatical analogies, as in this interesting case:

"Underachiever": "pupil who does not perform as well as he can."
"Overachiever": "pupil who performs better than he can."

The second definition is plainly inconsistent.

It is easier to fall into inconsistency in developing a set of definitions. You can, if you like, define:

"Novelette": "short novel";

but then you can't define:

"Novel": "long work of prose fiction."

For then, if you substitute the defining term of the second definition in the first definition, you get the inconsistency:

"Novelette": "short *long work of prose fiction.*"

You may argue that there is only an apparent contradiction here, since "long" and "short" originally had different contexts (a short novelette isn't the same length as a short novel). But if "short" means, say, under 20,000 words, and "long" means 20,000 words or over, there is a contradiction. However, it can easily be avoided by correcting the first definition. What this pair of definitions does is divide prose fictions into two subclasses:

"Novelette": "short work of prose fiction."
"Novel": "long work of prose fiction."

That is the correct way to put it.

One who makes definition proposals claims the freedom to change language to suit his own ends, and this freedom carries with it certain responsibilities. By all odds the chief among them is the duty to stick by his own rules, once he has laid them down. If he insists on giving a new sense to a particular word, then he must continue, throughout his discourse, to use it in this sense; he must not fall back on the usual sense when it suits him, or lead us to confuse the new sense with the old one. Whether through unscrupulousness or carelessness—whether fooling others or fooling himself—the definition proposer sometimes falls into a fallacy. Aiming to prove a particular statement, but not finding adequate deductive or inductive support, he introduces a definition proposal that makes the statement *appear* to be true, though it is not. In short, he introduces a **question-begging definition.**

There are two distinguishable ways of doing this, and it is well to note the difference. Suppose the conclusion to be proved is of the form "*A* is *B*"—never mind for the moment whether it is all or some or one. One device is to redefine the subject-term "*A*" in such a way that, by the new definition proposal, it *is* true that *A* is *B*. As long as it is made perfectly clear that *A* is *B* only in the new sense of "*A*," there is no deception. The writer may say:

> For my special purposes, I am redefining the term "federal government"; and by my new sense it becomes true that federal governments may have unlimited powers. This does *not* follow from the usual sense, in which federal governments must have limited powers. . . .

Of course, we may wonder why he goes to all this trouble to change the meaning of a perfectly good word, rather than find or invent another word: it is a somewhat arbitrary procedure. But there is no confusion in it.

However, suppose we read in a letter to the editor:

> I wish Senator Douglas would define monopoly. One might well say that the ministerial profession is a monopoly because no one except a minister is a minister. Certainly no one except a lawyer is a lawyer, therefore the ministry and the legal professions are monopolies.

We need not inquire what meaning Senator Douglas's original book review gave to the word "monopoly"; in any case, it is clear what this correspondent is doing. In opposition to the senator, he wants to argue (the conclusion is only suggested) that monopolies are not against the public interest. But instead of presenting evidence based on economic studies, he turns to the word "monopoly" itself and offers a new and very broad definition proposal, with the casual words "one might well say." According to *his* definition, a group of people have a monopoly if no one who is not a member of the group is a member of the group. This makes the word apply to *every* group of people, as he suggests, and since there are many groups of people whose existence does not conflict with the public interest, the generalization which is his implicit conclusion is apparently supported. This is a lesson in how to prove something without giving any reason: it is done by verbal sleight-of-hand; you merely make it true by redefinition.

The second device for "proving" that *A* is *B* by a question-begging definition is to redefine the predicate-term "*B*" instead of "*A*." Again, a careful writer who introduces a new sense of "*B*" may point out that by his new definition proposal, *A* turns out to be *B*.

> Perhaps you people didn't know it, but by our new enlarged definition of "depressed area," you are living in a depressed area. This of course makes you eligible for special funds. . . .

We might not object to being redefined into such benefits. In any case, it is made perfectly clear that a meaning is being changed, and why. But consider:

> Traditionally, creation was God's act in bringing the world into being, or, following Genesis, giving form to chaos. One unabridged dictionary gives as its first meaning of "creation": "the act of creating from nothing; the act of causing to exist; and especially, the act of bringing the world into existence."
>
> A change has occurred. Nowadays all sorts of undertakings are described as being creative. There are courses in creative writing in colleges, books on creative thinking, and the rest. "Creativity" is the O.K. word. Invention, discovery, innovation, artistic endeavor and social thought are now called "creative." And what is involved here is not just a matter of semantics. If merely producing or altering something, like painting a painting or thinking up a new (and probably useless) law, is creation, then man becomes equal to God, and the concept of man embodied in pseudophilosophies like pragmatism, positivism, existentialism, scientism, and the rest seem to be vindicated.

This writer is objecting to what he considers to be a question-begging definition. He says that modern thinkers (beginning with the Romantic period) have introduced a new and very broad definition of "create," which was not the original (theological) sense, and have thereby made it seem plausible that man is a creative being. Now this charge might be sustained if it were leveled at those who first made this definition proposal—providing they did not make clear that they believed man to be creative only in their new sense, which is different from divine creation. But once the broad sense of "creation" has become a standard sense—simply one of the designations of the term, which the unabridged dictionary also includes—then it is not the pragmatists, and so forth, but rather this writer, who may be in the position of offering a question-begging definition. For his argument can be put this way:

> I insist that there is only one proper sense of "create," and I propose that we keep to this one. It follows that only God creates, and therefore, the pragmatists are wrong when they speak of man as "creative."

The equivocation is apparent in this form, for the sense in which the pragmatists assert that man is creative is not the sense in which the writer denies that man is creative.

Since, as this writer remarks, "creative" is an O.K. word, there are elements of a further complexity in this example—though another example will bring them out more fully. Sometimes in the second form of question-begging definition, the redefined predicate "*B*" has a marked emotive force, positive or negative. Then what happens is this: In the original, or usual, sense of "*B*," *A* is not *B* at all. "*B*" is now given a new sense, and in this sense it means something a good deal less emotion-evoking (less admirable or less detestable) than what it meant before. But the writer keeps that old emotive force alive, so that when we accept his "proof" (by definition) that *A* is *B*, we find ourselves nudged toward approval or disapproval of *A* by means of the emotive force of "*B*." This is called a **persuasive definition.**

Here is an example:

> Modern psychiatry, among its many other benefits, has given us a broader conception of human behavior and human nature. In line with its work, I believe we should define "mental health" and "mental illness" so that they take into account the important factors. A man, for example, may be angrily opposed to racial equality, world government, public housing, and the preaching of the social gospel rather than salvational religion. Such people may appear "normal" to the untutored eye, in the sense that they can hold a job and preserve their status by exchanging their feelings with like-minded people; but they are actually well along the road toward mental illness, which I define as "a state of insecurity and fear marked by unusual opposition to social welfare and international cooperation."

Again, it may be up to the writer if he wants to adopt this broad definition of "mental illness," making political attitudes, rather than more strictly specified clinical manifestations, the marks of mental illness. But it amounts to calling anyone who happens to disagree with his own political and social views "mentally ill." The trick is that they *are* mentally ill by his new definition (if we allow him to get away with it), but that is a comparatively harmless charge, if "mental illness" is taken so broadly; the harm comes in because the old meaning of "mental illness" is not really wiped out, and the old negative emotive force is still active.

We must not conclude, of course, that all definitions, or even redefinitions, of emotive terms involve this fallacy. A newspaper might editorialize:

> A demagogue is one who, in disregard of truth and order, seeks to enflame mass passions to his own advantage by appeals to irrational prejudice. This is precisely what the president of the City Council is doing, and he is a demagogue.

This is a quite good definition report of "demagogue"—not a new definition proposal. So there is nothing question-begging about it. The political dictionary mentioned previously has an interesting entry on

> TERRORIST . . . The word is often used by the supporters of a particular regime to describe and to vilify any of its opponents who resort to acts of violence.

This seems to say that anyone who calls someone a "terrorist" must be guilty of persuasive definition, and hence of name-calling. But what else *can* a regime call a terrorist (asked W. S. Schlamm in the *National Review*) if not "terrorist"? No doubt "terrorist," like other highly charged words, lends itself readily to the persuasive form of definitional question-begging. By arbitrarily broadening the sense a little, say to include "cryptoterrorists," one could get to apply this word, with all its emotive force, to pacifist picketers, members of rifle clubs, and the most sincere followers of various Christian crusades.

Our defense against these verbal ploys is, as always, to keep our eye on what is happening: to see that when new rules are made, they are at least followed consistently so long as they are in force.

A Check-up Quiz Point out circularities and inconsistencies in the following sets of definitions.

1. (a) "River": "large moving stream of water."
   (b) "Pond": "enclosed body of water smaller than a lake."
   (c) "Brook": "small creek."
   (d) "Creek": "small river."
   (e) "Lake": "large pond."
2. (a) "Ravine": "depression worn by running water, larger than a gully and smaller than a valley."

(b) "Gully": "miniature valley or gorge excavated by a temporary stream."
(c) "Coulee": "deep bed of stream, with inclined sides."
(d) "Ditch": "trench for drainage."
(e) "Trench": "gully dug by man."

3. (a) "College": "institution of higher education in which undergraduates obtain B.A. degree."
(b) "University": "institution of higher education comprising a college plus graduate school."
(c) "Undergraduate": "student who does not attend graduate school."
(d) "Graduate school": "that part of a university that awards advanced degrees."
(e) "Junior college": "college that does not award B.A. degree."

4. (a) "Iamb" $\approx$ "syll with one gil."
(b) "Dac" $\approx$ "premise required to complete an iamb."
(c) "Tyl" $\approx$ "conclusion of an iamb."
(d) "Syll" $\approx$ "argument with two premises and one conclusion."
(e) "Gil" $\approx$ "missing premise."

5. (a) "Lawsuit": "legal action."
(b) "Litigant": "party in a lawsuit."
(c) "Plaintiff": "litigant who brings a lawsuit against a defendant."
(d) "Defendant": "litigant who is required to defend himself."
(e) "Legal action": "action involving a trial of justice between a plaintiff and a defendant to determine the legitimacy of a complaint."

For Further Study James MacKaye, *The Logic of Language*. Hanover, N.H.: Dartmouth College Publications, 1939. Max Black, *Critical Thinking*, 2nd ed., Ch. 11. Englewood Cliffs, N.J.: Prentice-Hall, Inc., 1952.

OUTLINE-SUMMARY: chapter six

A *definition* is a rule of synonymy between a term to be defined and a defining term: " 'Scale' to have the same designation as 'balance for measuring weight.' " It may be introduced into a discourse by a *definition report,* which is a statement that this rule is actually observed in a range of contexts by a certain group of people: " 'Scale' (in musicological discourses) has the same designation as 'ordered series of pitches used as the basis for musical compositions.'" A definition report is complete when its defining term specifies all the necessary conditions for applying the term to be defined, and it may be checked by testing to determine whether the defining term is too broad or too narrow for the term to be defined. A definition may be introduced into a discourse by a *definition proposal,* which is an imperative sentence stipulating that this rule shall be observed in a certain context or range of contexts: "'Fallacy of unequal negation' (in *Thinking Straight*) shall have the same designation as 'violation of the logical rule that in a syllogism the number of negative premises is to be equal to the number of negative conclusions.'"

A set of definitions is a group of definitions in which the defining terms in some are the terms to be defined in others. A *circular definition* is one in which the whole of the term to be defined appears in the defining term; and a circular set is one in which at least one of the definitions can be made circular by substituting according to the others. (Example: if "true" is defined as "not false," then "false" cannot without circularity be defined as "not true.") An *inconsistent definition* is one in which the defining term contains logically incompatible predicates; and an inconsistent set is one in which at least one of the definitions can be made inconsistent by substituting according to the others. (Example: if "fact" is defined as "proposition known to be true," then "misinformation" cannot consistently be defined as "false facts.")

A definition is *question-begging* if it is introduced into an argument as a definition proposal to make a certain statement true (for example, "Do-gooders are neurotic"), by presenting a new definition of either the subject or the predicate (for example, "By a 'do-gooder,' let us understand someone who has an abnormally strong compulsion to manipulate the lives of others for his own satisfaction"). When the predicate has emotive force, and the new definition broadens its designation to make it apply to the subject in the *new* sense, while at the same time the emotive force (positive or negative) of the *old* sense remains active, it is a *persuasive definition* (for example, "traitor" might keep its strong disparaging flavor even if momentarily broadened in meaning so that the charge of treason *in the new sense* is not nearly as serious as in the older and usual sense).

Exercise 24

For each of the following words, taken in its most usual sense, list some of the necessary characteristics and some of the nonnecessary criteria. Where possible, give a complete definition.

1. Watch
2. Holocaust
3. (The game of) football
4. Sonnet
5. Stew
6. Magazine
7. Graft
8. Betrayal
9. Picnic
10. Spy

Exercise 25

Criticize the following definition reports. Point out where the defining term is too broad or too narrow, and where it is ambiguous or very vague, and point out circularities and inconsistencies.

1. "Carpenter" = "one who practices carpentry."
2. "Carpentry" = "the art of working with wood."
3. "Plumber" = "one whose vocation is the practice of plumbing."
4. "Plumbing" = "the art of installing and repairing the plumbing."
5. "Skeptic" = "one who doubts the achievability of knowledge."
6. "Broker" = "one who deals in the buying of stocks and bonds from, or selling them to, private investors, other brokers, and investment houses."
7. "Excessive force" = "more force than is desirable."
8. "Dropout" =" a pupil who is no longer attending school."
9. "Boor" = "ill-mannered person."
10. "Tent" = "portable canvas building designed for camping."

Exercise 26

Analyze the use of definition proposals in the following passages. Point out ambiguity, excessive vagueness, and the need for further definitions. Point out question-begging definitions (including persuasive definitions).

1. I was shocked to hear the senator refer to the local chairman of the ADA as a "liberal," until I read his magazine article and found

out how he defines this term. He writes: "To lay a ghost at the outset and dismiss semantics, a liberal is here defined as one who believes in utilizing the full force of government for the advancement of social, political, and economic justice at the municipal, state, national, and international levels." Why, a benevolent dictator could be a liberal by that definition. I'm afraid the senator didn't lay any ghosts, and semantics are not so easily dismissed. In my opinion, a liberal ought to be defined as one who is unalterably and irrevocably opposed to allowing the government to do anything unless the people are incapable of doing it themselves; this is the true meaning of "liberal" as of "liberty."

2. To THE EDITOR: By what argument can Professor Sidney Hook, in his review of Ayn Rand's *For the New Intellectual,* deny her contention that a free mind and a free market are corollaries? Thinking is just a prelude to action, it is no end in itself. For freedom to be of any use, it must signify absence from restraint in putting ideas to the objective test. If one chooses to have certain ideas about economics and the best way of securing a market, he must be allowed to effectuate those ideas, or to the extent that he is forbidden he is not really free.

3. To THE EDITOR: I have one minor objection: Mr. Miller asserts that religion and morality are not necessarily related, and offers as proof the existence of "good" people who are not "religious" and vice versa. Is he perhaps equating "religion" and "Christianity" here? Is there anyone who is not "religious"? The fact that a person belongs to no church and even objects to the religiosity of some church members does not make him irreligious. The basis for an individual's morality is his religion; indeed, the nature of his morality is determined by the nature of his religion. (Which is to confess that not all moral truth is the sole possession of Christianity.)

4. The fact that the tiresome child, the lawbreaker, and the unhappy lover now pass through [the doctors'] consulting rooms implies the belief that people in these predicaments are, or may be, ill. The concept of illness expands continually at the expense of the concept of moral failure. . . . The significance of this question of who is sick and who is sinful cannot be laughed off as "merely semantic." . . . No verbal tricks with definitions will alter the practical consequences, in our culture, of drawing the boundary between health and illness in one place rather than another. . . .

Who, in fact, amongst the many who get into messes deserve to be fussed over as invalids and who should be required . . . to carry for themselves the responsibilities of normal healthy men and women . . . ? [Barbara Wootton, in *Twentieth Century*].

5. I yield to no man in the world . . . in a hearty goodwill toward the great body of the working classes; but my sympathy is not of that morbid kind which would lead me to despond over their future prospects. Nor do I partake of that spurious humanity, which would indulge in an unreasoning kind of philanthropy at the expense of the independence of the great bulk of the community. Mine is that masculine species of charity which would lead me to inculcate in the minds of the laboring classes the love of independence, the privilege of self-respect, the disdain of being patronized or petted, the desire to accumulate, and the ambition to rise. I know it has been found easier to please the people by holding out flattering and delusive prospects of cheap benefits to be derived from Parliament, rather than by urging them to a course of self-reliance, but while I will not be a sycophant of the great, I cannot become the parasite of the poor . . . [Richard Cobden, 1836].

6. [From a proposed amendment to the Arizona state constitution, forbidding the teaching of evolution in the public schools of that state.] Atheism is defined as a disbelief in the existence of God and the divine creation of man in God's image as recorded in the Bible and embracing, rather, the theory that man has evolved from a lower order of animals. . . . [This] shall be declared a sectarian doctrine . . . and it shall be unlawful for any course of study to be prescribed or taught in the common schools which is atheistic or sectarian.

7. It will not be difficult or time-consuming, I believe, to prove to the satisfaction of all fair-minded people that the humanities are of all disciplines in the college curriculum the most worthy of our attention and devotion—far more, at any rate, than the sciences of brute nature and the so-called "sciences," or rather studies, of gross human behavior—when we pause to reflect profoundly upon the true meaning of the word "humanities," as it has emerged in the course of the foregoing inquiry: namely, the humane studies of the highest and greatest achievements of human nature in every aspect of human culture.

8. The first [erroneous assumption] is that world government would stop wars and bring peace. It is essential that we adopt the usual meanings of the words "war" and "peace," for if this is not done, we may say that there is perfect peace in Russia. Peaceful slavery, how-

ever, is not the kind of peace any of us desire, as illustrated by none other than Franklin Roosevelt when he said, "It is better to die standing up than to live on your knees." In like manner, a "police action" or a "resistance to aggression" or such similar phrases do not make a war not a war. Otherwise, we may eliminate war and create peace by simple semantic expedient. There are types of "peace" in the world today as destructive to the human personality as the atom bomb. Without laboring the point further, it should be obvious that peace is much more than the absence of armed conflict.

REVIEW

As technology advances, as the store of human knowledge about nature and about man continues to grow, as our horizons of awareness widen to include the problems and preoccupations of people of other nations, cultures, races, and social classes, the individual who is trying to cope rationally with his environment finds his task becoming harder and harder. And he needs a larger and more constant supply of reliable information about what is going on, and why.

The great media of mass communication arise to supply this information—newspapers, radio and television, magazines of every character and inclination. For most of us they are the main source of knowledge about the deep issues of politics and government, the predicted consequences of basic policies, the trends of official thinking and world opinions. Yet, despite their power, these media are subject to the control of such a bewildering variety of special interests, and the largest of them are so deeply affected by particular economic and political groups that have a large stake in forming public opinion in certain directions, that even at best they pose formidable problems from a logical point of view—problems of linguistic interpretation and of logical evaluation.

And communication in the other direction takes on new difficulties—when it is up to us to make our views known and to defend a conviction or a proposal, to try to exert influence on the local school board or on those who are working with us in a business or civic organization. For to make a good case, and an effective one, we not only have to compete with stronger opinion-molding forces that may be arrayed on the other side, but we have to be master of more facts, able to marshal and connect them and draw cogent and convincing conclusions.

These are the tasks that this book is designed to help with. It is not, of course, a complete compendium of principles of interpreting and reasoning; it is more like a little home manual, covering the common diseases of discourse, giving clues for diagnosis, methods of treatment, and some precautions against further infection. In the course of the discussion, we have touched on a number of things to keep in mind when you find yourself in the role of reader (or listener) or of writer (or speaker). By way of conclusion, it may be well to run over them once more.

As a reader, approaching any discourse from a logical point of view, you are looking for true statements. You may have some definite problem on your mind, or you may simply be reading for general knowledge about long-standing problems that are always on your mind. The task is a double one: to find out, as well as you can, what the discourse *says,* and to find out whether what it says is *acceptable*—that is, whether it is worthy of belief.

In answering the first of these main questions, you are interpreting the discourse. You begin by getting a good grip on the over-all structure of the discourse. Is it or is it not an argument? And if it is an argument, what are its main points and lines of reasoning? If the discourse is confusing, or its structure complicated, you may have to outline it or summarize it, so as to be able to keep the lay of the land in view while proceeding to examine the details.

Next you turn to the details of the language. Are there words or phrases that are ambiguous, highly vague, or indefinite? Do any of them appear to shift their meaning in the course of the discussion? It may be that the discourse will turn out to be so unsatisfactory at this stage that there is no point in pursuing it further. If you can't resolve the ambiguity, you can't even take the discourse as saying one thing or the other, and so the question of acceptance doesn't arise. If there is total obscurity in some part of the discourse, then you have to set it aside. But usually, even if certain words are behaving rather strangely, when they are cleared up there still remains something to be considered further.

Are there words or sentences that have more in them than first meets the eye—connotations or suggestions that are important to make explicit to yourself? Metaphors may call for special analysis. And if there is heavy reliance on emotive language or emotive devices, you may have to try to neutralize the discourse to do a careful job of analyzing it. If the argument hinges on technical terms that are defined in the discourse, you will have to look over those terms and their definitions with particular care to be sure you understand them clearly.

In answering the second main question, you are making a logical evaluation of the discourse: that is, you are estimating its success as an argument. And you begin by asking: what kind of argument is it?

If the argument is deductive, you want to know two things: (1) Is it valid? To answer this question, you have to examine its logical structure: is it a syllogism, a conditional argument, or what? Then you have to apply the rules of validity for that kind of argument. (2) Are the premises true? If they are themselves supported in the discourse, then you have another argument to consider, and the same procedure must be used. If they are not defended there, you must decide, on the basis of your own experience and knowledge, whether you think it safe to assume them.

If the argument is inductive, you must again classify it further before you can say how convincing it is—that is, how much probability it gives the conclusion. If it shapes up as an argument for a generalization, you ask whether the sample chosen as evidence is perhaps too small or too biased. If the argument supports a hypothesis, you make sure you understand exactly what the hypothesis is, and then ask whether the facts at hand can be explained by an alternative hypothesis that has greater simplicity or frequency. Finally, if you are confronted with an argument from analogy, you know that in itself it does not give a proof, but it may suggest a generalization or a hypothesis for which some evidence can be supplied.

There is, of course, no guarantee that a discourse that passes even these tests will never let you down. But it will be a good deal more reliable than one that is not critically examined at all.

Let us turn now to the problem of the writer. As an argument-maker, rather than an argument-receiver, you usually begin with a question, too: perhaps a question raised by someone else, or perhaps one you have posed to yourself.

The first phase of your thinking is the imaginative search. Perhaps an answer to your question can be deduced or induced from facts already known to you; perhaps it can be established with the aid of further facts you must then proceed to acquire; or perhaps it will come only through free and adventurous creative thinking. As soon as you think of an answer, and regard it as supported in some way, then your task immediately shifts from discovery to critical examination. At this stage, you step back and examine your own argument just as if it were someone else's, applying the same tests we have just been reviewing.

When you write out an argument for others' eyes, you are working out its details. If it is complex, you should probably outline it before you write, so that the main points can be kept before you. And as you work out the sentences, you must as far as possible look at them objectively—reading them over with an eye for semantical and syntactical ambiguities, obscurities, excessive vagueness or indefiniteness—matters you can still correct, before it is too late, by changing the grammar here, shifting paragraphs there, adding, refining, making more precise—perhaps with the help of carefully constructed definition proposals.

Throughout the process, you must be careful always to maintain authority over your words—to watch the connotations and make sure they are the relevant and desirable ones in the context, to watch the suggestions and make sure that they do not go beyond what you want to say, to guard metaphorical expressions against extravagance and looseness, and to keep the emotive force of the language within due bounds. There are many temptations along the way for the writer to let himself go—but perhaps it will help you to avoid them, when you recall some of the examples of wild and woolly thinking and writing that we have examined in this book. Here is where writing and thinking are intimately connected: as you correct your writing, you are forced to sharpen your thinking. And the more clearly you can say what you believe, and why, the better you—as well as others—can see whether what you say is worth believing.

By way of final review, to run over the principles discussed throughout this book, there are several things you might do. For one thing, you may want to turn back to the preliminary quiz at the end of the Preview, and see what you would say about those passages in the light of what you have been studying. It may be helpful to remind you of the sections in which the relevant principles appear:

See §5 for principles applying to items	7, 17
§6 "	13, 18
§7 "	14
§8 "	1, 6, 20
§9 "	3, 23, 25
§10 "	5

§11	"	9, 15
§13	"	10
§14	"	16, 19
§16	"	2
§17	"	4, 11, 22, 24
§20	"	8, 12, 21

Another project would be to tackle a whole article from one of the magazines especially designed to present interpretations of current issues and opinions about them. You may be surprised to find how much it can illuminate what is going on in the article, and how much it can help in making up your own mind what to believe, to go over it with this sort of fine-tooth comb.

Finally, since the examples analyzed in the course of this book have generally been short, so that we could focus our attention on specific problems, it may be well to add here some general exercises, in which a variety of fallacies and confusions are combined. These passages are not offered as hopeless, for there may be good and bad arguments (or better and worse ones) in each. Nor are they designed to persuade you to any conclusion—though they deal with controversial matters, to make it harder for you to be detached and judicious about them. But if you can detect and expose the examples of bad reasoning and misleading use of language, you are able to put the principles of logic to good use.

Exercise 27

Analyze the fallacies and confusions in the following passage.

POLICE ADVISORY BOARD

It is high time that we citizens interested in law and order (and I speak as a retired law-enforcement officer) should take a cold hard look at the rising clamor for setting up a Police Supervisory Board in our city. According to the ideas being kicked around by the bleeding-heart alphabet boys—the ACLU, the NAACP, CORE, and the rest of them—they would have the mayor appoint a panel of five "leading citizens," which they call a "Police Advisory Board." Then people who want to complain about what some policeman did to them would write to this Board; the Board would have its investigator look into the case; and if necessary, the Board could hold a hearing. In the end, they might dismiss the complaint, or they might make a recommendation to the chief of police that the officer involved be reprimanded or suspended or whatever.

I want to tell you that no better device could possibly be invented for crippling, undermining, weakening, and discouraging the police department. If the Communists tackled the problem *directly* (and who has more to fear from law enforcement than they?), they could not do a better job of police-wrecking.

Why do I say this? For many reasons.

In the first place, to have a group of supervisors or advisors—call them what you will—breathing down his neck is humiliating for the police officer. They don't have civilian boards keeping an eye on firemen, mailmen, and other city employees. Obviously the same should be true of policemen. That's only straight thinking.

Second, there is the problem of morale. Frankly, I'm worried about the image of the police, and the disrespect it would cause among the populace to learn that complaints against policemen are actually upheld. Of course I do not mean that legitimate, verified, fully established, and sincere grievances should be hidden and ignored. But these grievances should be taken directly to the police department, which is fully capable of disciplining its own members if necessary; and if the department finds that the complaint is one of those frequent gripes, without substance or merit, then obviously it should be given no further publicity. Publicity can only do harm. In fact, merely to set up the Supervisory Board would be to admit that there might be some need for it; and this I will never admit.

They always yell about "police brutality." But there is no police brutality in this city. I speak from experience. Maybe there is a little roughness from time to time, or extra force used to subdue a mean and contrary person who resists arrest, or a blow or two in the course of interrogating a particularly hard-boiled and unwilling prisoner—but no "police brutality." Police do not, except in isolated cases, use excessive force.

The case against civilian control over the police is overwhelming. It abrogates the autonomy of decision that the police should have. It bears the stigma of reversion to the days of the Tweed Ring and the then mayor, the "elegant Oakley" Hall, when the Police Department was controlled by civilians, and vice and immorality flourished. We have come a long way since those days; but we could fall back. Various pressure groups would work insidiously through the Board, trying to make the police serve their special interests, instead of upholding the law impartially for all.

Besides this, the police could not do their proper work. They are trained in police procedures, and all who are trained know their job. But civilians are not trained. It follows that they do not understand the problems of police work, which are too intricate for the lay mind.

I can only pity the poor policeman, who is attacked by a vicious thug, afraid to use his nightstick or raise his gun, for fear that he will later be hailed before the kangaroo court and charged with "brutality," maybe lose a week's pay, which his six children need. In 1963 alone, 16,793 policemen were assaulted in the performance of their duty, and no less than 55 were murdered. These figures speak for themselves. The policeman must be allowed to defend himself—actually, that is the heart of the issue.

Police work is essentially simple; it is symbolized by the nightstick. The policeman exists to prevent crime, and to punish it. It is the other people who confuse things. There is the Supreme Court, with its ridiculous insistence that when we arrest the suspect we have to let him see his lawyer before we grill him. There is the coddling judge—likely as not, after we bring in some young punk, caught red-handed with a dangerous weapon, the judge will let him off as a juvenile, and give the policeman a lecture on how he should not have arrested the boy but taken him home to the parents and tell them how to bring up their children—when in fact the parents are more delinquent than their children. Since these so-called children would be found guilty if the judge brought them to trial, in dismissing the case against them he is really letting guilty persons go unpunished, which in my book is being an accessory after the fact.

The secret of success in police work is basically force, And the effectiveness of punishment is proportional to the severity of the force. That is self-evident. And the proof of it is an interesting experiment last year. We had a particularly bad district, and the commissioner sent in 100 rookies with big clubs and orders to use them. Suddenly that district became quiet and orderly. Even a tough kid understands a whack with a nightstick; it is a convincing argument.

It is this kind of effective police work that would be hamstrung by a Supervisory Board—they would call it "brutality," or something like that. I know they will argue against this with their statistics, but everybody knows you can lie with statistics. For example, they will point out that according to the FBI's crime index, Philadelphia (which in some recent years has had an active Police Advisory Board) has had a lower crime rate, while the national average has gone up, and other big cities which don't have such Boards have a higher rate. But this proves nothing. The true explanation is that the influence of the Quaker tradition in that city, as expressed in its very name, has given a strong support to peace.

The whole idea of destroying the freedom and independence of the professional law-enforcement agency is sickening—especially when obviously done to gain political support among the minority groups, the very ones who commit the most crimes. The truth is that nobody can define such things as "excessive force" or "unreasonable force." These words are completely vague. It's O.K., they say, for the policeman to seize the prisoner—what if he seizes him tightly, or pushes, or shoves? You can't draw a sharp line here; and therefore you can't make any rule. You have to leave it up to the policeman himself. If he knows his business, he will do the right thing.

And if, on some very rare occasion, the policeman doesn't do the right thing, why then the department itself can discipline him. No outside interference is needed.

Exercise 28

Analyze the following dialogue between an ex-schoolteacher and the dean of a school of education. Point out all fallacies and confusions.

TEACHER CERTIFICATION

TEACHER: I suppose I should begin by admitting that, after making a successful career of teaching in elementary and high school for many years, I have finally been driven out by the totalitarian methods of the educational hierarchy, with their nagging requirements and hamstringing restrictions.

DEAN: You refer to . . . ?

TEACHER: I refer, among other things, to the enormous proliferation of teacher-training programs, topheavy with "how-to" courses in educationism and pedagogy, and the whole certification racket. To get a raise in rank and pay, it doesn't matter how good you are, or how much experience you have—you have to keep going back every summer, or winter nights, to take more and more of these "Mickey Mouse" courses on how to teach. Then automatically, as you pile up the credits—all you need is a *C*—you get your raise. It is a system designed for the incompetent and the drudge.

DEAN: I don't know what you mean by "Mickey Mouse."

TEACHER: That's what the students call them, because they are so easy. In one course I took, Education 201: Human Development, there were twenty-four hours of school observation. Lesson 1 was to make a diagram of the classroom, noting size and position of door, windows, lights, and so forth. What a bore! Genuinely superior teachers will simply not submit to these humiliating requirements, and

I predict that we are on the verge of an even more drastic decline—a terrifying descent—in the quality of our teaching. I shudder to think how the next generation will be taught.

DEAN: How do you know that the good teachers will refuse to submit to these requirements? Maybe the ones who get out or stay out are simply the poor students who are afraid they cannot pass the courses. You can't go by their opinion, when it's evidently based on a fear of doing advanced work.

TEACHER: There is one way to tell who good teachers are: anyone who would be willing to bow to the educationists and accept the system of piling up hours of credits doesn't have the brains and ability to be a good teacher. Why, Admiral Rickover once said that even Albert Einstein could not legally be a teacher of first-grade arithmetic, because he never had enough credits for courses in education.

DEAN: Well, Einstein always said he was not very good at arithmetic, anyway. And of course the Admiral did not examine the teacher certification codes of the various states. The truth is that any superintendent of schools in any state could have hired Dr. Einstein immediately under the temporary provisional certification structure.

TEACHER: But at the end of the year, Einstein would get a little note saying that if he wished to continue to teach in that state, he would have to take six credit hours of education in the summer, or something like that. Imagine that poor old man having to put his intellect on a course in audio-visual aids, telling what kind of chalk works best on a blackboard, and what kind of colored balls make the best demonstration materials for teaching subtraction. It's pathetic.

DEAN: Your argument is fallacious. You seem to say that if the certification system allowed Einstein to teach in the first grade, it would be acceptable; but it does not, therefore it is not acceptable. The fallacy here is that Einstein might not want to teach in the first grade, and anyway he was unique.

TEACHER: What worries me most is that as teacher training is more and more dominated by educationism, it becomes harder and harder to maintain standards in schools. So many of the principals are ex-coaches, and such like, because they were the ones who had time to take all the education credits. One teacher I know resigned when her principal turned over her physics laboratory to a driver-training course and student activities. Pupils take less and less history, mathematics, languages, and so forth. What is happening to the standards?

DEAN: Of course we maintain standards. There is no slackening in the number of hours of work pupils have to take, or the number of days they have to go to school. We have rules in force. And remember that we must also maintain standards for the teachers—that is the purpose of education requirements, to prevent untrained people from ruining the minds of our pupils. For many years the states have recognized the need for accrediting professional personnel in veterinary medicine, chiropody, library science, and many other fields. Can you honestly say that the man who treats our dumb animals must undergo a more careful program of preparation and certification than the man who is responsible for molding the mind of our youth?

TEACHER: That is what concerns me—the idea of "molding minds," as though they are like putty in the hands of the teacher. I am amazed at the extent to which educationist thinking has taken over the accents of authoritarianism and tyranny. But it's all of a piece with the educationists' work. What worries me most is the way the national and state educational associations, putting the bite on their members to build up huge slush funds for lobbying, have manipulated the state legislatures to protect their interests. They have built up a closed shop—that's what it comes down to. Though we have organized to counteract them—our organization is called We The Parents (WTP)—and strongly solicited our members for contributions to support our effort to persuade legislators, we have not been able to accomplish much against the entrenched educationist powers.

DEAN: I hate to hear you speak that way. We educators welcome constructive criticism, of course, but these pernicious attacks can only undermine public confidence on the teaching profession and bring harm upon our teachers, schools, pupils, and the national welfare.

TEACHER: A lot the educationists care about the general welfare! We all know there is a serious teacher shortage; and we know how restrictive the certification requirements are. It is evident that it is these very requirements, which drive good people out of the profession and prevent new teachers who come into the state from teaching, that cause the shortage. It is the closed-shop principle.

DEAN: But certification cannot be the cause of the teacher shortage. The shortage is recent—it grew with the coming to school of the war babies. Before that, teachers were begging for jobs. Yet the certification standards have not been tightened. How do you account for that?

TEACHER: I don't think you need to put me on the witness stand for cross-examination. Some causes take a long time to achieve their effects, you know. But that's not my main point. I'm not against having teachers go back to school, take more courses, refresh their knowledge. I am against the fact that when they do go back to school, they are not supposed to take real content-courses, but only method-courses.

DEAN: Now this is a gross distortion of the facts, as I could prove to you if you were willing yourself to take the 135 education courses taught at our state university. We *have* content-courses, just as we have method-courses; and we encourage our returning teachers to get credit in subjects like history, mathematics, science, languages, that are related to what they are teaching. We see no inherent opposition between content-courses and method-courses; in fact, we see no basic distinction between them, for every course, if it does anything at all, has a content, doesn't it? If something is taught, then something must be learned.

TEACHER: It is learned, if the pupils are capable of learning. But you know yourself that the students who are attracted to schools of education are generally the poorest students. Why, aside from the two friends of mine I mentioned earlier, the three teachers I got to know best in my last school had low I.Q.'s, and were admitted to state education colleges with College Board scores of under 400.

DEAN: I don't agree with your evidence here. The best test of ability in studying is the grade a student gets; education students get just as good grades in their courses as other students do in theirs; it follows that they are just as good students.

TEACHER: My argument is perfectly clear and convincing. All poor students avoid taking many courses in the hard subjects, such as mathematics, philosophy, economics; most education students avoid taking many courses in these subjects; therefore, most education students are poor.

DEAN: I can see that your prejudice against educators and students of education goes far too deep to allow rational arguments to prevail upon you, and so, with sadness and regret, I suggest that we draw this discussion to a close.

Exercise 29

Analyze the logical relationships between the review and the reply in the following exchange of opinions.

THE STRATEGY OF DESIRE [1]

In "The Hidden Persuaders," Vance Packard called attention to Ernest Dichter, head of the Institute for Motivational Research. Mr. Packard identified Mr. Dichter as the grand panjandrum of the new

---

[1] From *The New York Times Book Review*, September 11, and October 9, 1960, © 1960 by John Keats; reprinted by permission of The Sterling Lord Agency.

breed of advertising men who dabble in psychiatry in order to sell soap, and suggested there was something both dangerous and immoral about this peculiar pastime. "The Strategy of Desire" is Mr. Dichter's lengthy reply. Apparently, he meant his book to be a refutation of Mr. Packard, a fuller explanation of what he, Dichter, was doing, and a blueprint for American victory in the cold war. Since the latter objective obviously makes the others seem trivial, it is that which chiefly concerns us here.

Briefly, the author urges the State Department to sell America to the world exactly as Mr. Dichter would sell liquor, hair-oil, automobiles, detergents, or anything else. By employing his techniques, Mr. Dichter says, we can also eradicate juvenile delinquency and racial animosities, perpetuate prosperity, and—to use a favorite literary construction of the author's—"etc."

Mr. Dichter's argument might be summarized as follows. Almost everyone is irrational. Therefore, to persuade a man to do something, to learn something, to vote for a certain candidate, or to think in a certain way, we must never appeal to his reason. Instead, we must capitalize upon his irrationality and appeal to his selfish desires, emotions, and whims. The "only debatable question" is how best to do so. This method of psychological "persuasion is good if there is a correct goal," Mr. Dichter says, calmly adopting as his Golden Rule the premise that the end justifies the means.

Throughout his text, the author makes clear that he is not concerned whether any product he sells is absolutely good or bad. He simply wants to sell it. If Mr. Dichter can persuade a man to believe that an absolutely bad product is absolutely good, if the man can be persuaded to have the illusion he is happy with it, why, then, what is all the fuss about? Persuasion, Mr. Dichter says, is "education."

The inescapable conclusion is that by Dichter's Dicta, we do not really have to eradicate juvenile delinquency, etc., nor do we really have to create a good America in order to sell America abroad. Instead, we have only to persuade our irrational citizency to believe delinquency does not exist. We have only to convince an irrational world that America is bountiful, generous, great, a land of heroes—a thing to be loved. To accomplish these ends, we have merely to create a "good image" of America by advertising techniques. The image may be a mirage, but so what? All we're trying to do is sell it. And if they buy it and are happy with it, that's all right, isn't it?

In a book that lacks the slightest literary grace, Mr. Dichter redundantly explains how best to cater to whims, to create illusions, and to trade on fears in order to take selfish advantage of the character defects of our neighbors. This, essentially, is his contribution to Western thought in our time. Throughout, he claims to be realistic, unemotional, and scientific. If he were half as scientific as he thinks he is, or if his efforts were half as efficacious as Mr. Packard fears they are, we would, indeed, have something to worry about. Happily enough, however, Mr. Dichter's evidence is unimpressive.

There is nothing to suggest that Mr. Dichter's "science" is one whit more valid than Gallian phrenology, nor that it is supported by more reliable data. His text burgeons with begged questions, dubious conclusions, and reiterations that he does not need conventional statistical support because statistics can be unreliable. Even more appalling are his omissions. For instance, he is at some pains to convince us that he has probed deeply into the childhoods and sexual lives of *X* number of people in order to construct a Freudian advertising campaign for a brand of soap. But nowhere does he mention all the people who refused to take part in his questionnaire.

On the basis of what Mr. Dichter says about himself in "The Strategy of Desire," it may be just as well that he is not presently the Secretary of State. For his philosophy leads to Miltown, and his science seems to be compounded of two parts Barnum to one part Freud. As Mr. Packard suggests, his advertising techniques constitute "a matter of justifiable public scrutiny and concern."

—John Keats

To the Editor:

John Keats' New York Times review of my book, *The Strategy of Desire,* is a careful strategy of deceit. Keats, of course, is the Johnny-come-latest-but-probably-not-last in the lengthening line of Packards, Gibneys, and others. These are the morality hucksters. They pound their royalty-stuffed chests and weep bitter tears over tailfins, then step into their sports cars and roar out to their Connecticut homes to cool off with a drink iced from a 1961 refrigerator engineered by the waste makers.

According to Keats, the Dichter view is that the end justifies the means. Actually, I said the exact opposite. My point—developed at considerable length—is that we have not accomplished very much in the past 2,000 years by preaching morality. If we had, the morality hucksters would not make capital of it so easily. I suggested, therefore, that we try modern social-science techniques. We have discovered that telling a man to be moral does not make him so. On the other hand, we recognize that parents use reward and punishment every day to persuade their children to adopt the rules of the society in which they live. Is it, then, so audacious to suggest that similar, if more refined, techniques be used to nudge an adolescent society toward goals of morality and maturity?

Nor is Keats correct in implying that I would change the image of the United States abroad without changing what is wrong with our country. What I really said was: "The success and failures of states and empires have reflected both physical and psychological forces. To a large extent, however, it was the psychological strategy people and nations exerted upon each other which resulted in final success."

I think it is criminal naïveté to suggest as Keats does that we should sit by and let Russia win the propaganda war. The facts which he sneeringly mentions, "that America is bountiful, generous, great, a land of heroes" are good enough to be praised right now. This does not mean that I or anybody else in his right mind would not want to see things improved. It is plain stupidity to advertise nothing but the bad things about this country. Why consistently attempt to portray a bad image and yell when someone tries to suggest that there are quite a few laudable things in this country? Keats feels that for us to employ methods to show a better face to the world is trying to sell a mirage.

Keats accuses me of capitalizing on man's irrationality rather than appealing to his reason. This, again, is a neat double-twist of my argument in *The Strategy of Desire*. What I actually said was: "I am indeed in favor of rational actions; it is unreasonable, however, not to see ourselves as we really are. Although I believe in rationality as the goal of man, I have to look at the real man, and the real man is both rational and irrational."

What seems to bother Mr. Keats most is that I recognize and accept advertising—annoying though it is at times—as a part of our free enterprise system. Truth is usually a better, a more convincing, and a more lasting form of persuasion even in advertising.

—Ernest Dichter
Croton-on-Hudson, N. Y.

To the Editor:

If Mr. Dichter is to continue to write books, he will have to face up to the possibility that not everyone will agree with him. His book impressed me as being stuffed with begged questions, shaky hypotheses, random selection of data, and unwarranted conclusions. Nothing in his letter suggests to me that this is not his usual practice when composing prose.

I understand Mr. Dichter's pain over a bad review, but this is something he will have to learn to live with; it is an occupational hazard of writing.

—JOHN KEATS
Philadelphia, Pa.

Exercise 30

Analyze the fallacies and confusions in the following passage.

PORNOGRAPHY ON THE BOOKSHELVES

May I say, to begin with, that I not only appreciate the invitation to address the Ladies' Auxiliary this evening, to help launch the Anti-Smut Drive for this year, but I also admire the dedication and high morality that has impelled you to carry on your mission to rid the city of pornographic literature, in whatever shape or form it may appear. You motto, "A Clean Book in a Clean Hand," so deftly combining concern for the mind and body, is a truly inspiring one.

You have already made a name for yourselves that will not soon be forgotten in the annals of the war against obscenity. You demonstrated forcefully last year, in your own ladylike fashion, how drug-store owners with questionable paperbacks on their racks could be led to see reason and right by surreptitiously pasting stickers on their books reading "I am obscene; do not read me." (I have never ceased to admire the virtue and self-control you constantly exercise in living in such close proximity with the books you condemn without yielding once to the temptation to read any of them.) And your battle this past year against the public library for circulating that vile book, *The Voyeur of Peyton Place,* showed what can be done by the mobilized forces of goodness. By powerfully wielding the instruments of public protest—writing to the newspapers, picketing the library with signs bearing quotations from the book, and presenting a petition to the Library Board signed by thousands of persons of good will—you made every citizen of our city aware of the nature of this book.

One of the fruits of your work has been the recent ordinance passed by City Council giving a new and more precise, but broadened, definition of "obscenity," which has served to put the smut-peddlers on notice that we will root them out. "Obscenity," according to this carefully worded definition, "is when a piece of writing exploits, is largely devoted to, is made up of, stresses, emphasizes, or otherwise places prominently on view, descriptions of illicit sex or sexual immorality." One of the clarifying features of this definition is that it makes obscenity a species of description, along with descriptions of other aspects of human life, such as Western stories and science fiction; obscene fiction then becomes a special category, containing those books filled with sex, and any bookseller who places such books on sale, whether knowingly or unknowingly, can be severely fined.

The weepers and gnashers of teeth of the Civil Liberties Union, who are always more concerned to protect so-called "rights" than to protect the public against harm, have argued that the law could be applied against many works of genuine literary merit, even classics, like *Anna Karenina* and *Nana*. But these literary works can easily be distinguished from hard-core pornography, which is what the law prohibits. Hard-core pornography has a tendency to corrupt and deprave: look, for example, at the memoirs of Casanova and Fanny Hill, the books of the Marquis de Sade, the *Life and Loves* of Frank Harris, and so forth. All these are definitely harmful. Now, I realize that some highbrow psychologists disagree here—I don't know what their secret motives are, but I do know that scientists are always eager to experiment on poor human beings. I suppose that the psychologists would be happy to see what happens if you expose innocent people to filth; and so I wouldn't put much stock in what they say. Anyway . . . they argue that these books are not necessarily harmful, and may even be beneficial to some poor misguided souls. But take any one of the books I mentioned—or rather, don't take it, of course, but just consider it. It is easy enough to see that reading the Marquis de Sade is not good for you, when it is so obviously pornographic.

The attraction to obscenity is like a disease that is obvious on the face of it; it is socially undesirable; a book can be a carrier, like an infected object; it can spread its influence as it is passed from hand to hand. Therefore, it must be quarantined like an infectious disease; and the way to contain it and prevent its spread is censorship—official and unofficial. And this must be rigorous and complete. The line must be drawn sharply. Critics of censorship are always trying to draw red herrings across the path and pull the wool over our eyes—they like to point out, for example, that a few years ago a man in Uniontown, Pennsylvania, was fined $100 for carrying a placard with a verse from the Bible written out on it (Isaiah 36:12), as part of his antiliquor campaign. They argue that if censorship is justified, then even the Bible is obscene, but since that is absurd, censorship is not justified. The fallacy in this argument is that obscenity is indeed a matter of degree; if you let a man carry vulgar words around that way, you can't deny his right to publish stories with them, and then you have no reason to prohibit any kind of filthy writing. Therefore, it's all or none. And I say—you say—we good citizens say—it is *none!*

You recall the dispute we had over *Catcher in the Rye,* when it was shockingly discovered that this book was on the senior high school reading list—even though it contains one very bad word and some disgusting and prurient scenes. Mrs. Annabelle Anniston, long-time president of the Federated Women's Social and Sewing Clubs of our city, spoke out promptly: "In my judgment, this book is a bad book through and through, and can only corrupt every student who reads it." That is important testimony, coming from her. It's true that the chairman of the high school English department replied that on the contrary the book is a "good novel, acclaimed by literary critics." She said that 95 per cent of the high school graduates go to college, and that this book appears on almost all college freshman reading lists, including those of church schools like Ohio Wesleyan University. The trouble with these arguments is that they miss the point, which is after all an elementary one that anyone should be able to grasp: the high school pupils should never be exposed to verbal sewage. That's all there is to it!

The gist of our argument is this: Everybody agrees that morally uplifting books should be published; but pornographic books are not morally uplifting. It follows that they should *not* be published. There's no getting around that. It's no use trying to make exceptions. Some people will argue that maybe certain books are pornographic, but after all they are also great literary works, and their aesthetic value outweighs their possible danger. This is absurd. I follow George P. Elliot in adopting this definition: "Pornography is the representation of directly or indirectly erotic acts with an intrusive vividness which offends decency without aesthetic justification." It follows that pornography can never have aesthetic justification.

But why should we quibble about definitions? I am tired of the way the federal courts have been handling the obscenity problem. Completely ignoring the real issues—the flood of smut being printed and sent through the mails, amounting to a vast business of millions of dollars, supplying an apparently inexhaustible demand for dirt, dirt, and more dirt—completely ignoring all this, the courts go on playing their semantic games, fussing about distinctions and verbal definitions, and making it harder and harder for the law-enforcement agencies to stem the evil tide. The police and magistrates are hamstrung at every point. When they see obvious pornography lying on the drugstore shelves—with titles like *Lust King* and *Sex Kitten* and *Bed and*

Broad—to titillate the prospective buyer, their hands are tied, because they are not sure they can prove that the books are really obscene by some fancy definition of the Supreme Court. I tell you the time will soon come when the general public will rise up to claim its rights here. The great mass of our citizens are solidly against obscenity—in fact, all but a very tiny percentage of warped and twisted minds—and they are getting impatient with this hairsplitting. The time is not far off when you will see the bonfires. When every church will have a portable charcoal broiler in front of it for burning the bad books, when every library will be stripped clean of filth, and every school reading list purged of anything that might offend delicacy. Then you will see a blaze whose light will shine throughout the land as a symbol of goodness and decency.

I can only say, Carry on!

EIGHTEEN FALLACIES

(A checklist of common errors in reasoning analyzed in this book, with definitions and examples.)

1. Affirming a Disjunct (§5) An invalid form of the disjunctive argument, in which the second premise ("He will work hard") affirms one of the disjuncts in the first premise ("He will either work hard or be fired"), and the conclusion denies the other disjunct ("Therefore, necessarily, he will not be fired").

2. Affirming the Consequent (§5) An invalid form of the conditional argument, in which the second premise ("He will work hard") affirms the consequent of the first premise ("If he wants to keep the job, then he will work hard"), and the conclusion affirms the antecedent ("Therefore, necessarily, he wants to keep the job").

3. Argument from Analogy (§11) An unsound form of inductive argument, in which two things of different sorts are asserted to have a number of characteristics in common ("My love is like a red, red rose, being lovely, sweet, fair, healthy, and so forth"), one of the two things is then asserted to have a further characteristic ("The rose will soon fade and wither"), and it is concluded that other thing has the same characteristic ("Therefore, probably, my love will soon die").

4. Begging the Question (§8) A form of deductive argument in which the conclusion is already assumed (not necessarily in the same words) as a premise ("We can believe what it says in the college catalog, because the catalog itself says that it is the official publication of the college"). Such an argument is also said to be **circular.** A special kind of circular argument is that in which a **question-begging definition** (§20) is proposed in order to make the conclusion true by definition ("By my definition, 'unbreakable' means 'requiring an unusual degree of force to break'; therefore, these dishes are unbreakable").

5. Black-or-White Fallacy (§14) An unsound form of argument, in which it is held that there is no difference, or no notable difference, between two things (for example, between waking and sleeping), because the difference is one of continuous degree, and therefore the difference is the sum of many small and trivial differences (for example, between being "half-asleep" and being very sleepy).

6. Cross-Ranking (§11) A fallacy of classification, which consists in using more than one basis of division in dividing a class into subclasses (as when a restaurant menu lists its offerings under the categories of dinners, sandwiches, salads, beverages, and desserts).

7. Denying the Antecedent (§5) An invalid form of the conditional argument, in which the second premise ("He does not want to keep the job") denies the antecedent of the first premise ("If he wants to keep the job, then he will work hard"), and the conclusion denies the consequent ("Therefore, necessarily, he will not work hard").

8. Distraction (§17) Turning the course of an argument or a dispute away from the point at issue by means of an emotive device, and bringing in irrelevant considerations ("You say that you are against raising the sales tax; far be it from me to cast aspersions, but I certainly would like to know what is your personal stake in seeing that retail businessmen do not suffer any diminution of their profits").

9. Equivocation (§13) Changing the sense of a word or phrase in the course of an argument in such a way as to make the reason offered appear more convincing (or more relevant) than it really is ("That is an artificial lake; what is artificial is spurious; therefore, that lake is spurious").

10. Far-Fetched Hypothesis (§10) A hypothesis accepted on the support of a particular body of evidence when that evidence can be explained by an alternative hypothesis that is simpler or more frequent ("The little Negro church was set afire after the civil-rights meeting was over; therefore, it must have been done by the leaders and the minister in order to cast suspicion upon local segregationists").

11. Hasty Generalization (§9) A generalization accepted on the support of a sample that is too small or biased to warrant it ("I had a bad time with my ex-husband; from that experience I learned that men are no good").

12. Inconsistency (§6) A discourse is inconsistent, or self-contradictory, if it contains, explicitly or implicitly, two assertions that are logically incompatible with each other (Advertisement of Florida motel: "Indoor cook-outs every Saturday night"). A special case of inconsistency is **special pleading,** which consists in appealing to a general statement in refuting another person's assertion, and then ignoring that statement in defending one's own.

13. Maldistributed Middle (§7) An invalid form of the syllogism, which violates the rule that the middle term must be distributed exactly once ("All schoolhouses are fireproof; some brick buildings are fireproof; therefore, necessarily, some brick buildings are schoolhouses").

14. Oversimplification (§17) Excluding relevant considerations from an argument or a dispute by means of an emotive device that makes it appear that the point at issue can be settled more easily than is really the case ("The D.A.'s campaign for mayor raises again the ugly specter of boss control, as the clubhouses once again renew their efforts to get a stranglehold on the voters; to me, this is the only issue of the campaign: are you for or against bossism?").

15. Post Hoc, Ergo Propter Hoc (§9) A form of hasty generalization, in which it is inferred that because one event followed another, it must be the effect of the other ("You notice how the sales went up after we instituted our new advertising campaign; our success is obvious").

16. Slanting (§16) A form of misrepresentation, in which a true statement is made, but in such a way as to suggest something that is *not* true ("Oh, I admit that our space program will cost a certain amount of money," which suggests that the amount is not great), or to give a false description through the connotations of the terms ("Money is being poured into the space program," in which "pour" connotes heedless and unnecessary spending).

17. Unequal Negation (§7) An invalid form of the syllogism, which violates the rule that the number of negative statements in the conclusion must equal the number in the premises ("No churches are fireproof; no schoolhouses are churches; therefore, necessarily, all schoolhouses are fireproof").

18. Uneven Distribution (§7) An invalid form of the syllogism, which violates the rule that an end term be distributed in the conclusion if and only if it is distributed in the premise ("All schoolhouses are fireproof; this building is not a schoolhouse; therefore, necessarily, this building is not fireproof").

INDEX